THE BIG BOOK OF Science

A CHILDREN'S ENCYCLOPEDIA

Brown Watson
ENGLAND

Project Editor: Cristina Drago
Editorial Assistant: Maria Pia Arciuli

Book Editor: Antonella Meiani
Artist: Pier Giorgio Citterio

Production: Aurion S.r.l., Milano
Editor/Writer: Paola Cocco
Designer: Adriano Tallarini

Il Grande Libro degli Esperimenti

ISBN 978-0-7097-2222-9

Reprinted 2015, 2018
Printed in China

Air

What is air? Does air weigh anything? Can it exert any force? How much force has the wind? Which shape is the best for flying? How do sounds travel?

You will find the answers to these and many other questions by doing the experiments in the following pages, under the following headings:

Air is everywhere • Air pressure • Hot and cold air
Flight • Air and combustion • Sounds

Air is everywhere

Air is everywhere, taking up every free space. There is air in water, in objects and in plants, in the human body and in animals. And although air is light and invisible, we can still find ways to weigh air and to see it.

Where can we find air?

IN WATER WITHOUT GETTING WET

What you need
- a clear glass jar
- ping-pong ball
- piece of kitchen paper
- transparent bowl or basin (deeper than the jar) containing water

What to do

1 Place the paper in the bottom of the jar so that it cannot move about.

2 Place the ping-pong ball on the surface of the water in the bowl.

3 Turn the jar upside down over the ping-pong ball. Press down with the jar until it touches the bottom of the bowl.

What happens?
The water does not get into the jar and the ping-pong ball is resting on the bottom of the bowl, almost dry.

Because...
... the air in the jar stops the water from getting in and making the paper wet. Lift the jar straight up out of the water and you will see that the paper is barely wet, almost as if the jar has just been drained!

4 Immerse the jar once again.

5 When it touches the bottom, tilt it a little.

What happens?
Bubbles of air escape from the jar.These rise to the surface and burst. Water gets into the jar, the ball rises higher inside and the paper gets wet.

Because...
... the air inside the jar finds a way of escape and rises upward. Now the water takes up the space which has been left by the air.

Vacuum-packed products
If you read the information printed on jars of coffee, you may see the words 'vacuum packed'. This refers to a special manufacturing process which takes out the air inside the jar so that the smell of the coffee is better preserved. When the seal is opened, you can hear a noise which is almost like a breath: this is the air taking up its space again inside the jar.

Air in water
Water contains air too. You can see that by leaving a glass full of water near a source of heat. When the water begins to warm up, you will notice tiny bubbles full of air collecting together on the inside of the glass.
But human beings cannot breathe the air which is in water. Underwater we have to use a snorkel to take air from the surface, or cylinders full of oxygen.

Air is all around. It occupies every free space, however small.

Does air have weight?

HOW TO WEIGH AIR

You need:
- two plastic sticks, one 15cm and one 30cm
- balloons of equal size, each slightly inflated
- two cans of drink
- sticky tape
- pencil

What to do

1 Mark the centre of the 30cm plastic stick with the pencil.

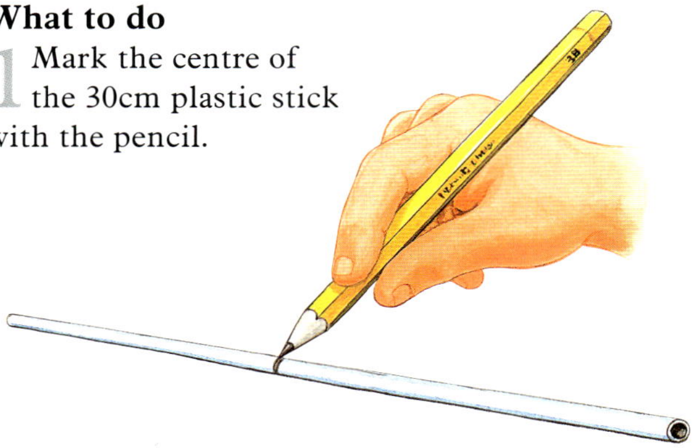

2 Fix one balloon at each end of the stick with the sticky tape.

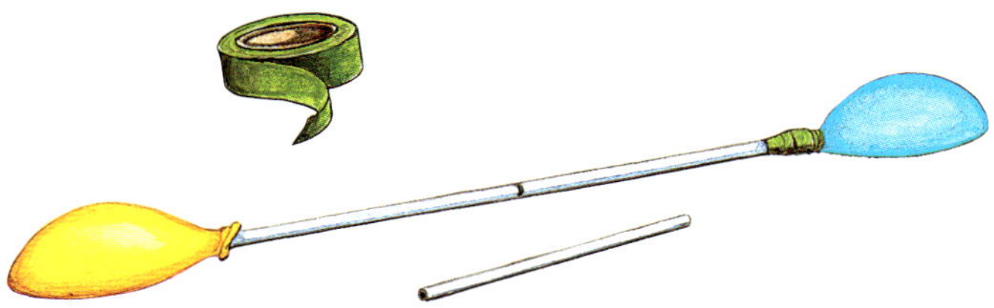

3 Tape either end of the 15cm plastic stick to a can. Place the centre mark of the 30cm stick on top.

What happens?
The stick with the two balloons stays horizontal.

Because...
... the ballons are of equal weight.

4 Remove one balloon and inflate it fully. Re-attach it to the 30cm plastic stick, making sure that this is balanced the same as before.

What happens?
The fully-inflated balloon weighs down the long plastic stick at one end.

Because...
... the air inside the fully-inflated balloon makes it heavier than the other one.

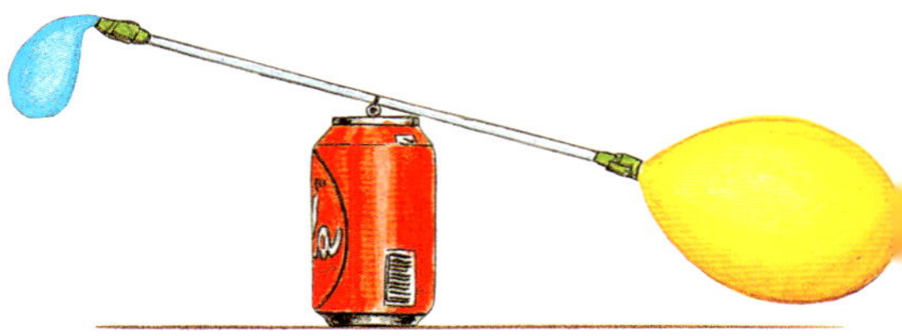

THE AIR IN A ROOM

You need:
- a metre rule (or tape measure)
- pen and paper
- bathroom scales

What to do

1 Take the measurement of a room in metres. (This is best done from corner to corner.) Measure the width and the length of the floor and the height of one wall.

2 Multiply the three measurements together to obtain the volume in cubic metres (volume = width x length x height).

3 Scientists have calculated that one cubic metre of air weighs approximately 1.2kg: so if you multiply the volume of a room by 1.2 you will obtain the weight in kilograms of the air in the room.

4 Now weigh yourself. Compare your own weight with that of the air in the room. Which is the most?

What happens?
You will find that the air in the room weighs more than you do.

Because...
... the air in a medium-size room is equal to that of an adult person (about 70 kg.)

Bubbles of air to attract prey

A ping-pong ball springs up from under the water and breaks free. Then you will see it spinning rapidly on the surface, because it is lighter than the water on which it floats. And that is why bubbles of air in water always rise up.
The pilot whale uses this phenomenon (something happening naturally, which we can see, feel or hear) to capture its prey. It moves in circles below a shoal of fish, making air bubbles which rise up towards the surface of the water. These bubbles attract the fish towards the whale, ready for the whale to swallow them up.

Even something which may seem as light as air has weight.

Air pressure

The atmosphere is the thick layer of air which surrounds the earth (about 1000 km). It exerts its pressure on bodies and objects, but nobody is aware of it. Yet 15 tonnes of air presses against a grown-up person! We can discover the great strength of air pressure. Although we cannot feel this on us, it is possible to measure it, increase it, and use it to operate machines and to overcome the force of gravity.

Does air exert a force?

AN INVISIBLE FORCE

You need:

- a ruler
- a large sheet of paper
- a board to work on

What to do

1 Place the ruler on the board so that it sticks out over the edge by about one third.

2 Put the sheet of paper on top of the ruler, so that the paper lays flat on the board.

3 Strike the sticking-out part of the ruler to make the paper jump up in the air. (Take care that the blow is not hard enough to break the ruler!)

What happens?
The paper stops the ruler from lifting up.

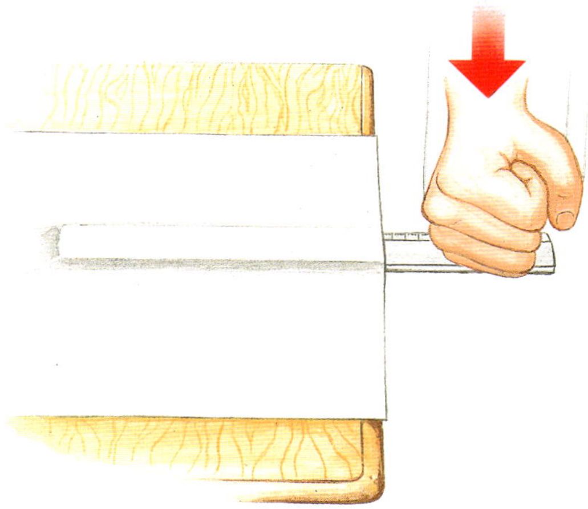

Because...
... air is pressing down on the paper. And because the surface of the paper is very wide, the quantity of air on it is enough to stop the paper from rising up, despite the force of the blow.

AIR MAKES WATER RISE

You need:

- a bowl
- a drinking glass
- water

What to do

1 Put the glass into the water and turn upside down.

2 Lift up the glass, but without the rim going above the surface of the water.

What happens?

The level of water in the glass rises, so that this is higher than the water outside the glass.

Because...

... the pressure of air on the surface of the water in the bowl pushes the water up into the glass. If the rim of the glass were raised above the surface of the water, air would enter and push it outside. Then the glass would empty.

Air exerts a force of pressure on all surfaces with which it comes in contact.

Does air only press downwards?

STRONGER THAN WATER

You need:
- a glass with a smooth rim
- a picture postcard, or a piece of glossy card, postcard size
- water
- a sink in which to work

What to do

1 Fill the glass with water.

2 Carefully place the glossy side of the postcard down on the rim of the glass. (You will eventually make it a little bit wet.)

3 Keeping the palm of your hand on the card, turn the glass upside down.

4 Take your hand away from the card.

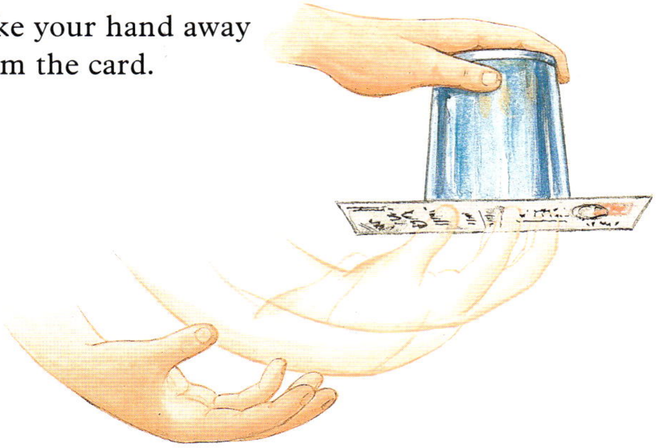

What happens?
The card remains attached to the rim of the glass and the water does not fall out.

Because...
... the air pressure exerted on the card from underneath is greater than the weight of the water inside the glass. This is why the card sustains the water and the water does not spill out.

The power of suction

When a suction pad is pressed down on a surface, the air which is inside escapes. Because of the air pressure outside, the rubber of the suction pad stays firmly attached to the surface, completely airtight. But if you lift the edge of the rubber, the air gets in and the suction pad no longer works, because the air pressure both inside and outside the suction pad is the same. You can prove this for yourself by testing which surfaces the suction pad will stick to and those on which it will not stick.

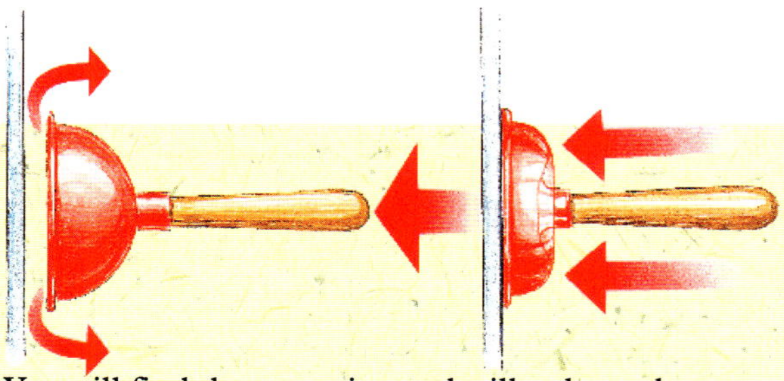

You will find that a suction pad will only work on surfaces which are perfectly smooth. On surfaces which are rough, the air presses down on the suction pad and immediately gets into any gap between the surface and the suction pad rubber.

Air pressure is exerted in all directions, as well as from the bottom to the top.

Does the air which surrounds the Earth press down on us?

THE PRINTS

You need:

- plasticene or modelling clay
- a glass bottle full of water and sealed with a cork

What to do

1 Soften the plasticene and mould into a fairly thick, round base the same size as the base of the bottle.

2 Place the bottle on the plasticene base, taking care to keep it upright.

3 Remove the bottle. Turn it upside down and put it on the plasticene base again.

What happens?

The print left in the plasticene by the upright bottle is not as deep as the print left by the upside down bottle.

Because...

... the surface on which the weight of the upright bottle is distributed is larger. But with the upside down bottle, the same weight is concentrated on a surface which is smaller. This exerts greater pressure and so the upside down bottle leaves a print which is much deeper. The pressure exerted by a human body also depends on how large the surface of contact is. That is why skis prevent skiers from sinking into the snow!

A balance of strength

Atmospheric pressure is determined by the weight of the air which is above us, and which presses down on everything found on the surface of the Earth. So, how is it that it never crushes us? Because the human body has many different surfaces on which air pressure can be distributed in different directions; and, most importantly, because inside our bodies, as with the bodies of all animals and objects, there is air which presses towards the outside to equal the atmospheric pressure. Due to this balance of strength, we can withstand the atmospheric pressure which is exerted on us.

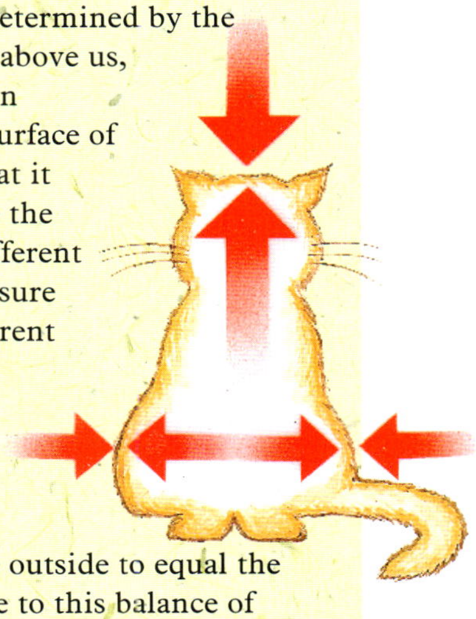

Variations in pressure

Atmospheric pressure in the mountains is less than the atmospheric pressure at sea level. The lower you go, the thinner the layer of air which is above – therefore less atmospheric pressure is exerted. The same applies under water. The deeper you go, the more you would feel the weight of the water getting heavier. Atmospheric pressure also changes in temperature (hot air weighs less than cold air) and with humidity or dampness. (Air which carries drops of vapour is heavier than dry air.) Because of these variations we need to use instruments to measure atmospheric pressure, such as the barometer and the altimeter.

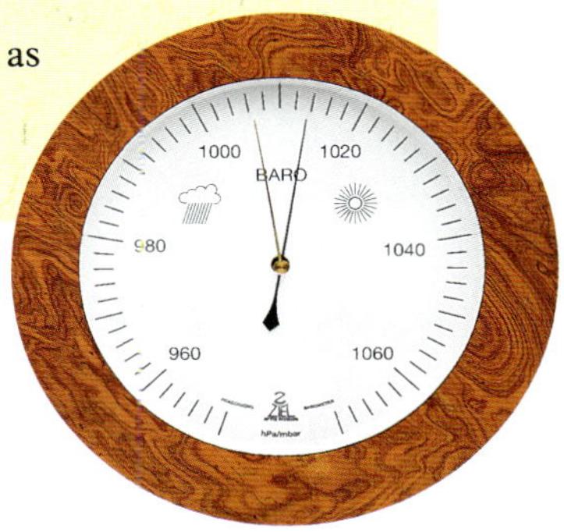

A barometer is used to measure atmospheric pressure and so predict changes in weather conditions.

The atmosphere presses down equally on bodies and objects. It is balanced by the pressure of air within them.

Can air be compressed?

SQUASH THE AIR

You need:
- a plastic syringe without a needle

What to do

1 Take the syringe and lift the plunger, so that the syringe fills with air.

2 Cover the hole of the syringe with a finger and press down hard with the plunger. Then let it go.

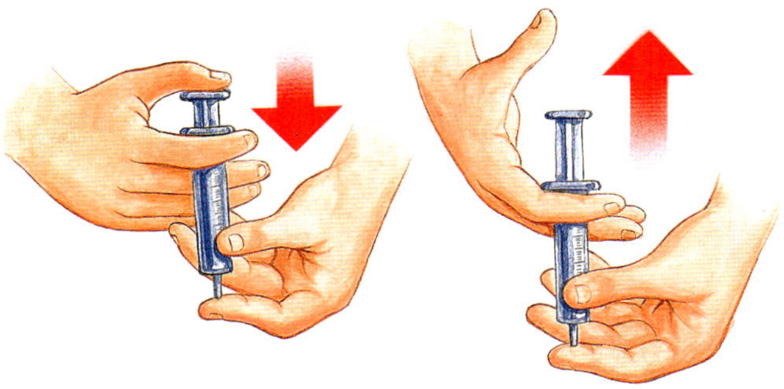

What happens?
The plunger shoots up, as if by an unseen force Then it stops: you feel a strong push against your finger. Take your finger away and the plunger returns to its original position.

Because...
... the air is compressed, because the plunger makes it occupy a much smaller space. This compression increases the air pressure – that is the force with which it presses against the inside of the container and on your finger. The plunger returns to its original position because the compressed air tries to expand. Then the pressure diminishes and makes a depression (dent).
If you try to repeat the experiment with a syringe full of water, you will find that the plunger does not shoot up.

The strength of compressed air

The compressed air inside a pneumatic tyre is able to support the weight of a bicycle, car or automatic train. Due to the tyre's flexible, springy surface, it will cushion the vehicle when the wheels go over bumps or any unevenness in the ground.

The helicopter and the parachute work by making use of air pressure. As the rotor blade of the helicopter whirls, it pushes the air downwards, compressing it and so getting a force to help it take off and push up into the sky.
The shape of the parachute is designed to gather and compress under it a great quantity of air which presses upwards: this is sufficient to counteract the force of falling and so slows down the descent.

The hovercraft is a means of transport which can move on the ground and on water, suspended on a cushion of air.
Instruments as simple as an eye-dropper and as complex as a jet engine work due to air pressure being compressed in a reduced space. You use compressed air each time you let go of an inflated balloon to see it rise up into the air.

JET-PROPELLED BALLOONS

You need:

- string
- sticky tape
- a medium-size balloon
- drinking straw

What to do

1 Thread the string through the straw and tie the ends tightly between two points at equal height in a room (e.g. handles or hooks).

2 Inflate the balloon and keep the neck closed between your fingers.

3 Fix the balloon underneath the drinking straw with the sticky tape and pull the balloon along to one end of the string.

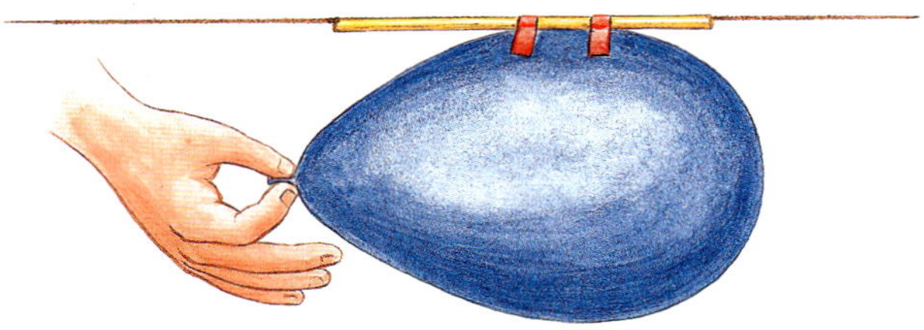

4 Pull your fingers against the mouth of the balloon, then let go.

What happens?

The balloon shoots along the thread at speed.

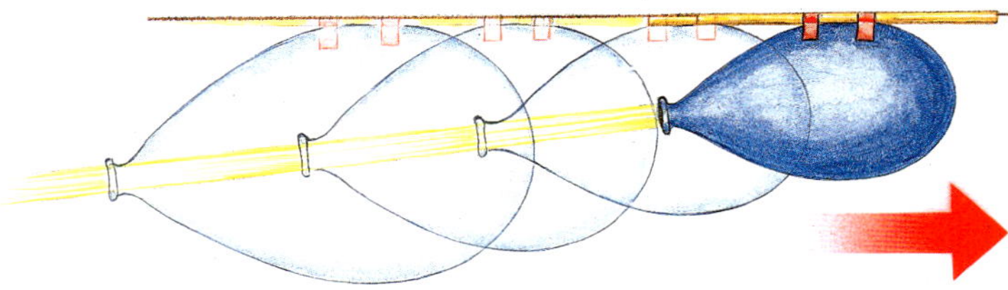

Because...

... when the balloon is closed, the air inside presses equally against the inside surface. When the balloon is let go, the air inside expands. This creates a backward thrust, and the reaction is that the balloon is pushed forward.

The force of reaction

The arm strokes of a swimmer or the blows from the oar of a rower shows us how, for each force of action, there is a force of reaction. The push from behind of the arm or the oar on the water causes a push of equal strength in the opposite directon, which makes the swimmer or the oarsman move forward. This is how the jet aircraft works. Its reactor engines shoot out bursts of very hot exhaust gases behind it, and the reaction to this is powerful enough to propel the aircraft forward.

Air can be compressed; the force of compressed air can support and move considerable weights.

Hot and cold air

Great masses of hot and cold air move around in the atmosphere. Weather satellites take photographs of these for meteorologists to study, in order to forecast rains and hurricanes. These masses of air are rather like the wind, flowing constantly all around the Earth, depending on the reaction of the air and the heat of the Sun.

What happens to air which is re-heated?

HEATING AIR AND COOLING AIR

You need:
- a balloon
- an empty bottle
- a basin with hot water. (Take care: hot water must be handled with caution!)

What to do

1 Inflate the balloon slightly and place on the neck of the bottle.

2 Hold the bottle for a minute or two in the hot water.

What happens?
The balloon inflates.

Because...
... the air, like all substances, is made up of tiny, moving particles called molecules. The heat makes these molecules move apart. This means that the air inside the bottle spreads and therefore it needs more space. So it enters into the balloon and inflates it.

3 Now run the cold water tap on the balloon.

What happens?
The balloon deflates.

Because...
... the air, now affected by the cold, contracts (that is, the molecules come closer together). And so the air occupies only the space in the bottle.

THE MAGIC GLASS

You need:
- a glass
- a book
- a board with a smooth surface
- cold and hot water

What to do

1 Balance the board on the book so that it is slightly tilted. Rinse the glass in cold water and put it upside down on the highest point on the board.

2 Now take the glass and rinse in hot water. Put it once more on the highest point of the board.

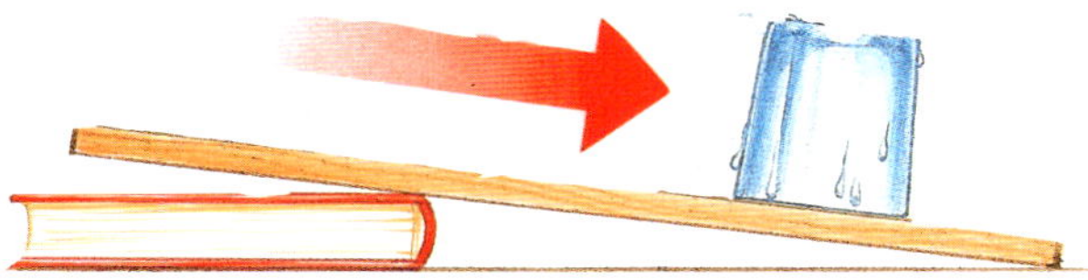

What happens?

When the glass is rinsed in cold water, it moves slowly towards the bottom of the board, then stops. When the glass is rinsed in hot water, it slides rapidly to the bottom and falls.

Because...

... the air contained in the glass, heated by the water, expands and the glass rises very, very slightly from the board, so it can slide towards the bottom without any resistance (anything to stop it).

Beware of air expansion!

On any aerosol spray you will find this warning: 'Keep out of direct sunlight. Do not expose to temperatures above 50°'. After the experiments on these pages, you can understand the reason for these words. The gas compressed in the areosol that we use to spray the product is like air: if it heats up, it will expand and make the aerosol explode!

When it is hot, air spreads out and so occupies more space than when air is cold.

Does air weigh the same cold as when it is hot?

THE SPIRAL

You need:
- a square of paper (at least 13cm square)
- a pencil
- scissors
- a piece of string, about 20cm long
- a source of heat, such as a very hot radiator – or you can use an electric pan under the supervision of an adult.

What to do

1 Draw a spiral on the paper as shown in the picture. Cut along the spiral lines.

2 Make a little hole in the centre of the spiral. Thread the string through and fasten with a knot.

3 Hang the spiral above the source of heat.

What happens?
The spiral begins to spin round on its own.

Because...
... the air is warmed up by the source of heat and rises up. As it comes in contact with the spiral, the air is channelled between the strips, pressing against them and making it spin round.

Hot air for flying

The hot air inside a hot-air balloon is less dense than the colder air of the atmosphere. So the balloon will remain in flight for as long as the air inside it is heated. The first people to invent a method of rising up in the sky using hot air were two French men, brothers Etienne and Joseph Montgolfier. In the 18th century, they built their first models from greaseproof paper, heating the air inside by burning straw. In 1783 another two French men, Jean-François Pilâtre de Rozier and the Marquis d'Arlandes, became the first to travel in a hot-air balloon built by the Montgolfiers.

Free flight

The flight of sailplanes, (aircraft without engines) is called gliding. This is made possible by the presence in the atmosphere of thermals – currents of hot air which rise up faster than the sailplane, or glider, can descend.

After being towed into the air either by an engined aircraft or a winch, the glider rises on a spiral path by using a thermal, then proceeds to glide (that is to say, it is in free flight), until it meets another thermal. The skill of the pilot is knowing exactly the conditions in which these thermals form and change, in such a way that it is possible to find another thermal for the glider to make use of, and so continue to fly.

This type of flying is also sometimes called 'thermal soaring', because it uses air thermals.

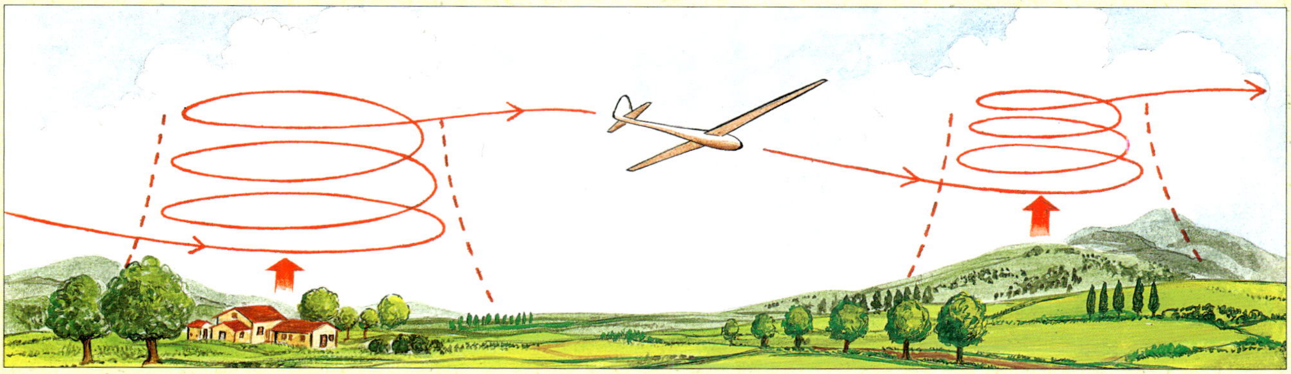

Hot air is lighter than cold air and therefore rises up.

How does heat spread in the air?

THE CIRCULATION OF AIR

You need:
- tissue paper
- scissors
- string
- sticky tape

This experiment must be done in a warm room in winter.

What to do

1 Use the sticky tape to stick strips of tissue paper to a piece of string at least one metre long.

2 With another two pieces of sticky tape, stick the ends of the string to the lower corners of a window, as shown in the picture.

3 Open the window just enough to pull the string tight. Watch the movement of the tissue paper strips.

What happens?
The strips bend towards the inside of the room.

Because...
... the cold air which enters, strikes them.

4 Now repeat the experiment, this time fastening the ends of the string to the top corners of the window.

What happens?
The strips bend towards the outside.

Because...
... as cold air comes in below, hot air from the top part of the room escapes out, bending the strips as it does so.

Heating up a room

Heat can get through cold and hot things. In a room, a hot radiator warms the air nearby, then the air around it. As the hot air rises, its place is taken by cold air, which is heavier. This air in turn is warmed up and rises. When air is high up, it comes in contact with air which is colder and warms up this air. So the hot air becomes cold again and descends, and this hot air-cold air-hot air cycle continues. This movement of air from the bottom to the top and from the top to the bottom is called the convector (meaning 'transmission') current.

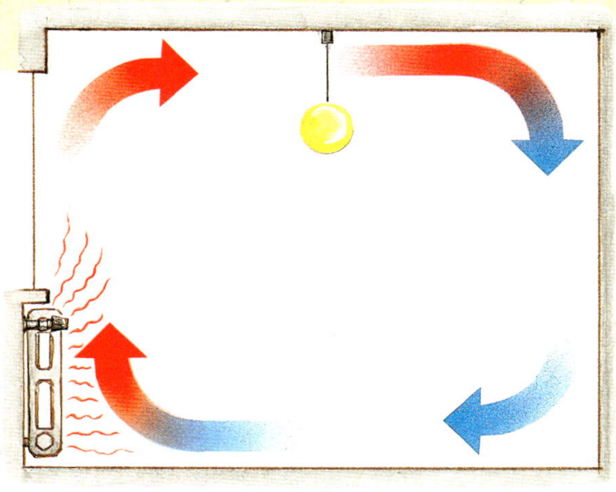

TEST TO CONSERVE HEAT

You need:
- three glass jars
- three lids
- something woollen
- sheets of newspaper
- a box as deep as the jars
- hot water
- a thermometer which can be used in water

What to do

1 Wrap the first jar in the woollen material. Put the second jar in the box, and pack crumpled-up newspaper all around it. Leave the third jar uncovered.

2 Fill all three jars with hot water. Take the temperature of each and screw the lids on top.

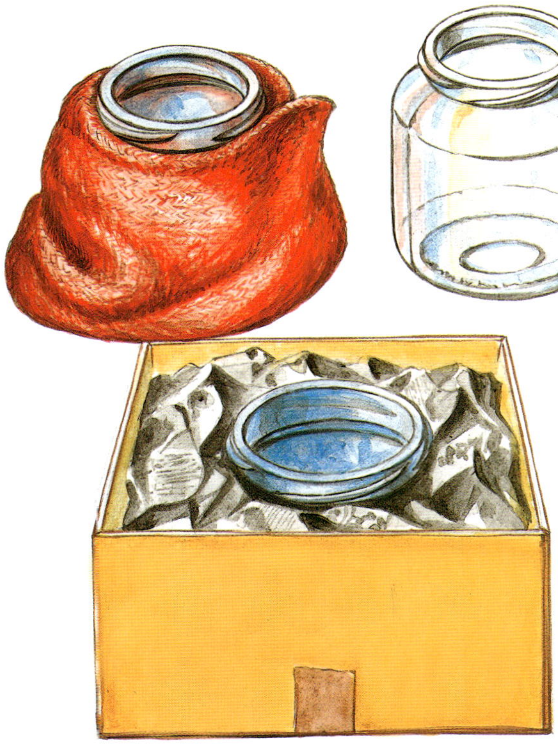

3 Place the jars somewhere cold (for example a balcony or in a cold room) for 30 minutes.

4 Use the thermometer to check which jars of water have cooled the least.

What happens?

The water which cooled the most was in the jar that was uncovered. The water which had cooled the least was in the jar inside the box with the crumpled-up newspapers, also the jar wrapped in woollen material.

Because...

... the quantity of air trapped inside those two jars was more, because they were insulated against the cold air. This slowed the cooling-down of the water.

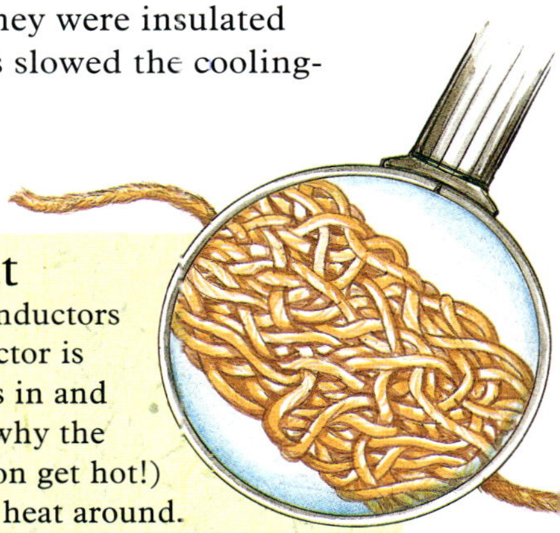

Conserving heat

There are many good conductors of heat. One such conductor is metal, because this keeps in and throws out heat (that is why the metal handles of pots soon get hot!) Free-flowing air spreads heat around. But metal traps the heat and stops it spreading, which is why it is such a good conductor.

Also, we use double glazing to prevent the heat inside the home from escaping. Between the two panes of glass there is a gap which traps the air, creating a barrier between the warm air and the cold air. The fibres of woollen clothes, padding, feathers of birds and the coats of many animals work in the same way, by trapping the warm air. Even snow can work as insulation, protecting animals and seeds from harmful frosts.

In the air, heat is transmitted through rising and falling movements called convective currents.

Does hot air and cold air exert the same pressure?

WHAT IS SQUASHING THE BOTTLE?

You need:
- an empty plastic 1.5 litre bottle with the stopper
- hot water

What to do

1 Fill the bottle with hot water.

2 After a few seconds, empty the water and put the stopper on at once.

What happens?
At once you will see the bottle flatten lengthways, as if two hands were squeezing it!

Because...
... the air inside the bottle, light and expanded because of the heat, has a lower pressure than the air on the outside. It is the pressure of the air outside which squashes the bottle.

A view from up high

There are enormous convective currents around the Earth, caused by the heat of the Sun. Air continually moves from areas of high pressure, where the air is colder and heavier (as at the North and South poles), to areas of low pressure, where the air is hot and therefore light (as at the Equator). The movements of these great masses of air determine the winds and changes in temperature. That is why meteorologists and weather forecasters study them carefully. In an area of low pressure we can predict rainy weather because the air rises and condenses to form clouds. In an area of high pressure, dry weather is predicted, with clear skies and radiant sunshine, because the winds push the clouds towards the outside of the area.

A satellite picture of Europe showing a cyclonic swirl over the United Kingdom.

Hot air expands, weighs less and therefore exerts a lower pressure than cold air.

How much force does the wind have?

THE THRUST OF WIND

You need:
- a piece of cartridge paper
- a pencil
- scissors
- a drawing pin
- a small stick

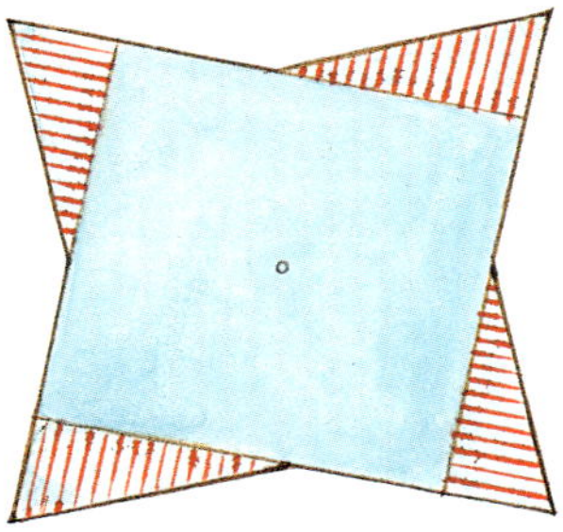

What to do

1 Cut the cartridge paper as shown in the picture.

2 Fold the parts shaded in the picture.

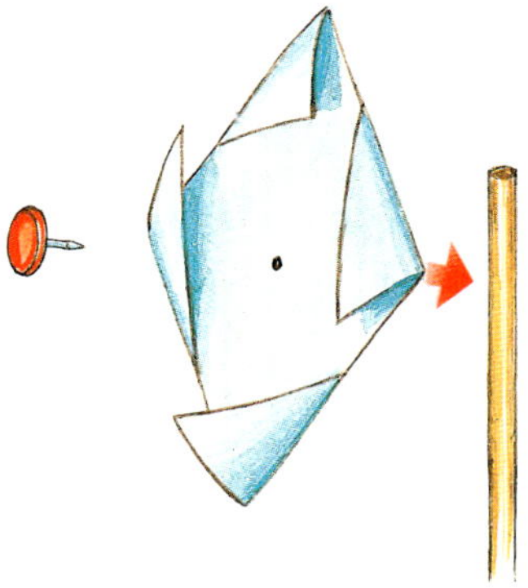

3 Fix the centre of the wheel to the stick with the drawing pin.

4 Make sure that the wheel spins freely. Hold it so that the wind catches it.

What happens?
The wheel spins fast.

Because...
... as the air strikes the card, it is gathered up towards it, but it is stopped at each of the four corners. The thrust of the wind against the four corners pushes the wheel around. Windmills and machines on wind farms work in the same way. Wind blows on to the obstacles that can be pushed, i.e. the sails, making them turn. On wind farms, the energy of the wind is transformed into electrical energy.

Sailing their yachts, the crews use the energy of the wind.

Cyclones

Areas of low pressure are also called cyclonic. These areas are more changeable than those of high pressure and can cause cyclones, also called typhoons or hurricanes according to the geographical zone in which they form. Tropical cyclones are the most violent meteorological phenomenon known on Earth. They can create total devastation, destroying everything in their path. In cyclones, the wind spins at speeds which can reach over 500 kilometres an hour, around a central point called the 'eye of the cyclone' where the pressure is lower, the sky is clear and the air calm.

The wind has great strength. This can be used as a source of energy, but it can also have devastating effects.

Flight

When we see an aircraft taking off, we may often wonder at the power by which it overcomes the force of gravity, rising up into the sky and flying in the air by means of its strong wings. How must those wings be constructed so that they support the great weight of the aircraft? What is the best shape to go through the air? What features of the air can aeroplanes make the most use of? What speeds can an aircraft reach?

How does a wing work?

BLOW A SURPRISE

You need:
- a strip of paper 10cm wide and 20cm long
- a sheet of paper
- two books

What to do

1 Hold the sheet of paper under your bottom lip and blow on the top surface.

What happens?
The sheet of paper rises.

Because...
... the air which flows across the top surface of the paper exerts a pressure which is less than the pressure underneath, where the air is still. It is the pressure underneath which makes the paper rise.

2 Place the sheet of paper across two books which are set about 10cms apart. Blow on the paper.

What happens?
The paper sinks down between the books.

Because...
... air is moving underneath the paper, exerting a pressure which is less than that which presses down on the top surface of the paper.

A MAGIC BLOW

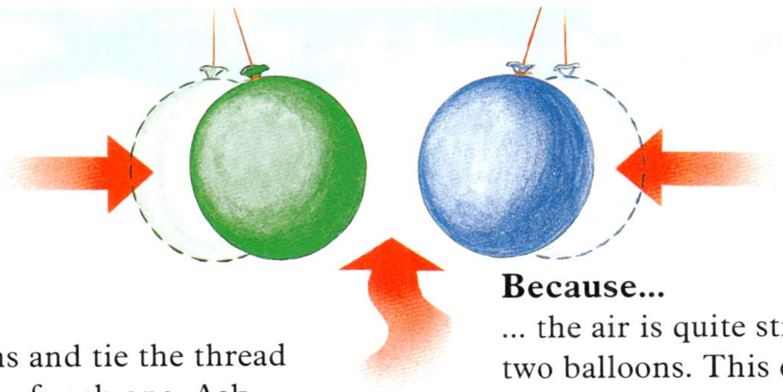

You need:
- two balloons
- thread
- a drinking straw

What happens?
The balloons come near each other.

What to do

1 Inflate the balloons and tie the thread around the mouth of each one. Ask someone to hold them in front of you with a distance of about 30cm between the two.

2 Blow through the straw between the balloons.

Because...
... the air is quite still around the outside of the two balloons. This exerts a greater pressure than the air which flows between them, and so it pushes one balloon towards the other.

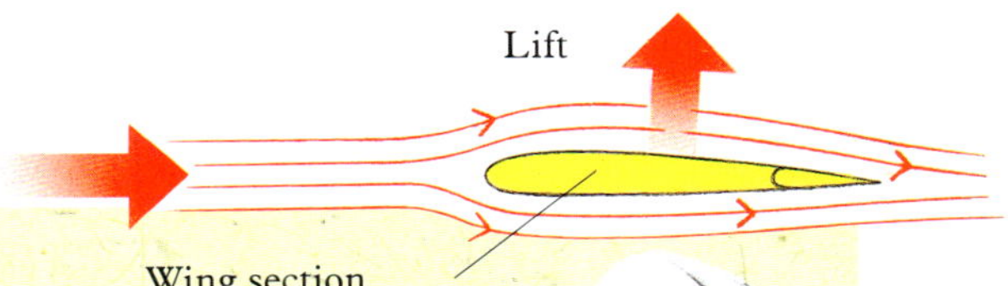

Air on the wing

The top surface of the wing is curved and the rear end is lower than the front edge, helping the air to flow more quickly over the top surface. This means that the pressure of air on the underside of the wing is greater and it pushes the wing upward. The force of this air also supports the wing, which means that the aeroplane is lifted up as the air moves past it. This force is called 'lift'. The flow of air on the wing can be deflected by fins or by control panels called *flaps* which allow the aircraft to take off, to turn and to remain at altitude.

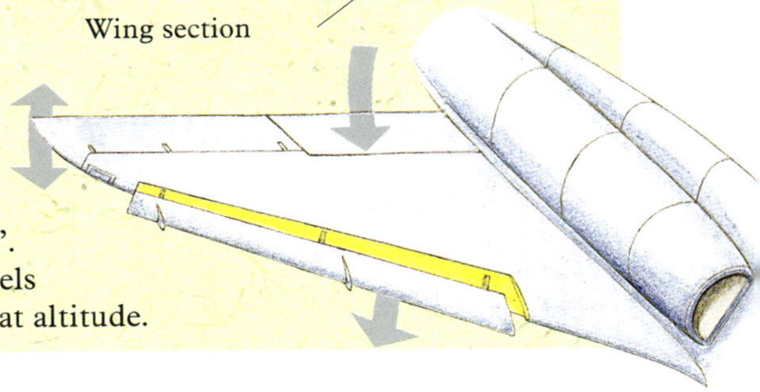

The wing of an aircraft in flight is sustained by a force called 'lift', caused by the air pressure underneath the aircraft.

Which shape is best for flying?

A PAPER AEROPLANE

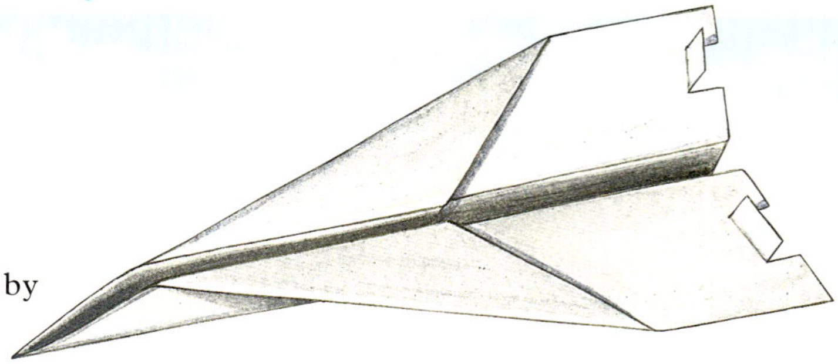

You need:
- two sheets of A4 paper

What to do

1 Make a paper aeroplane from one A4 sheet, by carefully following the instructions underneath each drawing below.

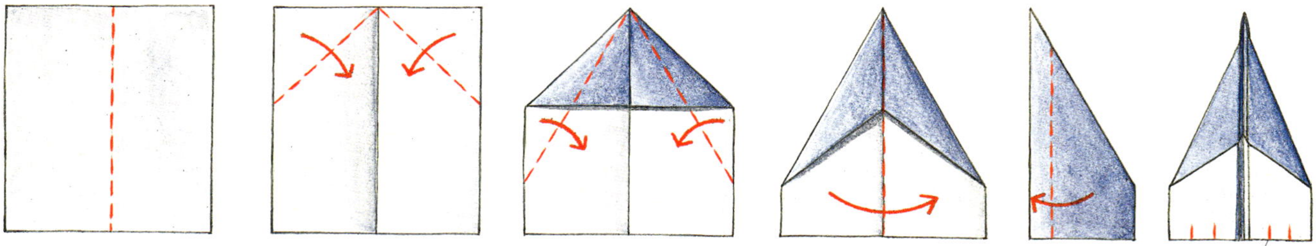

Fold paper along the dotted lines, then open it out.

Fold along the dotted lines shown, in the direction of the arrows.

Make two cuts either side of the centre fold

2 Throw the flat sheet of paper into the air and watch what it does.

3 Now throw the paper aeroplane into the air, and watch what it does.

What happens?

The flat sheet of paper flutters haphazardly in the air, and soon falls to the ground. But the paper aeroplane keeps in the air much longer and follows a proper path.

Because...

... the shape of the paper aeroplane is made to break through the air. It uses the 'lift' to remain in flight, until it exhausts the force of the thrust from your hand. But the flat sheet gives the air a wide surface to press down on, and so does not fly.

The wind tunnel

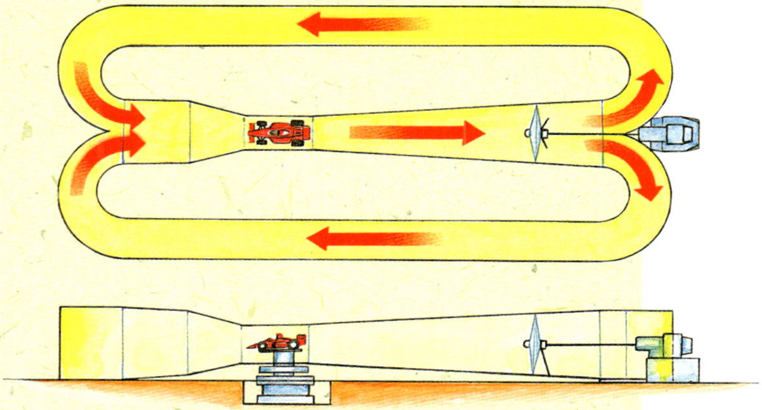

Can you imagine a cube-shaped aircraft? Or a racing car with the front part completely flat? When things which travel at speed are built, they are shaped to reduce the resistance of air to their movement.

A wind tunnel is built to measure and observe their aerodynamic (the ability to move through the air) features. In it, the prototype or working model of an aircraft or racing car is kept stationary, and subjected to strong currents of air, similar to those which it would meet if it were moving. One test is to fix strong threads to the model to show the movement of the air against it; another is to treat the model with chemical substances which react by changing colour according to temperature. Such procedures, together with special equipment and the careful observation of the technicians, make it possible to study the force with which the car or aircraft can break through the air – that is the ratio between its speed and the power necessary for it to move at that speed. The more aerodynamic the shape, the less the strength needed to obtain a particular speed. These studies have led to important changes and improvements in the design and building of civil and military aircraft. The straight aeroplane wing has given way to the delta wing, or a variable geometric (which can adapt to different speeds). Also, the aerodynamic shape of the fuselage (body of the aircraft) has become increasingly important.

Supersonic speed

Passenger aircraft liners fly at an average speed of 800-850 kilometres an hour (km/h).

Those which can fly at a speed which is faster than sound are called supersonic aircraft. Their speed is measured in Mach. Mach 1 equals the speed of sound, which is about 1050 km/h.

The fastest civil aircraft in the world is Concorde, which flies at a cruising speed of 2330 km/h (Mach 2.2). The fastest military jet aircraft in the world is the Lockeed SR 71, which flies at a speed of Mach 3.5.

An aerodynamic shape is one which penetrates easily through the air and the air flows quickly over its surface.

Air and combustion

It was only at the end of the 17th century that scientists found that the air is made up of many gases. By observing a flame with a limited quantity of air to use up, they discovered the different ways in which each of the gases in the air plays its part in the process of combustion (or burning). When you light a fire, it will burn more if air is blown on to it. But if you blow on the flame of a candle, it will go out! In these pages you will discover more about the conditions in which things burn, experiment with the features of gases which make up the air and find out where these gases come from.

What is in the air?

USING UP AIR

You need:
- a soup plate
- a candle
- a clear glass jar which is taller than the candle
- water
- ink
- a match
- modelling clay

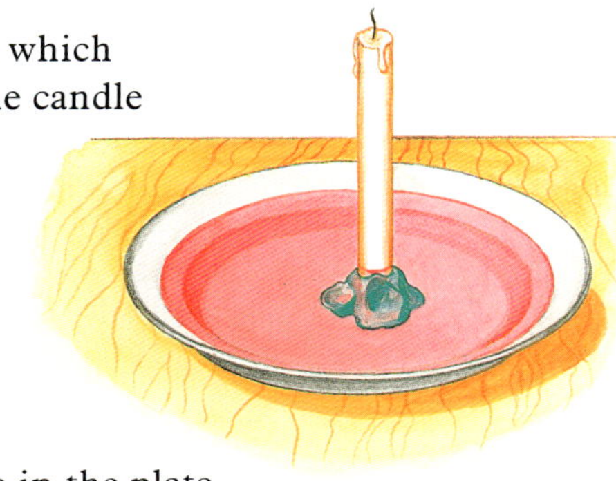

What to do

1 Fix the candle in the plate with a little modelling clay.

2 Pour a little water into the plate. Add a few drops of ink so that the water is easier to see.

3 Ask an adult to light the candle. Then cover it with the glass jar.

What happens?
After a few moments, the flame goes out and the water from the plate rises up into the jar, taking up about a fifth of the space.

Because...
... the candle, as it burns, uses up one part of air, called oxygen. The water, pushed up by the pressure of the air outside, enters into the jar, taking up the space left by the oxygen. But it cannot fill the jar completely because the rest of the air, which is mostly nitrogen, still takes up space inside.

The components of air

Air consists of oxygen (21%), nitrogen (78%), water vapour, carbon dioxide and other gases. Nitrogen is an inert (non-moving) gas which plays no part in the process of combustion.

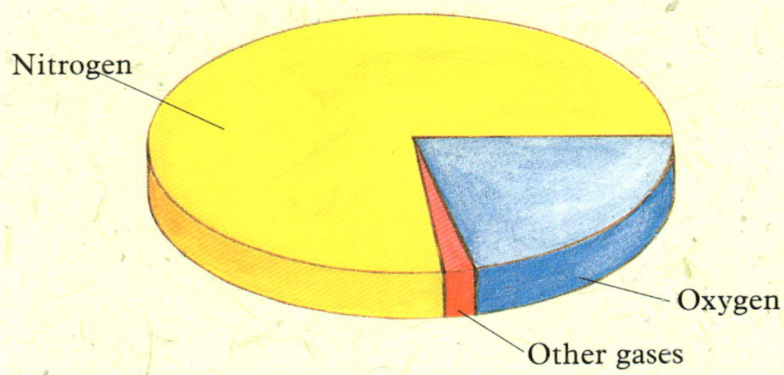

Combustion

When something burns, this demonstrates a chemical reaction which is called combustion. Combustion can only happen with three things present – heat, fuel and the combustive agent. If one of these is missing, the flame goes out. When we light a candle with a match, we produce the heat which is necessary so that the oxygen (the combustive agent) burns the wax (fuel) which covers the wick. By blowing on the flame, we take away the heat of the combustive agent, so that the combustion is interrupted. This does not happen with a fire in the hearth, because the air which can be blown on it does not have the power to blow it out. Instead the air feeds the flames with more oxygen, making the fire burn more.

Air is a mixture of gases: of these, oxygen and nitrogen have the largest share.

How is oxygen and carbon dioxide made?

A PLANT AT WORK

You need:

- a few sprigs of a water plant
- a bowl
- a clear glass jar or vase
- water

What to do

1 Fill the bowl with water.

2 Place the sprigs in the jar then fill this with water.

3 Cover the mouth of the jar with a card. Keeping your hand on the card, carefully turn the jar upside down, and lower gently into the bowl.

4 Place the bowl in sunlight. Remove the card carefully.

What happens?

Little bubbles of air (these are full of oxygen) collect on the leaves. The bubbles rise to the surface.

Because...

... the leaves of the water plant, just like plants on the ground, release oxygen in the presence of sunlight. Oxygen is invisible, but we can see the leaves releasing it under water.

Photosynthesis

Plants are able make all the nutrients that they need for growth from the Sun. They absorb sunlight and carbon dioxide which, together with water and chlorophyll (the substance which gives plants their green colour), they produce oxygen and glucose, the sugar which constitutes their food. This process is called photosynthesis, and happens during the day. By night, plants absorb oxygen. Without plants, no human or animal life would be possible.

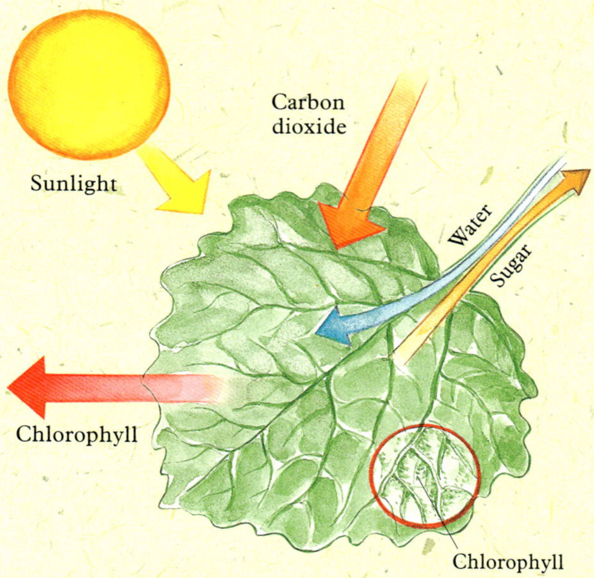

Why do we breathe?

When we breathe in, we introduce into our bodies air which contains oxygen. Our lungs pass the oxygen into the blood, where it is used for the chemical reaction of combustion of food. The waste substance produced by this process is carbon dioxide, which we get rid of when we breathe out. Plants then use carbon dioxide in their photosynthesis. Oxygen and carbon dioxide continue to be breathed in and out for as long as we live.

A CARBON DIOXIDE EXTINGUISHER

You need:
- a plate
- a glass
- a match
- a candle
- a teaspoon
- vinegar
- bicarbonate of soda
- a cardboard tube
- modelling clay

What to do

1 Fix the candle on to the plate with a piece of clay. Ask an adult to light the candle.

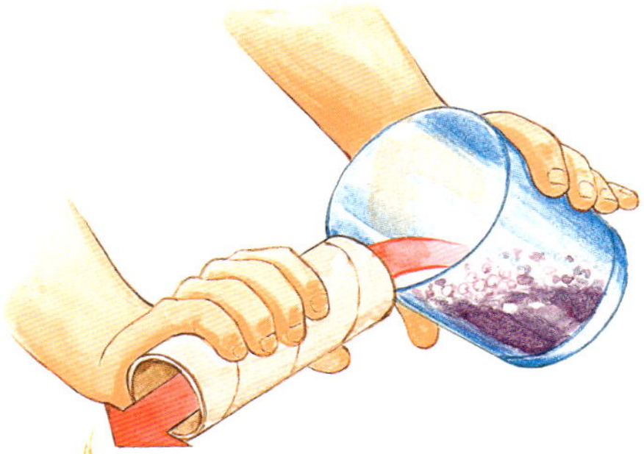

2 Hold three fingers against the glass and pour in this measure of vinegar. Add one teaspoon bicarbonate of soda.

3 When bubbles of gas form in the glass, hold the cardboard tube a short distance from the flame (be careful not to hold it too near!) Tip the glass slowly against the tube, as if you were pouring air from the glass into the tube.

What happens?
The flame goes out.

Because...
... the bubbles of gas which you saw forming when the bicarbonate of soda and the vinegar were mixed together are carbon dioxide. This gas is heavier than the air and so goes down along the tube and on to the flame, taking away the oxygen and so interrupting the combustion. Fire extinguishers used to put out other types of fires, such as those arising from faulty electrical appliances, contain carbon dioxide.

Carbon dioxide in food and drink

The holes which we see in some cheeses are caused by carbon dioxide which develops as milk curdles and becomes sour. The spongy appearance of bread is due to the bubbles of carbon dioxide which develops as yeast makes the dough rise. Carbon dioxide can be used to make drinks fizzy. In its solid state, as dry ice, it keeps foodstuffs and other things cold. If ever you try putting dry ice in water, you will see it giving off a strange sort of mist and making lots of bubbles...

Oxygen is produced by plants. Carbon dioxide is mostly breathed out by humans and animals.

Sounds

Our life is surrounded by sounds and noises which help us to understand what is going on around us. They are 'de-coded' by the brain, even if we can see what has made the noise. Sounds are produced by objects which vibrate. If you place a hand on your throat whilst you are speaking, you will feel the vibration of your vocal chords. But how can sounds reach our ears? And what is needed to make sounds spread?

How do sounds spread?

SEE SOUND

You need:
- a sheet of plastic (cut from a carrier bag)
- an elastic band
- a plastic bowl
- a saucepan
- a wooden mixing spoon
- coarse grain salt or rice

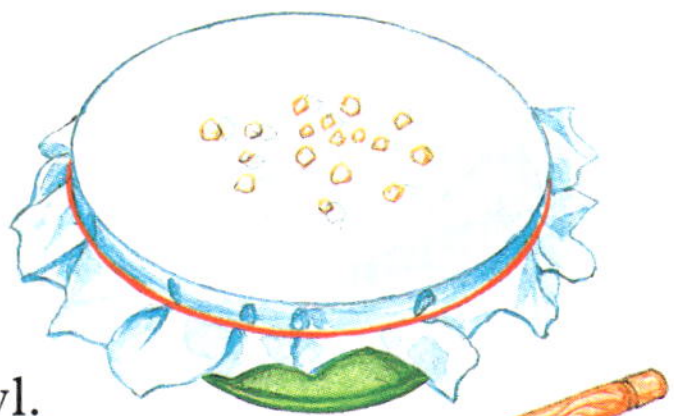

What to do

1 Put the plastic sheet over the top of the bowl. Keep in place with the elastic band so that the plastic is tightly stretched.

2 Place the salt or the rice on the plastic.

3 Hold the saucepan near the plastic bowl (but not close enough to touch) and hit it a few times with the wooden spoon.

What happens?
The grains of salt or rice jump about.

Because...
... when the saucepan is hit, it makes a noise which vibrates. This makes the air around it vibrate as well, producing sound-waves. When these waves hit the bowl, the bowl vibrates and makes the salt or the rice jump about.

How do we hear sounds?

The human ear is the ideal shape to receive sound-waves and carry these to the eardrum. The eardrum is a highly sensitive membrane (thin skin). It vibrates as the sound-wave reaches it, and these vibrations pass to the liquid inside the cochlea in the inner ear. From here the sound 'messages' are sent along the auditory nerve to the brain, which then 'de-codes' them, so that we hear.

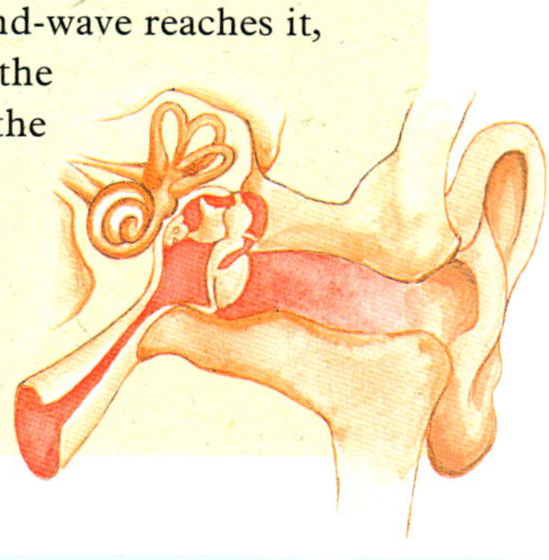

SEE VIBRATIONS

You need:
- a broom handle
- six ping-pong balls
- six pieces of string, each 50cm long
- two chairs
- sticky tape

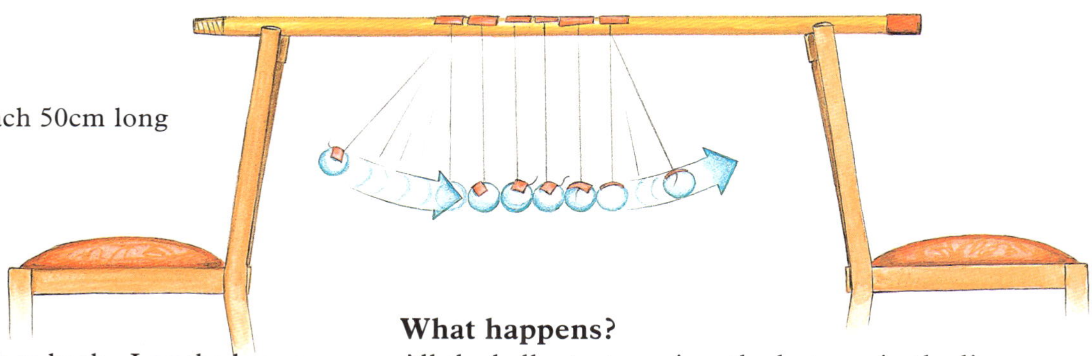

What to do

1 Place the chairs back to back. Lay the broom handle across the backs of the chairs.

2 Fix a ping-pong ball on each length of string with the sticky tape. Then tape the loose end of each piece of string to the broom handle, so that each ping-pong ball will touch the one on either side.

3 Pull back the first ping-pong ball, so that the string is tightly stretched. Then, let go, so that the ball will touch the next one.

What happens?

All the balls start moving, the last one in the line swinging as far out as the first.

Because...

... the first ball passes on the movement to the second, which transmits the movement to the third, and so on. Air molecules which are hit by sound vibrations behave in the same way. Vibrations from an object spread into the air around it. These vibrations are then transmitted from one layer of air to another, due to the way a sound-wave can curve and bend.

Sounds spread and reach our ear through air which vibrates.

Are sounds transmitted only through the air?

LIKE A TOM-TOM

You need:
- a wrist watch (not digital)
- a table

What to do

1 Hold the watch to your ear and listen to the ticking. Then gradually move it away until you can no longer hear the sound.

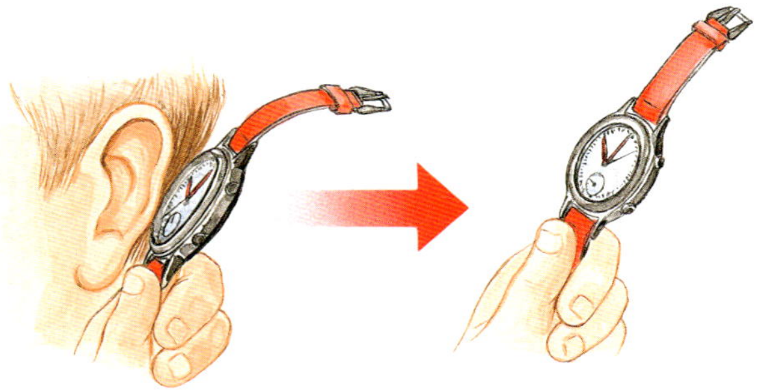

2 Place the watch on the table. Put your ear on the table at the same distance which you measured first.

What happens?
The ticking of the watch is distinctly heard by your ear.

Because...
... sounds are better transmitted through solids than through the air. Sounds also travel easily through bricks and glass. That is why sounds can be heard through walls and windows.

Sounds in water

Sounds under water seem louder. When you swim on your back and your ears are under the surface of the water, you will hear the sound of your breathing amplified (louder); if you try to beat two stones in water you will hear the sound they make very strongly. In water the speed of sound is almost five times more than in the air!

At different speeds

In the air, sound travels at 340 metres per second, whilst, in the same second, sound travels 1500 metres through water, 5000 metres through steel, 4800 metres through iron. In one second, light travels a good 300,000 kilometres: that is why during a storm we first see the lightning and then hear the thunder.

Sounds can also be transmitted through solids and liquids more quickly than through the air.

How do string instruments work?

ELASTIC BAND SOUNDS

You need:
- an aluminium dish
- elastic bands of various thicknesses
- two pens

What to do

1 Put the elastic bands around the length of the dish at about 1cm between each one. Try making some sounds by plucking them.

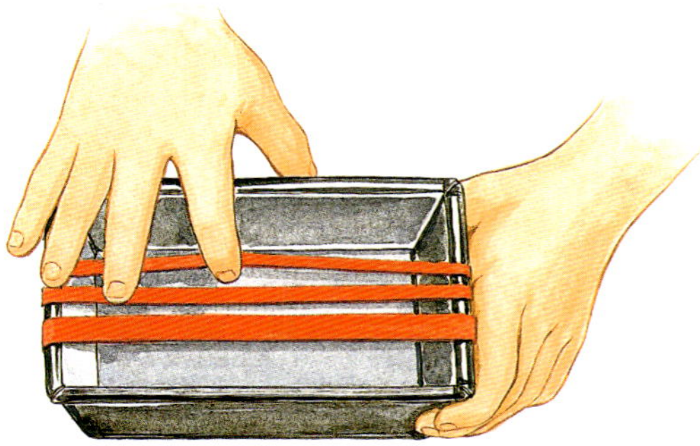

2 Now insert the two pens under the elastic bands, one at each end of the dish. Pluck the elastic bands again.

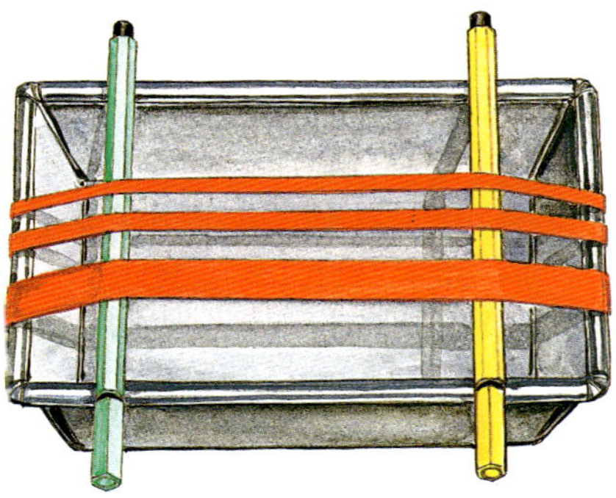

What happens?
When you plucked the elastic bands the first time, the sounds you heard were rather flat and not very clear. The second time, the sounds were much clearer.

Because...
... the first time, the vibrations of the elastic bands were obstructed by the bands rubbing against the edges of the dish. But the pens acted like the bridge of a guitar, keeping the elastic bands raised up, so that they vibrated more easily. The bands produced vibrations by resonating the air in the dish, making sounds which were clearer and deeper. The effect of resonation is also used by instruments such as violins, mandolins and pianos, all of which have a space which resonates with vibrating sound.

Dangerous resonation

The two prongs of a tuning form produce the same note by making the same number of vibrations at the same time. If you were to vibrate only one prong, after a little while the other would also vibrate, struck by vibrations in the air produced by the first prong, and vibrating in sympathy. The second prong will resonate with the first.
Each object which is able to vibrate has a natural frequency which is set in motion when the object is struck by a sound-wave which has the same vibration frequency.
A bridge may collapse if the oscillations (vibrations) of a wind, or from the movement of people and transport across it are equal to the vibrations which the bridge makes on its own. If this happens, all the vibrations resonate together at the same frequency, putting the whole structure in serious danger.

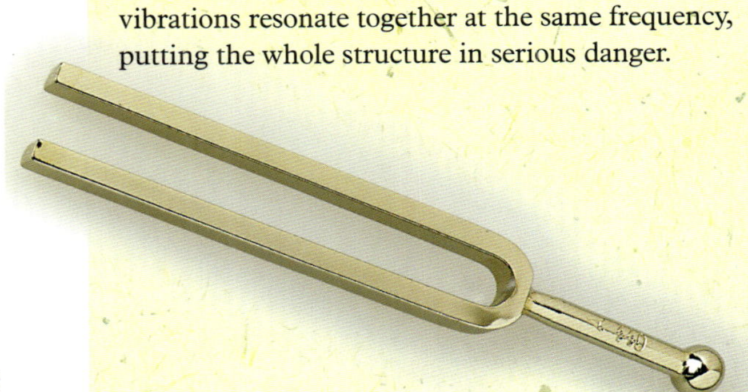

Instruments with strings have a space for resonation, in which the air vibrates, amplifying the sound.

Fact-Finder

Weather stations

Forecasting the changes in weather has always been very important, especially for agriculture, shipping and aviation.Daily weather predictions are easily available and people follow forecasts on television and radio to help plan their work and their travel. Technology means that weather forecasting is increasingly more detailed and almost entirely accurate up to five days ahead. This is because there are about 9000 weather stations all over the world, and approximately 800 above the Earth's surface, all sending and receiving data sent from special aircraft and ships, meteorological balloons and satellites in space which photograph the movement of the masses of air and take note of the temperature from these. This information is then analysed by special computers which can then forecast possible developments.

The hemispheres of Magdeburgo

In the seventeeth century a physicist from Magdeburo in Germany, Otto von Guericke, used a special pump to remove all the air from a copper container which had been made in two halves. Due to a total lack of air pressure from the empty interior, the pressure on the external walls united the two halves with such strength that eight horses attached to each half could not separate them.

Man and flight: important stages

1783 – in France the first manned flight, a hydrogen-filled balloon with two men on board. A hot-air balloon is often called a 'Montgolfier', the name of its inventors.

1852 – French aviator Henri Giffard built and piloted a dirigible (airship) powered by a propeller which was activated by a steam engine: a non-rigid airship has a floppy covering which keeps its shape because of the gas (hydrogen or helium) inside it.

1900 – German inventor Graf von Zeppelin built the first rigid airship.

1903 – in North Carolina, USA the Wright brothers Orville and Wilbur built the first aeroplane powered by a petrol engine. It flew for 59 seconds.

1927 – American Charles Lindberg completed the first non-stop transatlantic flight in 33 hours and 29 minutes in a single-engine monoplane.

1931 – two American pilots, Post and Gatty, completed a round-the-world flight in a single-engine aircraft.

1939 – Russian-born engineer Igor Sirkorsky designed the first helicopter.

1952 – an American military helicopter completed a transatlantic flight in 42 hours.

1957 – the military aircraft Boeing B52 completed the first non-stop round-the-world flight in 45 hours and 19 minutes.

1976 – supersonic aircraft Concorde, built by the French and English, linked London and Paris with Washington in 3 hours, 35 minutes.

Torricelli's barometer

It was the Italian scientist Evangelista Torricelli who discovered in 1643 the true meaning of air pressure. He filled a glass tube closed at one end with mercury. Then he turned the tube upside down, closing the other end with his finger and immersed the tube in a vase with other mercury. When he removed his finger the mercury rose to 76cm, then stopped: at that moment the external atmospheric pressure which was pressing on the vase was the same as that inside the tube which held the mercury. Since the weight of 76cm of mercury was 1.033kg and the tube had a base of 1 square centimetre, Torricelli estimated that the atmosphere exerted a pressure of just over one kilogram for each square centimetre surface (1kg = 1 cm square). The instrument invented by Torricelli to measure air pressure is called a barometer.

Water

How does water move? Why are drops of water round? Why do some things float and not others? Why does it rain? What happens to a substance when it dissolves in water? Find the answers to these and many more questions by doing the experiments in the following pages, under these headings:

The force of water • The surface tension of water
To float or not to float? • The transformation of water
Water solutions

The force of water

Water, like all liquids, has no shape. It can occupy any space which is available.

It can flow downwards, drawn by the force of gravity, and when water falls, the force is so strong that this power can be converted into electrical energy.

Yet, delicately and slowly, water can also to rise up through the stem of a plant, keeping it alive.

The following experiments demonstrate many other features of water – the way it can seep through substances, its force of pressure and the way it moves when it becomes warm.

How can water move?

WATER RISING UP

You need:
- a stick of celery complete with leaves, about 20cm long
- a glass jar
- water
- blue or red ink

What to do

1 Put water in the jar. Colour the water with a few drops of ink.

2 Put the celery in the coloured water. Then put the whole thing somewhere warm.

What happens?
After a few hours the stick of celery and its leaves take on the same colour as the ink.

Because...
... if you cut the celery, you will see that the ribs are like little tubes. The water has risen up through these narrow tubes and into the leaves, as if drawn towards the top. This is called capillary action. This is how plants absorb water from the ground through their roots, with the water rising up until it reaches the ends of its leaves. White flowers can sometimes be coloured in the same way.

FLOWERS WHICH FLOAT ON WATER

You need:
- a sheet of paper
- coloured pencils
- scissors
- a soup plate with some water in it

What to do

1 Draw the shape as you see in the picture. Colour it in, then cut out.

2 Fold the ‘petals’ inwards along the dotted lines, as shown.

3 Place the paper flower on the water very carefully.

What happens?
Slowly, the flower opens.

Because...
... the water penetrates by capillary action into the little empty spaces between the fibres of the paper. This makes the fibres swell, including those along the folds. This swelling makes the lines unfold, and so the flower opens out.

Water not only moves downward, it can also rise up by means of capillary action.

Can you increase the force of water?

THE WEIGHT OF WATER

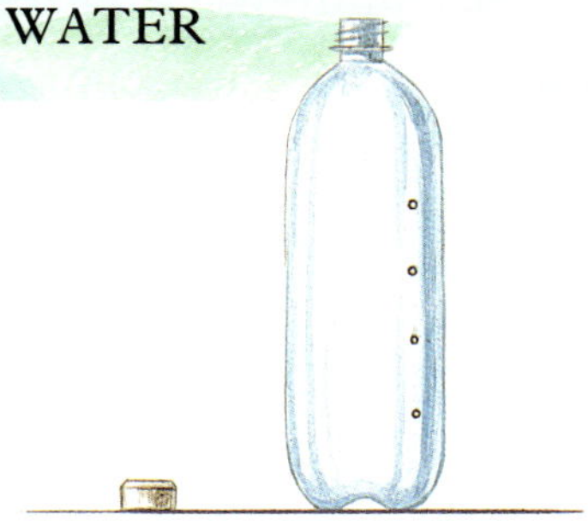

You need:
- two plastic bottles
- one nail
- sticky tape
- water

What to do

1 Using the nail, pierce a vertical line of holes on one bottle. Pierce a horizontal line of holes on the other bottle, as shown in the picture. (Do this with the help of an adult.)

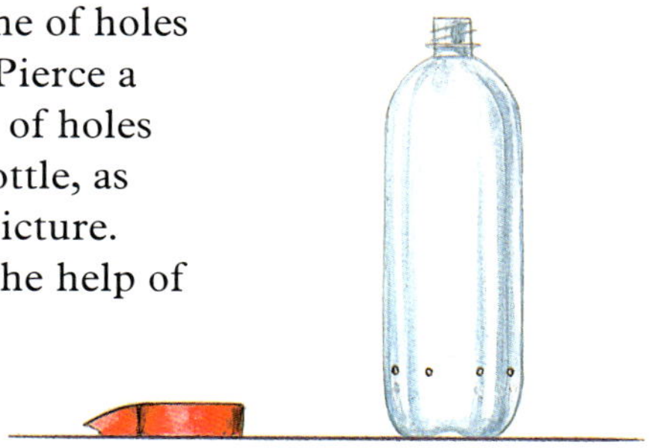

2 Cover both bottles with sticky tape.

3 Fill the bottles with water. Remove the tape first from one bottle, then the other.

What happens?

Water spurts out at an equal distance all around the bottle with holes in a horizontal line. But, from the bottle with the holes in a vertical line, water spurts out at different distances. The nearer the base of the bottle, the greater the distance.

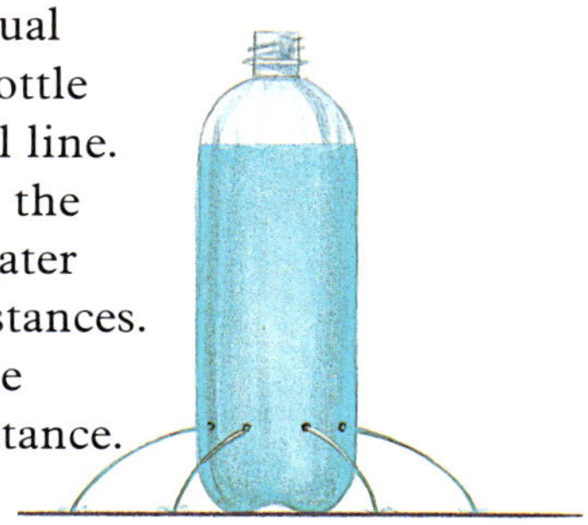

Because...

... the water weighs heavily against the inside of the bottles, and so it escapes through the holes with considerable force. This force is stronger where a lot of water weighs against the inside of the bottle (or where the water is deepest) and so the spurt here is longer.

Deep Sea Exploration

A bathyscaphe is a submersible (underwater vessel) which is used for exploration and research at great depths of the oceans. The hull of the bathyscaphe houses the engine and the tanks. As the bathyscaphe dives, these tanks are gradually filled with water to balance the internal pressure with the external pressure of the waters. Beneath the hull is a sphere of steel, strong enough to withstand the pressure of the waters at great depths. This sphere is for the crew and their observation instruments. In 1960, Jacques Piccard (son of Auguste Piccard who invented the bathyscaphe) and Lt. Don Walsh of the US Navy went 11,022 metres (35,800 feet) in the bathyscaphe Trieste III to the sea bed of the Pacific Ocean, as deep as it is possible to go.

A SIMPLE FOUNTAIN

You need:
- a plastic tube
- sticky tape
- the glass (or plastic) part of an 'eye-dropper'
- a funnel
- water

What to do

1 Using the sticky tape, bind the funnel to one end of the plastic tube and the dropper at the other.

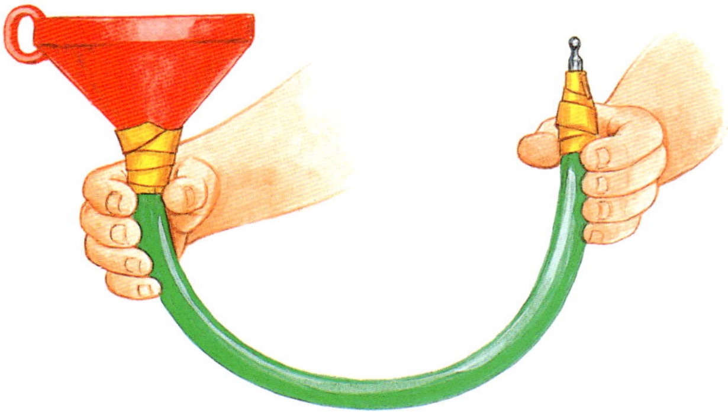

2 Close the opening of the dropper with your finger and fill the tube with water through the funnel. (Work over a sink.)

3 Lower the end with the dropper and take away your finger.

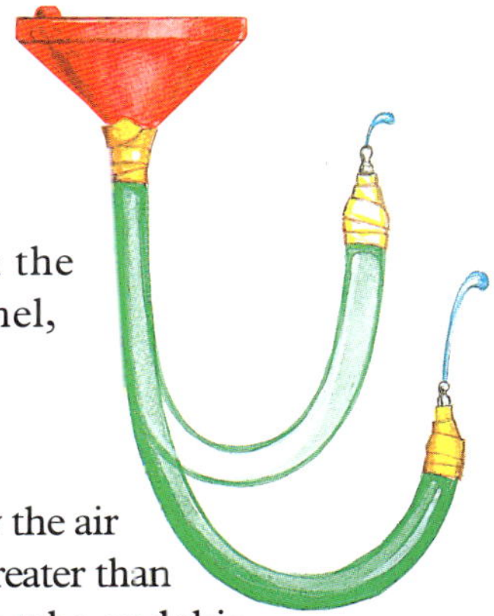

What happens?
A spurt of water escapes from the dropper. The higher the funnel, the higher the spurt of water.

Because...
... the force of pressure exerted by the air on the opening of the funnel is greater than the weight of the water inside the tube, and this produces an upward jet. Raising the funnel makes the spurt of water higher, because the water in the tube is falling from a greater height. Raising an object's height above the Earth's surface gives that object additional potential energy.

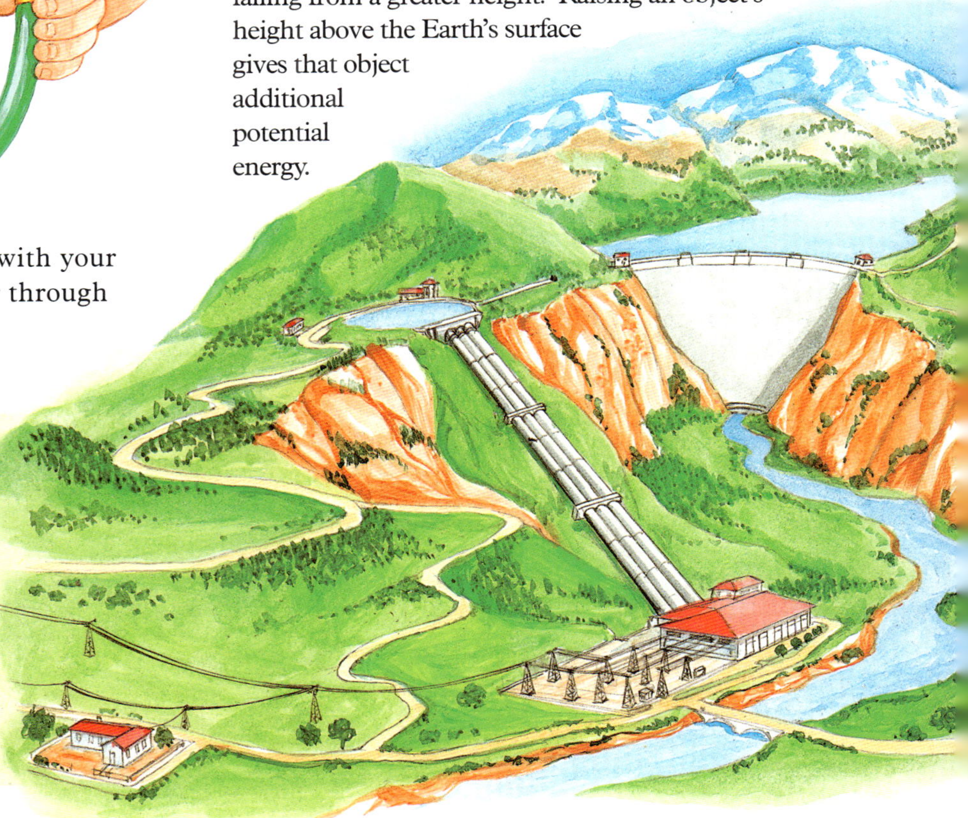

The natural force of water

The energy of water has been used for centuries to drive watermills. This energy may be by water falling from a height or by water flowing below. The power from the force of water falling from mountain zones is used by hydroelectric stations to produce electrical power.

Water subjected to the pressure of other water or air adds to the strength of its force.

Why does heat make water move about?

WATER AND HEAT

You need:

- a see-through bowl or basin
- a little glass jar with a lid
- coloured ink
- water

What to do

1 Fill the bowl or basin with cold water.

2 Put a few drops of ink in the jar and fill with hot (not boiling) water.
(Ask an adult to do this for you.)
Then put the lid on.

3 Immerse the jar in the cold water and put it on the bottom of the bowl or basin.
Remove the lid.

What happens?

The coloured water escapes into the bowl or basin and rises up, spreading out towards the surface. After a few moments it begins to descend and to mix with the rest of the water.

Because...

... like all matter, water is made up of tiny, moving particles called molecules. Heat speeds up the movement of the molecules, and they move away from each other. As they spread out, they become less dense (less tightly packed together) and so lighter. That is why the coloured hot water 'floats' on the cold water. As the heat spreads and the coloured water begins to reach the same temperature as the cold, so it descends and begins to mix with the rest of the water.

How water heats up in a saucepan

Saucepans are generally made of aluminium or steel. Aluminium and steel are good conductors of heat, both containing and giving out heat. So, the saucepan heats up on contact with heat and heats up the water at the bottom. The heated water rises up, colder water takes its place, and this too gets hot and rises up. These movements of rising and falling allows the heat to spread through all the water in the saucepan. We call these movements 'convection'. In the air, heat moves around in the same way.

Why does the underwater diver use a wet suit?

Water, like air, is not a good conductor of heat. It cannot contain heat nor can it give off heat. The diver's wet suit creates a layer of water which prevents water coming in contact with the skin, so that the body heat is not lost. Also, the wet suit is made with insulating material. This is material which both keeps the heat in and helps it to spread.

Sea currents

Sailors travel continually through warm and cold currents. These are streams which run through sea waters and affect the state of the oceans and the whole Earth. These currents are generated by winds and the difference in temperature and salt content. Currents of cold water (which is more dense and heavier) and which come from the seas at the North and South Poles flow at the lowest depths of the oceans. Currents of warm waters (lighter and less dense) come from tropical and equatorial seas and flow more towards the surface of the oceans. The currents mix with the sea water, carrying oxygen to the deepest regions and evenly distributing the mineral salts to the living things under the sea. They also affect the climate and change the temperatures along the coasts on which they lap. For example, the warm Gulf Current comes from the Caribbean seas and towards Europe, where it warms the climates of the oceanic coasts. The cold currents from Labrador in Northern Canada cools the Atlantic coasts of the United States, bringing very harsh winters.

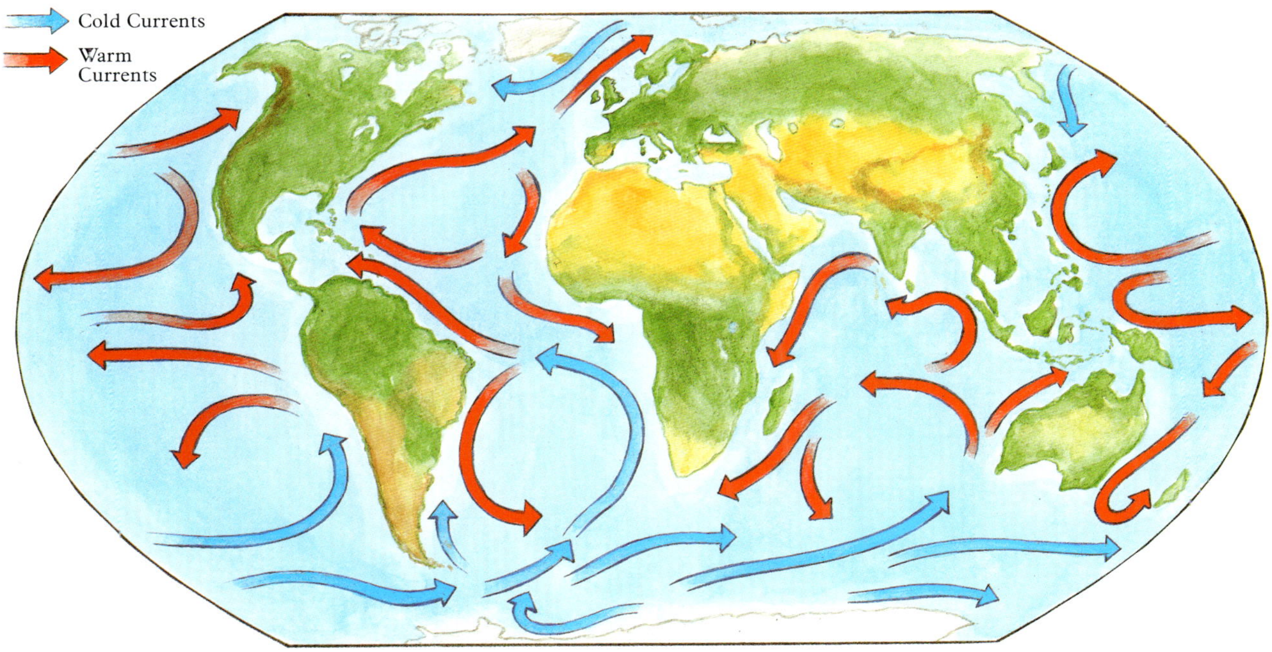

When heat spreads in water, it becomes light and will rise up in cold water.

The surface tension of water

Water is fluid; it can be poured and you can make things sink into it. Its molecules can make water move, but they do not separate completely because they are constantly attracted to each other.

The molecules on the surface of the water, not having other molecules to attract from above, bind together more strongly. It is this surface tension which makes it possible for some creatures to walk on water – and for us to make soap bubbles.

Why are drops of water round?

SUSPENDED ON WATER

You need:
- tweezers
- a needle
- a glass
- water

What to do

1 Fill the glass with water up to the brim.

2 Take the needle with the tweezers and let it down very gently on the surface of the water.

What happens?
The needle floats (you may find that the needle sinks to the bottom. Try again. It is very important to place it slowly and horizontally.)

Because...
... the molecules of water on the surface form a sort of film which is able to support a light object. This force which keeps the molecules together is called surface tension. When you fill the glass to the brim, look closely at the surface of the water. Above the brim, it bends slightly into a curve. This curve is the surface tension, pulling tightly to contain the water like a bag. So if there is only a little water, the surface tension will make it form into a round drop.

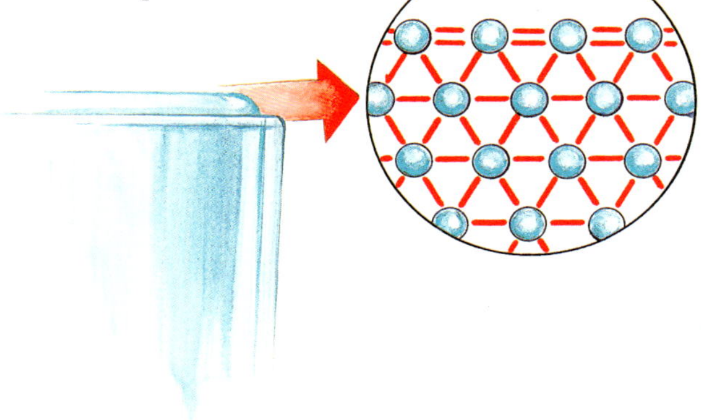

A BARRIER OF MATERIAL

You need:
- a handkerchief
- an elastic band
- a glass
- water

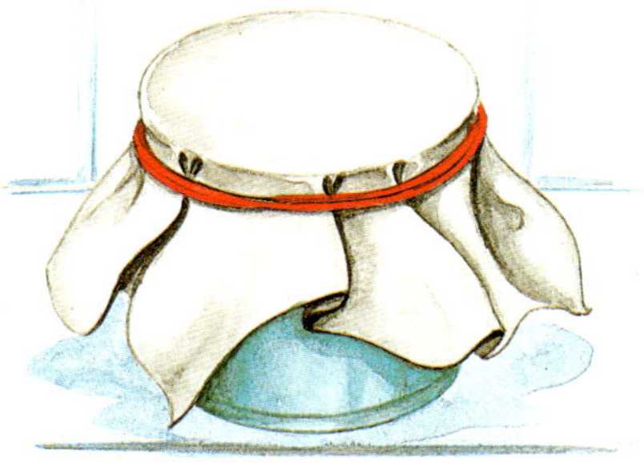

What to do

1 Put the handkerchief in water. Then wring it out.

2 Fill the glass with water.

3 Place the handkerchief over the glass. Stretch tightly and keep in place with the elastic band.

4 Quickly turn the glass upside down. (Work over a sink.)

What happens?
The water remains blocked in the glass, as if the handkerchief were waterproof.

Because...
... when you dampened the handkerchief, the water filled up the little spaces between the fibres of the material. Because of the surface tension, this creates a tight barrier through which the water cannot penetrate. Wet hairs clinging together in locks and damp sand which can be modelled without cracking are other examples of water binding fibres and particles together by filling up the spaces in between.

Walking on water

The water stick insect and pond-skater are small pond-dwelling insects. Their long, soft legs are coated with hair, so that they can jump or slide on the surface of the water in search of their prey without slipping. Under their feet, the 'skin' of the surface tension of the water bends inward, but this is strong enough to support the insect without breaking.

The surface tension of the water creates a membrane which can contain a small quantity in a little, round drop.

How does soap act in water?

HOLES IN WATER

You need:
- talcum powder
- water
- liquid soap
- a sink or a bowl

What to do

1 Fill the sink or basin with water.

2 Sprinkle the talcum powder on the surface of the water.

3 Dip your finger into the water here and there, as if you were making holes in it.

What happens?
The talcum powder shows up the surface tension of the water. So, as soon as your finger pierces the surface tension, you can see the 'hole' closing again.

Because...
... the surface tension is a strong force. It is broken only momentarily when you pierce it with your finger.

4 Now put a drop of liquid soap on your finger. (Take care: do this away from the sink to avoid soap getting into the water). Then put the soapy finger into the water, close to the edge of the sink.

5 Make holes in the talcum-powdered water with the soapy finger.

What happens?
The first time you dip in your soapy finger, the talcum powder moves away. But the next time you dip it into the talcum powder surface, your finger leaves 'holes'.

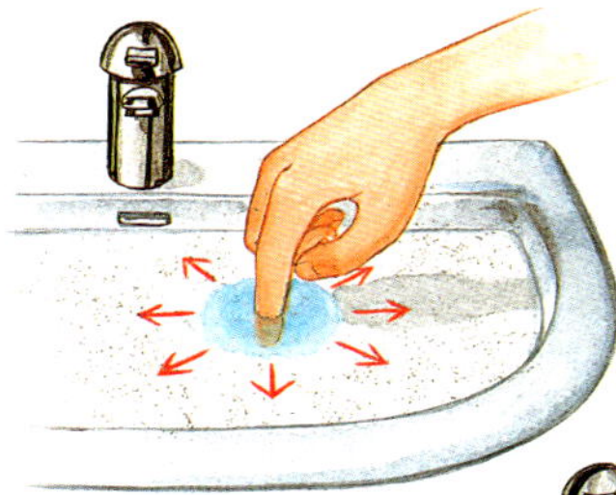

Because...
... the soap loosens the tension at the place where you dip your finger. On the rest of the surface, the tension is stronger and so this attracts and holds back the talcum powder. The holes left by the soapy finger do not close again, because in these places the soap prevents the water molecules from joining up together again. So the 'surface skin' cannot regain its unbroken state. If you want to repeat the experiment, you will need to change the water.

A SOAP BOAT

You need:
- a basin or a sink
- a piece of card
- scissors
- liquid soap
- water

What to do

1 Fill the basin or sink with water.

2 Cut a triangle shape from the card. When the water is still, place the cardboard triangle in a corner of the basin or sink, pointing towards the centre.

3 Put a little soap on the tip of one finger. (Do this away from the sink.) Then put the soapy finger in the water, behind your cardboard 'boat'.

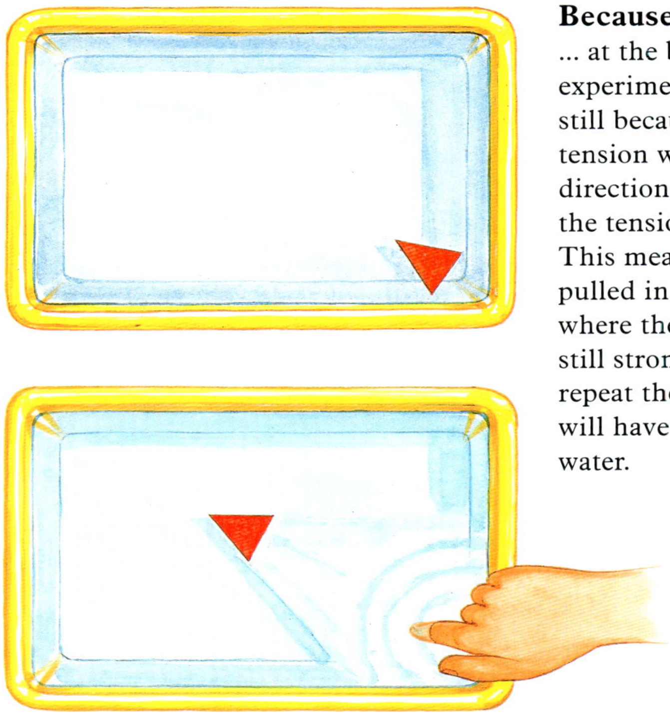

What happens?
The boat shoots forward towards the opposite side of the basin or sink.

Because...
... at the beginning of the experiment, the boat stayed still because the surface tension was pulling it in all directions. The soap lessens the tension behind the boat. This means that the boat is pulled in front, into the area where the surface tension is still strong. If you want to repeat the experiment, you will have to change the water.

How soap works

Water alone is not able to remove the dirt from clothes, plates or the skin, especially if the dirt is greasy. There are two main types of molecules in detergents – those which attract and cling on to the small particles of dirt and those which dissolve in the water, stopping the water molecules from coming together. This is how the detergent breaks up the dirt and removes it from the object being washed. Then it spreads the dirt out into the water, ready to be drained away.

Soap diminishes the force which keeps the water molecules together.

How are soap bubbles made?

CONCENTRIC DOMES

You need:

- liquid for soap bubbles (it is best if you keep this in the refrigerator for about an hour)
- a drinking straw
- a smooth surface to work on (something like glass, plastic or steel)

What to do

1 Moisten the work surface.

2 Dip the straw in the soap. Blow a bubble and slowly place this on the surface: the bubble will become a dome.

3 Dip the straw in the soap again, and also wet the outside with the soap. Insert the straw very carefully into the first dome and blow gently to form a second dome.

4 Make a third dome in the same way. (Work very carefully, so that each new dome does not touch the one which you made before.)

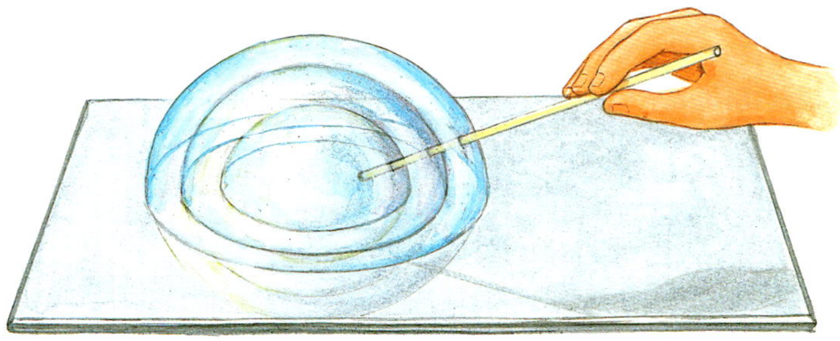

What happens?

Each bubble positions itself at the centre of the dome made before, and it makes the others grow bigger.

Because...

... there is air inside the bubbles. The introduction of a new bubble moves the air from the one before, which grows larger because of the elasticity provided by the soap. The more you try this experiment, the more different structures you will find you can create by placing the bubbles on the surface and seeing how much your bubble mix can expand.

Recipes for soap bubbles

To make lasting bubbles, you could try one of these recipes. Which one is the best?

❍ 600g water + 200g washing-up liquid + 100g glycerine

❍ 600g hot distilled water + 300g glycerine + 50g detergent powder + 50g ammonia. The liquid must rest for a few days, then needs to be filtered and kept in a refrigerator for 12 hours before use.

❍ 300g water + 300g washing-up liquid + 2 teaspoons sugar

❍ 4 tablespoons grated or flaked toilet soap in 400g hot water (better still if the soap can be dissolved in water over a source of heat). Leave the liquid for a week, then add two teaspoons of sugar.

BOUNCING BUBBLES

You need:

- something made of wool (a jumper or scarf)
- soap bubble liquid (best if you chill this in the refrigerator)
- straw
- a ping-pong bat (you can also use a little tray or a hard-back book)

What to do

1 Wrap the woolly around the bat.

2 Blow a bubble, so that it lands on the woolly.

3 Gently move the bat to bounce the bubble.

What happens?
The bubble lies on the wool without changing shape or breaking, and bounces!

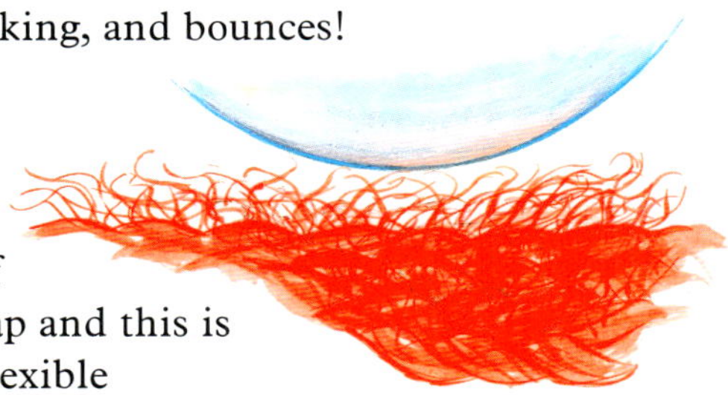

Because...
... the surface of the bubble is made up of water and soap and this is sufficiently flexible ('bendable') to land on the woollen, remaining suspended on it without breaking. If you want to play this game on a cold day, try taking your bat and wool outside with the bubble. The bubble will freeze and look like a crystal.

Are cube-shaped bubbles possible?

The tension 'skin' which soap makes for a bubble will stretch as far as it can. But this skin always wants to close up into a shape where the volume of air is less on the inside than on the outside surface – a sphere. So bubbles of other shapes cannot be blown naturally. But more unusual bubbles can be created using a piece of wire. If the soap solution is flexible enough, it may be possible to make soap bubble cubes or pyramids.

Soap reduces the surface tension of water, thus allowing the air inside to expand.

To float or not to float?

Swimmers know the feeling of weightlessness when they move or float in the water. But weightlessness is not just a sensation, it is a reality. Water supports solid objects, cancelling out some of their weight.

The following experiments show what is needed for an object to float, and how it is that some very heavy objects such as ocean-going ships keep afloat.

Why do things seem to weigh less in water?

WHAT THE DYNAMOMETER REVEALS

You need:
- a dynamometer (an instrument for measuring force)
- an apple
- thin string
- a deep bowl
- water
- pen and paper

What to do

1 Tie one end of the string to the stalk of the apple and the other end to the dynamometer. Write down how much the apple weighs.

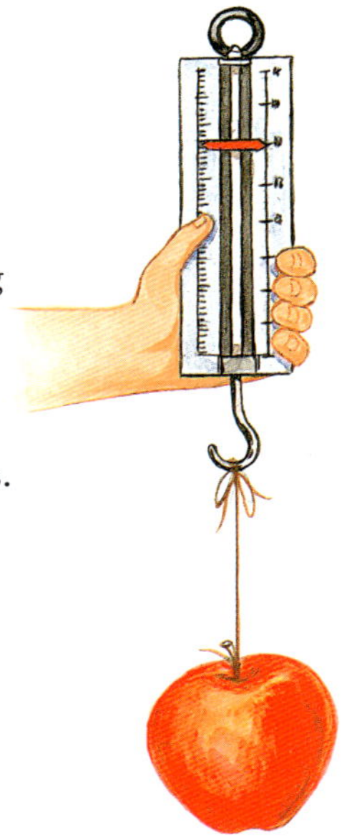

2 Fill the bowl with water.

3 Immerse the apple in water without taking it off the dynamometer. Write down how much it weighs now.

What happens?
When the apple is in the water, the dynamometer shows a lower weight.

Because...
... when the apple is immersed, it moves a certain amount of water. This water it moves tries to take up its position again, and presses against the apple, pushing it up towards the top. This push is called displacement and is the same as the weight of the water which the apple has moved. So if an object weighing 500g is immersed and moves 200g of water, it gets a push towards the top which diminishes its weight by 200g. Therefore, when immersed, that object will show a weight of 300g.

The Archimedes Principle

Have you noticed that when you get into the bath, the level of the water rises? This simple fact is said to be the inspiration for the Greek scientist Archimedes, who lived in Syracuse in the third century A.D. After noting the rising of his bath-water, he carried out many experiments, not only with water but also with other liquids to prove his theory of the displacement of water and establish the Archimedes Principle (or, the rule of Archimedes). This rule states that an object immersed in liquid is given a upward thrust, which is equal to the weight of the liquid which the object has moved.

Objects in water get an upward thrust which is equal to the weight of the water displaced by the object.

Why do some things float and not others?

A QUESTION OF SHAPE

You need:
- modelling clay
- a saucepan with a lid
- a bowl
- water

What to do

1 Fill the bowl with water.

2 Mould the modelling clay into a flat shape and place it on the water.

3 Now roll the boat-shaped clay into a ball. Place this on the water.

What happens?
The little boat settles on top. The ball sinks to the bottom.

4 Now place the saucepan lid on the water, first horizontally, then vertically.

What happens?
When horizontal, the saucepan lid floats. When it is vertical, it sinks to the bottom.

Because...
... the more water which is displaced by an object, the greater the thrust which the object gets towards the top. With the clay boat and the horizontal saucepan lid, a wide surface floats on the water, and therefore they each displace a lot of water. So they each get an upward thrust which is sufficient to keep them afloat. The clay ball and the vertical saucepan lid displaces only a little water, therefore the area which is immersed is reduced. So the thrust which they get is not enough to keep them afloat. This experiment shows that floating also depends on the shape of an object.

LIMIT OF FLOATING

You need:
- plasticene
- small objects, such as paper-clips, marbles, dice, pebbles
- a basin
- water

What to do

1 Mould the plasticene into a little tub, as you see in the picture.

2 Fill the basin with water and place the tub in the water. Make a notch on the tub to mark the level of the water.

3 Very slowly, put the objects in the tub and see if the notch becomes lower than the level of water.

What happens?
The more the tub is filled, the lower it sinks into the water.

Because...
... the tub is concave, which means it bends inward, and it contains air. When it becomes filled with objects, but keeps its same size, the tub weighs more, which means it has a greater density (density means the weight contained within a volume of space). As long as the displaced water is the same weight, which is more than the tub, the tub keeps afloat, even if it continues to sink down still more. When the weight of the tub is more than that of the water which it has displaced, the tub will sink. This experiment shows that the ability to float also depends on the density of whatever is put into the water.

Ships and submarines
Even when they are built from very dense materials, such as steel, ships do not sink because inside they have hollow areas full of air. Their density is therefore less than that of the water. Submarines are able to float and to enter into water whenever they need, by altering their density. This is done by tanks which can be filled with water for the submarine to dive into the water, then emptied when it needs to rise up to the surface again.

Which is denser, wood or iron?
A wooden marble will float when it is put in water; but an iron ball of the same size and displacing the same amount of water, sinks to the bottom. This is because iron is more dense than both the wood and the water. If the object is denser than water, it will sink, because it cannot displace more water than it weighs.

The floating of an object depends on its shape and its density.

Does gas and liquid float in water?

JUMPING MOTHBALLS

You need:
- mothballs
- vinegar
- bicarbonate of soda
- water
- a glass jar
- a spoon

What to do

1 Fill the jar with water, then add two spoons of vinegar and two bicarbonate of soda. Mix thoroughly.

2 Put the mothballs in the water. (If they feel very smooth, scratch them a little to make them rough.)

What happens?
At first, the balls go to the bottom. But after a short time, little bubbles attach themselves to the surface of the balls and they begin to rise, then descend and rise up a few times.

Because...
... the vinegar and bicarbonate of soda, mixed together, produce a gas, carbon dioxide. This is released into the water in the form of little bubbles. Like all gases, carbon dioxide is lighter than water and so it floats. When the carbon dioxide attaches itself to the mothballs, it takes them with it as it rises to the top, where it disperses into the air. At this point, the mothballs become heavy again and go to the bottom, then rise up, carried along by other bubbles of carbon dioxide.

TEST OF DENSITY

You need:
- a see-through container
- liquid honey
- linseed or corn oil
- water

What to do

1 Pour the honey and then the oil into the jar.

2 Pour in the water.

What happens?
The liquids do not mix, but separate into layers. The oil floats on the honey; the water sinks underneath the oil, but floats on the honey.

Because...
... the three liquids have different densities. The oil, which has the least density, floats on the water. But the honey settles on the bottom because this has the greatest density.

THE EFFECT OF BRINE

You need:
- table salt
- a large glass
- an egg
- a teaspoon
- a dessert spoon
- water

What to do

1 Half fill the glass with water. Then, using the dessert spoon, carefully put the egg in the water.

What happens?
The egg sinks to the bottom of the glass.

2 Take the egg out of the water. Add 10 tablespoons of table salt, and mix until it is dissolved. Now you have made brine.

A sea of oil

Whenever there are spillages of oil, this causes damage to the environment which is often impossible to clear up. Crude oil has a density which is so light that it floats on the sea. When it reaches the coast, crude oil will cover the beaches and rocks and is impossible to remove. There are substances which can be sprayed on crude oil before it reaches coasts. These force the oil to the bottom of the sea. Here, the oil will cause pollution, but the damage is less extensive than it would be on the surface.

3 Put the egg in the water once more.

What happens?
The egg floats.

4 Take the egg out of the water again. Slowly pour more water into the glass until it is full.

5 Put the egg in the water again.

What happens?
The egg remains suspended in the centre of the glass.

Because...
... the egg is more dense than the water, and so it sinks. The salt water (the brine) is more dense than clear water, and therefore makes it possible for the egg to float. In the last stage of the experiment, the clear water floats on the brine because clear water has a lesser density. So the egg stays in the middle, because it has more density than the clear water but is less dense than the brine.

There are some toys which use liquids of different densities. Because it is impossible for the two liquids shown here to mix, this produces a fascinating wave effect. In this toy, the boats have a density which is less than the blue liquid, but more than the clear liquid. This is why they remain suspended in the centre.

All substances which have a lesser density than water will float on it.

The transformation of water

Although water is a liquid, extreme cold will change it into a solid (such as ice, snow or frost). Heat will change into a gas which escapes into the air (such as steam vapour). The following pages set out the fascinating cycle of water, with experiments to demonstrate how it forms into clouds, rain or mist. Discover also what happens when water is in the air, and why windows steam up in winter.

How does heat dry something which is damp?

DISAPPEARING WATER

You need:
- two glasses, exactly the same
- a little plate
- a felt-tipped pen
- water

What to do

1 Fill the two glasses with water to the same level. Mark this level with the felt-tipped pen.

2 Cover one glass with the plate.

3 Put the two glasses near a radiator, or in direct sunlight.

What happens?
The day after, the level of water in the uncovered glass is lower. The level in the covered jar is almost the same.

Because...
... because of the heat, the water in the uncovered glass has evaporated – transformed into tiny, invisible drops of steam vapour which become absorbed into the air and 'float away'. This is how clothes which are hung up or spread out in the sun become dry. As well as heat, moving air (such as the wind or our breath) makes water evaporate. It moves the steam vapour which comes off wet objects and this makes it possible for the the air around to absorb it.

Boiling point

When water reaches 100°C, it begins to boil. Bubbles of steam form in the liquid and these escape into the air through the surface. The temperature of boiling varies with variations in pressure. In high mountains, for example, the mass of air which hangs over the Earth's surface is less, and so the atmospheric pressure is lower; therefore, water here reaches boiling point at a temperature of less than 100°C.

The strength and energy of steam

Steam takes up more space than water (1700 times as much!) Kept under pressure, steam is able to give off an enormous strength, which is able to power many machines.

The first steam engine was invented in the second half of the 18th century. Many were used to work machines in factories and made for locomotives which pulled trains. A century later, the steam engine became largely replaced by the internal combustion (petrol) engine.

Geysers

Geysers are jets of steam which come from the interior of our planet. They erupt through cracks in the Earth's surface and can reach a height of 10 metres. Their energy is called geothermal and this energy can be used to produce heat and electricity. There are many geysers throughout Iceland and in New Zealand and the United States.

The first steam locomotive was built in Great Britain at the beginning of the 19th century.

Heat makes water evaporate and disperse through the air.

Why does it rain?

RETURN TO THE LIQUID STATE

You need:
- a saucepan
- a steel lid
- a hot-plate
- water

What to do

1 Fill the saucepan with water. Ask an adult to put it on the hot-plate.

2 When the water boils, hold the lid up high in the cloud of steam which rises up from the water.

What happens?
Drops of water form under the lid.

Because...
... vapour rises up from the water as it boils and comes into contact with the cold lid. As this happens, the vapour loses heat and immediately returns to the liquid state. This phenomenon is called condensation.

Rain

With the heat of the Sun, water evaporates from lakes, rivers, seas, from plants and from our skins. The enormous quantity of particles of water vapour which rise up into the atmosphere cools and condenses into tiny, little drops of water which group together to form clouds. If a cloud meets with hot air, it disperses and evaporates. If it meets with cold air, the drops which form join together. They become too heavy to be sustained by the air and fall to the ground in the form of rain.

WATER FROM NOTHING

You need:
- a glass
- a freezer

What to do

1 Make sure the glass is perfectly dry. Put it in the freezer.

2 After 30 minutes, take the glass out.

What happens?
Immediately, the glass steams up; soon after, tiny droplets of water form on the glass. If you touch it, your finger is damp.

Because...
... in the freezer, the sides of the glass are very cold. When the class is brought into contact with the air, the sides of the glass cools the air, and the water vapour in the air changes into tiny drops of water which mist up the glass. In winter, the windows of cars steam up because our breath, rich in water vapour, condenses into drops of water as soon as it comes into contact with cold air.

Humidity in the air

In the hottest days of the summer, when we feel hot and sticky, you will hear weather forecasters say that the humidity of the air is high. This means that the quantity of water vapour in the air is rising. When there is not much water vapour, the air is dry and our perspiration quickly evaporates. But when the humidity is high, there is already so much vapour in the air that our perspiration cannot evaporate.

Mist is formed by tiny drops of water which originates from the condensation of water vapour in the atmospheric layers nearest the ground.

Cold air can hold only a little water vapour. If the night gets cold and the air is very humid, the water vapour condenses into tiny drops of dew which can be seen on leaves and on the ground in the morning.

When water vapour comes in contact with cold air, it condenses and becomes water again. This is how rain begins.

Why do water pipes sometimes burst in winter?

SOLID WATER

You need:
- a glass or plastic jar with lid
- water
- a freezer

What to do

1 Fill the jar to the brim with water.

2 Place the lid on top of the jar, without screwing it down.

3 Put the whole thing in the freezer and wait until the water in the jar has frozen.

What happens?
The water has become solid, and has risen above the rim of the jar, raising the lid.

Because...
... when the water becomes ice, it takes up more space than when it is liquid, and so the jar cannot hold it all. If we were to leave a firmly-closed glass bottle of water in the freezer, we would probably find it in pieces because of the pressure of the ice. The pipes which carry drinking water and water for central heating in the house must be protected in winter and insulated from the cold so that they do not burst because of ice forming inside.

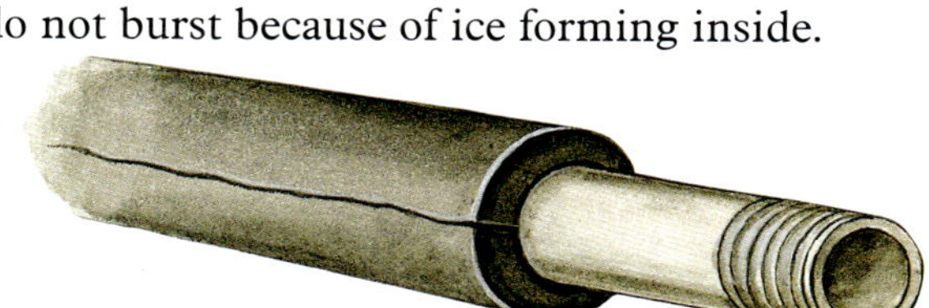

The structure of molecules

Almost all substances when they become warm spread out. When they become cold again, they contract, or come closer together. Water contracts up to 4°C, but if it becomes colder still, it begins to expand once again. This is due to the fact that the ice molecules increase the distance from each other, and arrange themselves in a hexagonal pattern.

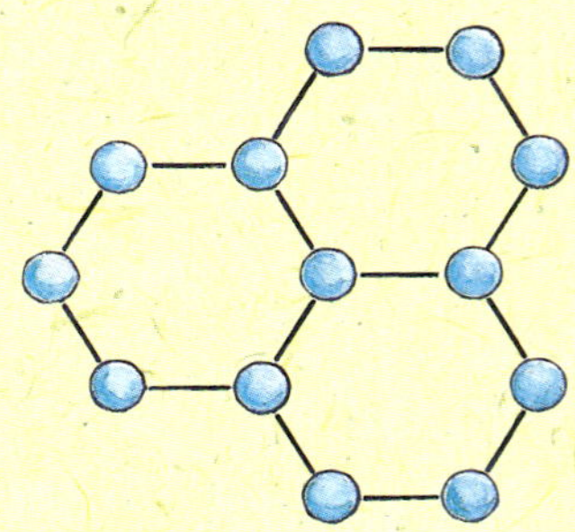

WHEN ICE MELTS

You need:
- a glass
- hot water
- ice cubes

What to do

1 Fill the glass almost to the brim with hot water.

2 Put one or two ice cubes in the water. Ask some friends if they think the water will overflow when the cubes have melted.

What happens?
The level of the water remains the same.

Because...
... water in its liquid state takes up less space than when it is solid. So, when the ice melts, the water does not spill over the rim of the glass.

Ice floats

The dilation (spreading out or enlargement) of water into the solid state means that ice is less dense than water, and so ice floats. In nature, this characteristic of water is very important. When ice floats on the surface of the seas at the North and South Poles, it makes a protective barrier so that many living things can survive the freezing cold until the ice thaws and the weather becomes less harsh.

Enormous icebergs float because ice has a lower density than water. Only one ninth of each great mountain of ice can be seen; the rest is submerged, below the surface of the sea.

When the temperature drops to minus 0 °C, dew becomes frost.

Clouds are made by drops of water coming together. If clouds come into contact with very cold air, these drops change into crystals, and join together to form snowflakes.

At 0 °C, water solidifies into ice, and takes up more space than water in its liquid state.

Water solutions

Water makes up 60 percent of our body. The major part of the water on our planet is a solution of salt and water; and although rivers and lakes are known as fresh water, these also contain a good quantity of dissolved salts. Spectacular underground grottos with their stalagtites (hanging down) and stalagmites (rising up) have been formed by countless drops of water rich in calcium carbonate constantly dripping, condensing and freezing.

What happens to a substance when it melts in water?

TO MELT OR NOT TO MELT

You need:
- 7 little glasses (not coloured)
- water
- a teaspoon
- small quantities of salt, sand, sugar, rice, honey, ground coffee and instant coffee

What to do

1 Fill all the glasses with water.

2 Put a teaspoon of one substance in each glass. Mix carefully with the water.

What happens?

Some substances (sugar, salt, honey and instant coffee) dissolve in the water, colouring it a little. Others (sand, rice and ground coffee) remain visible. They stay suspended in the water during the mixing, then sink to the bottom or float in the water.

Because...

... with substances which dissolve in water (seeming to disappear as they melt in it), the water molecules are able to slide between the molecules of the substance and separate them. In this way we obtain a solution in which the soluble ('dissolvable') substance does not succeed in settling down to a layer in the water in which it is dissolved (solvent). But if the molecules of the substance are impervious (can withstand) the water, these remain separated and easily visible. In this case we say that the substance is not soluble in water.

SATURATION LEVEL

You need:
- two glasses
- a teaspoon
- cane sugar
- hot and cold water

What to do

1 Half fill one of the glasses with cold water.

2 Count how many teaspoons of sugar you can put into the water to dissolve. Stop when sugar remains visible and sinks to the bottom.

3 Half fill the second glass with hot water.

4 Count how many teaspoons of sugar you can manage to dissolve in this glass.

What happens?

More sugar can be dissolved in the hot water than in the cold water.

Because...

... when no more sugar can be dissolved in water, we say that the solution is saturated. Due to the heat, the water molecules are still able to absorb more sugar molecules. The solution which is obtained in this way we call supersaturated. When the solution cools down, the excess sugar will be seen at the bottom.

Substances which are soluble in water dissolve in it.

Do soluble substances evaporate with the water?

SALT CRYSTALS

You need:
- table salt
- two glasses
- a length of cotton
- a small plate
- a spoon
- water

What to do

1 Pour cold water into the two glasses.

2 Put salt in both glasses, mixing it until you can add no more.

3 Link the two glasses with a thread, so that the two ends dip well into the water. Put the plate under the part of the thread which hangs down between the two glasses.

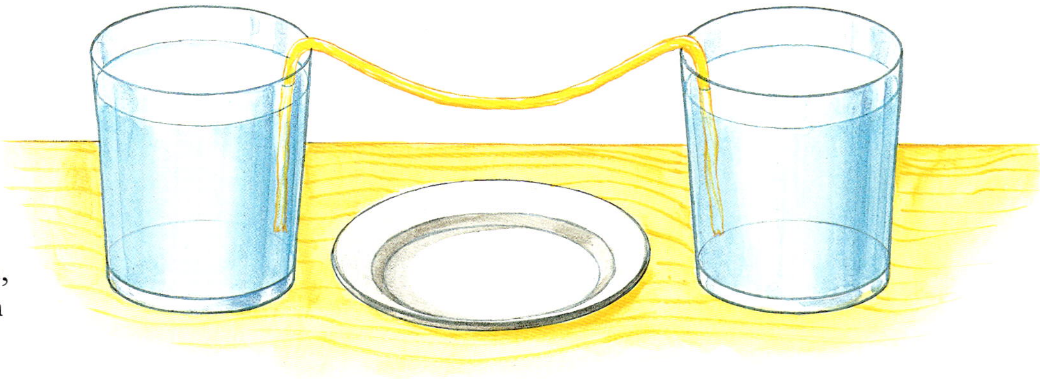

What happens?
After a day or so, salt crystals form on the thread and on the plate.

Because...
... the salt water rises along the thread by capillary action. The water evaporates from the thread (and from the plate where some droplets fall) leaving the salt, which solidifies into crystals – this means that the molecules join together to form a particular geometric pattern.

Salt in the home

The salt we use with our food is mostly extracted from salty seas. Big, shallow tanks are built in coastal regions and these fill up with sea water. The heat from the Sun makes the water evaporate, leaving the salt which forms in crystals on the bottom of the tanks. If we wanted to obtain pure water from the sea, we would have to reclaim the evaporated water by cooling it down to make it condense. The process by which the solvent (e.g. salt) is separated from the solution (e.g. sea water) is called distillation.

Salty and not so salty

Not all seas contain the same amount of salt. The saltiest seas are those where the rate of evaporation is high and there is very little flowing water or rainwater – such as the Red Sea. Seas which are less salty are those where the evaporation is poor and water constantly flows into it – for example, the Baltic Sea.

A very salty sea

The Dead Sea is not a sea, but a lake! It contains about 280g of salt for each kilogram of water. The Dead Sea is so salty because it is situated in a place with a very hot and dry climate and also because it does not have a river outlet. Therefore water escapes only by evaporation, causing a strong solution of salt in the water which remains. And since salt water is more dense than fresh water, anything and anyone can easily float in the Dead Sea, even without swimming!

On the banks of the Dead Sea, the levels of salt and the strong evaporation creates some spectacular salt structures.

SEPARATE A SOLUTION

You need:

- instant coffee
- a saucepan
- a spoon
- a hot-plate
- water
- a match

What to do

1 Ask an adult to boil water in the saucepan. Pour this into the cup and dissolve a spoonful of coffee into it.

2 Take a spoon (this must be cold and quite dry) and hold it in the steam which rises up from the cup.

What happens?

After a few moments, drops of water form on the spoon. Wait until these cool, then taste them. They will be pure water, not coffee.

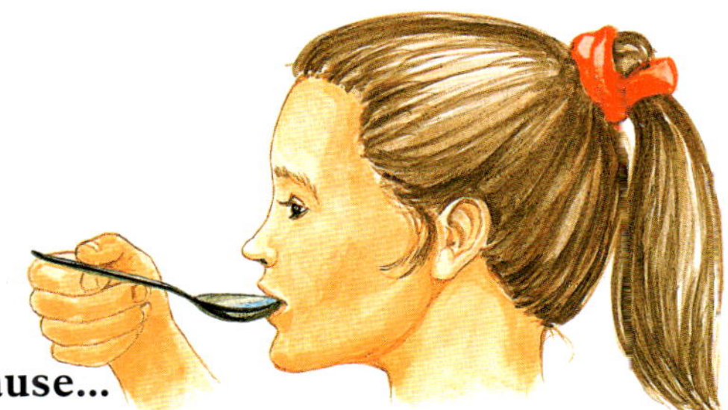

Because...

... heat makes the water evaporate, but not the coffee. When the steam comes into contact with the cold surface of the spoon, it condenses into drops of pure water. You can do the same test with clear water and salt. The drops which condense will always be pure water.

**With evaporation, water solutions separate.
But only pure water evaporates.**

Fact-Finder

Naval tanks

Naval tanks are specially-built basins or canals equipped to carry out experiments on miniature models of ships which have been designed but not yet built. For example, the shape of the prow (the part of the ship which goes first into the water) may be adapted for the best penetration of the water. Naval tanks are very large. They can be up to 900 metres long, with a width of up to 24 metres and up to 6 metres deep. The models of ships can be up to 9 metres long, and are towed into position, equipped with various systems to test how they move forward. The measurements of resistance of water on the progress of the ship is made with a large dynamometer (to measure the force of the thrust) connected to the model with a cable, or by an electrical instrument. The results of these measurements can be used to change or improve the design of the ship when it is being built.

Fish keep afloat

How do fish swim at different depths? Most fish have a 'swim bladder', a sac situated behind the stomach, which contains oxygen, nitrogen and carbon dioxide. Due to the increasing or the decreasing of the volume of this bladder and therefore its content of gases, fish can vary their specific gravity (the relationship between their weight and their volume) and so succeed in moving in a vertical direction in the water.

Water in the human body

60% - 70% of the human body is water. But which parts of the body have the greatest percentage of water? The most 'watery' part is the vitreous membrane in the eye which is 99.68% water. The parts with the least amount of water are the teeth and the skeleton which contain only 2% water.

Flotation

In some countries such as Sweden and Finland, the natural course of water can be used as a means of transport. Enormous quantities of tree-trunks cut down in the forests can be carried along by the currents of the rivers. In this way, the logs are transported to the valleys downriver, where the logs gather together against special barriers.

Rivers, seas, lakes:

The largest on our planet:
The longest river in the world: The Nile, 6,670km
The deepest sea: the Pacific Ocean, which in the Marianne Seas, reaches a depth of 11,022 metres
The largest lake: the Caspian Sea, 371,000sq. km.
And the highest waterfall in the world?
This is the Angel Falls in Venezuela and falls from a height of 972 metres!

Salter Ducks

The energy of the sea waves can be used to produce electricity, although not in very large quantities. The devices used for this purpose are called Salter Ducks, because they are shaped rather like a toy duck and are named after the English inventor, Salter. Each 'duck' is positioned on the surface of the sea in such a way that it is hit on its point by the waves, and these move the 'beak' back and forth. This action works a pump which is connected to an electricity generator.

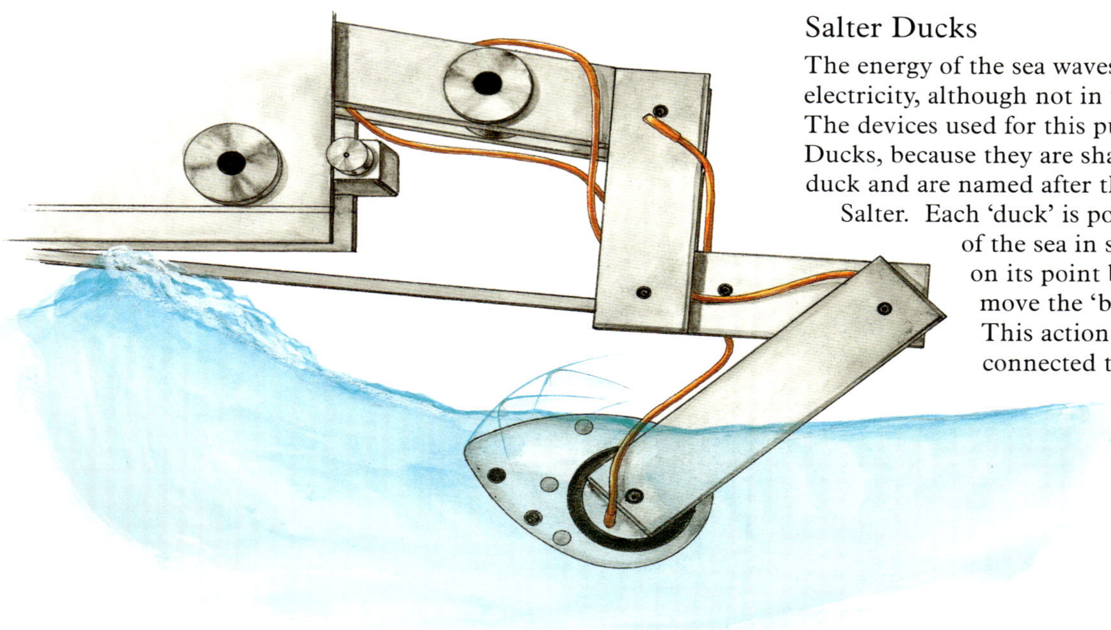

Light

How do shadows form? Why is it that the light enables us to see? How do lenses work? How do our eyes see things? Find the answers to these and many more questions by doing the experiments in the following pages, under these headings:

Rays of light • Reflection • Refraction • Colours
Capturing an image

Rays of Light

Nothing in the Universe is faster than the speed of light. It travels at the extraordinary rate of 300,000 km per second! But how does light travel from its source (whether this source is the Sun or a lamp) to the object on which it shines? Can light illuminate all the sides of an object? What exactly are shadows? How are shadows made? Can they change shape?

To answer these questions, we must discover some facts about light, finding out where it comes from, which things stops light from travelling and which things it can shine through.

How does light spread?

A STRAIGHT PATH

You need:
- two squares of cardboard
- a torch
- two strips of cardboard
- a few books

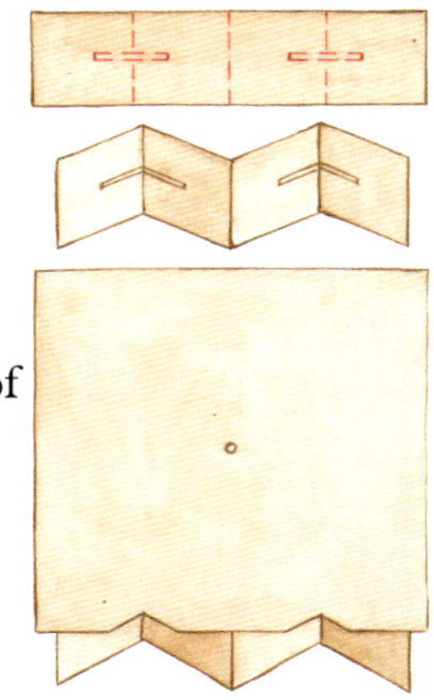

What to do

1 Pierce a hole in the centre of the two cardboard squares. Make supports for each square by folding the cardboard strips and cutting notches, as you see in the picture.

2 Place the squares in the supports and line up the holes. Put the torch on the books, with the light aimed at the hole of the first square. Kneel or sit down so that your eyes are level with the hole in the second square.

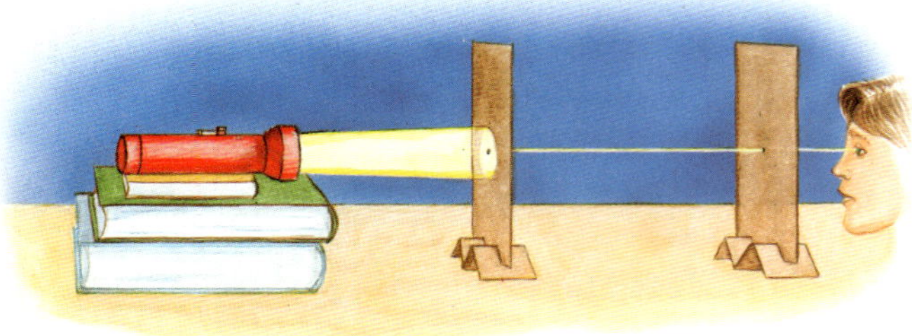

What happens?
Your eye sees the light through the two holes.

3 Move one of the squares so that the holes are no longer lined up.

What happens?
The eye can no longer see the light.

Because...
... light travels in a straight line. So it cannot pass through the hole if it cannot find the end of its path.

A LIGHT ON THE WORLD

You need:
- a globe
- a portable lamp
- a darkened room

What to do

1 Point the light directly at the globe.

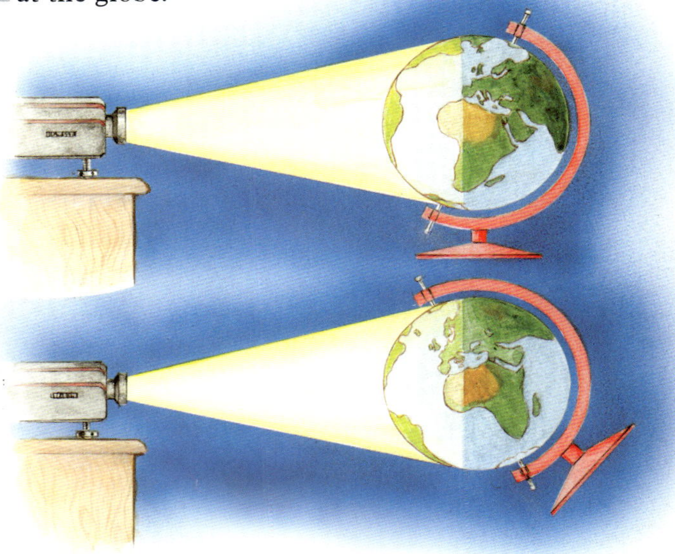

2 Move the globe downwards, from top to bottom, then side to side, keeping it in the light.

What happens?
The globe is illuminated only at the part which is turned towards the source of light. The opposite side always remains in the dark, no matter how you hold it.

Because...
... the rays of light follow a straight path. They cannot curve around an object and light up the side which cannot be seen. That is why the Sun can only shine on one side of the Earth, the side which is turned towards its rays; on the other side of the Earth away from the Sun, there is darkness.

Light travels in straight lines. If something blocks its path, it can only illuminate the part which is facing it.

What is the reason for shadows?

STOP THE LIGHT

You need:

- a torch
- a table lamp
- a piece of black card
- scissors
- sticky tape
- a stick
- a darkened room

What to do

1 Cut the black card into whatever shape you like. Fix the black shape on to a stick with the sticky tape.

2 Hold the shape between the beam of the torch and the wall of the room.

3 First, bring the shape nearer the light, then draw it back towards the wall.

What happens?
The closer the shape is to the torch, the bigger the shadow on the wall. The further the shape is from the torch, the smaller the shadow.

Because...
... when an object blocks the straight path of the light, a shadow forms behind that object. The closer the object is to the source of the light, the more light it blocks out, and so its shadow is bigger. But if the object is further away, it does not block out much light, and so the shadow is smaller.

4 Shine the lamp on the shape.

What happens?
The shadow has a more blurred outline than before.

Because...
... when the source of light is bigger than the object, the shadow which forms is dark at the centre and lighter towards the edges, where only part of the light can reach. The darkest part of the shadow is called the umbra. The area of light shadow is called the penumbra.

When the Sun, the Moon and the Earth are in a straight line,there is an eclipse, where the Sun or the Moon is wholly or partly obscured. When the Moon is between the Earth and the Sun, this is a Solar Eclipse. If the Earth comes between the Sun and the Moon, this is a Lunar Eclipse.

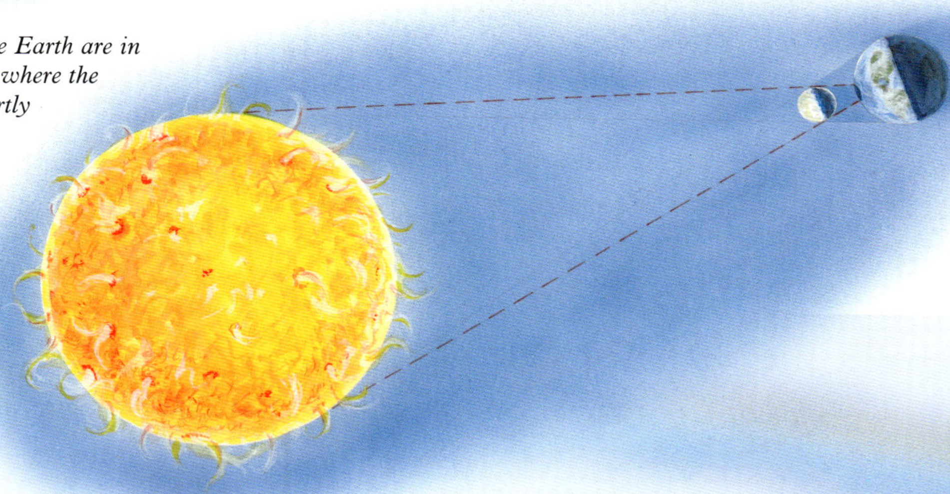

A GARDEN SUNDIAL

You need:

- a cardboard disc, about 20cm in diameter
- a stick about 10-15cm long
- scissors
- a pencil
- a watch
- a patch of ground where the Sun shines throughout the day

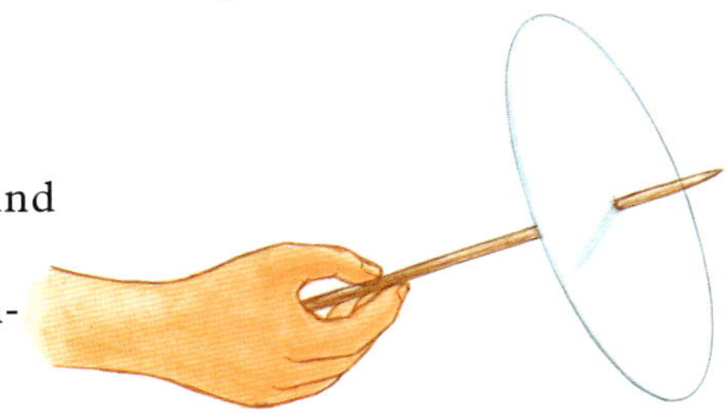

What to do

1 Make a hole in the centre of the disc. Push the stick through, to about one third of its length. Put in the earth, so that the disc is firmly on the ground.

2 As soon as your watch is on the hour, mark where the shadow of the stick falls on the disc with your pencil. Write down the time beside the line.

3 Do the same thing each hour, remembering to write down the time for each shadow.

What happens?

The shadow thrown by the stick is in a different position for each hour. The pencil lines spread out from around the stick towards the outer edge of the disc.

Because...

... the position of the stick's shadow changes as the position of the Sun appears to change. What really happens is that the Earth is rotating at a constant speed, either towards the Sun or away from it.

You have made a sundial, an instrument once used for the measurement of time. Sundials can still be seen today, on the walls of some old houses and in the grounds of ancient squares and gardens.

In the shadow of a tree

Within the space of one day, the position of the Sun in relation to the Earth changes (this is because the Earth is rotating on its axis). Therefore, the direction of the rays of the Sun also change. That is why shadows 'move'. When the Sun is high, it throws short shadows. When it is low on the horizon, the shadows are longer.

When an object blocks out the light, it casts a shadow, which is an area where the rays of light cannot reach.

Do all objects cast shadows?

TO PASS OR NOT TO PASS?

You need:
- a torch
- a book
- a cup
- a glass with some water
- a piece of thin glass
- a piece of thin paper
- a handkerchief
- a piece of tissue paper
- a darkened room

What to do

1 Line up the objects in front of a wall. Shine the torch on each of them in turn.

What happens?

Shadows form on the wall behind the cup and the book. Behind the glass and the sheet of glass, the wall is lit up. There is a blurred halo behind the tissue paper and the handkerchief.

Because...

... the cup and the book are *opaque* (cannot be seen through) and so these stop the spread of light. The thin piece of glass and the water are *transparent* (can be seen through). Materials like the thin paper, the tissue paper and the handkerchief are *transluscent* (letting some light through). So they only partially block out the rays of light. The light which remains spreads out to illuminate the wall slightly.

A halo around the Moon

The atmosphere around the Earth can also become translucent. When crystals of ice form at high levels of the Earth's surface, these spread the light which is reflected from the Moon. They reflect the light back, making it look as if there is a halo around the Moon.

THE TRANSPARENT EFFECT

You need:

- a sheet of paper
- drops of oil
- a drinking straw
- a torch
- a darkened room

What to do

1 Use the straw to shake one or two drops of oil on the paper.

2 Place the paper between the beam of the torch and the wall.

3 Switch on the torch. Shine the light on the oily patch.

What happens?

When you shine the torch on the oily patch, the light passes through it on to the wall and is much stronger.

Because...

... the paper blocks out large parts of the light rays. The oil penetrates through the fibres of the paper, making little transparent (see-through) chinks which allows the light to pass through. The same thing does not happen with water, because this cannot penetrate so easily between the fibres of most types of paper.

Why is it that we can see through some materials?

The normal eye is equipped to see things in light. If between the eye and the object in the light there is a transparent material, for example, a pane of glass or a shop window, or even a small quantity of water, then we can see the object perfectly. However, it is not only the type of material which lets the light pass through, or blocks it out, but also the thickness of that material. For example, although water in a glass is transparent, the water of the sea at certain depths is not, nor if the Sun is shining on the surface. In the same way, a glass just a few millimetres thick is transparent, but glass several metres thick is not.

Translucent materials, those which let only a certain amount of light pass through, allow us only to make out the shape of objects. Through a curtain or paper, for instance, we see only vague shapes.

Only opaque objects block out the rays of light and cast shadows.

Reflection

Why is it not possible to see anything in the dark? How can the Sun shine on everything that surrounds us?
Our eyes, in order to see, use the way that light rays reflect when those rays strike an object which is not transparent. We see all that is struck by the rays of light, because our eyes use the light reflected from things. And if we can receive those reflected rays well enough, we can produce images which are identical to the real thing.

How does light allow us to see things?

SHINING WHITE

You need:

- a sheet of white paper
- a sheet of black paper
- a torch
- a mirror
- a darkened room

What to do

1 Switch on the torch in a darkened room and stand in front of a mirror.

2 Hold the torch sideways to your face, so that the light shines on your nose.

3 Take the black paper in your free hand, and then the white paper, looking in the mirror all the time.

What happens?
The torch by itself only illuminates your nose. But with the black paper, the reflection of your face is almost completely obscured. With the white paper, almost your whole face appears illuminated.

Because...
... with the torch alone, the light reflects back only from the object it meets, which is your nose. With the paper, the effect depends on the colour. The black paper hardly reflects the light which shines on it. But the white paper reflects a lot of the light, so the rays of light reflect back on to the face, illuminating it.

FROM THE DARK INTO THE LIGHT

You need:

- a room full of different things (a storeroom, for example)

What to do

1 Go into the darkened room. Close the door and look around.

2 Open the door a little, so that there is only a tiny chink of light. Look around again. Then gradually open the door still more, until it is open wide and look around the room.

What happens?

When the door is closed, your eyes cannot see the objects in the room. With the first shafts of light, you begin to distinguish the objects a little more. Gradually, as more light enters, you see all the objects clearly.

Because...

... things are visible only by reflecting the light – that is, by the light being sent back to our eyes. Clear objects reflect a lot of light. Darker objects absorb a great deal of light, and so reflect only a little. So we need a lot of light to see darker objects.

We see objects only if the rays of light strikes them, bounces off and then returns to our eyes.

How do mirrors work?

TRUE REFLECTIONS

You need:
- a piece of strong black cardboard
- a small mirror, square or rectangular
- scissors
- torch
- a darkened room

What to do

1 Fold the piece of cardboard, as shown in the picture. Then cut three slots along one side.

2 In the darkened room, switch on the torch, and place it behind the slots.

3 Place the mirror at the opposite end of the folded card, as shown in the picture.

What happens?
When the rays of light strike the mirror, each ray bounces back at an angle on the card.

Because...
... the mirror reflects the light in the ordinary way, with the same angle of reflection with which the ray strikes the mirror (angle of incidence). But if a ray of light strikes the reflective surface in a perpendicular (straight up) direction, it bends itself back along the same path. If a surface is smooth, the light becomes reflected in an ordinate way – that is to say, all the rays go in the same direction. If the surface is rough, then the rays bounce back in a disordinate way.

MIRROR AGAINST MIRROR

You need:
- two flat mirrors

What to do

1 Look into one of the mirrors and move your hand.

What happens?
Your reflection is shown in reverse – if you move your right hand, this will be shown as the left hand in the mirror.

2 Place the two mirrors at an angle to each other. Stand between the two.

3 Move a hand.

What happens?
Your reflection is now correct. The movement of your right hand matches the movement of your right hand in the reflection.

Because...
... when the reflected light from your body strikes the mirror in front of you, it bounces back directly, creating the back-to-front image. But when you face two mirrors, each mirror reverses the back-to-front reflection from the other, and so the reflection is 'straightened out'!

MAKE A PERISCOPE

You need:
- a piece of strong cardboard, 32cm x 50cm
- scissors
- sticky tape
- two handbag mirrors, 6cm x 10cm
- a ruler
- pencil
- two pieces of cardboard, each 6cm square

What to do

1 Using the ruler, divide the cardboard into four equal parts, each 8cm wide. Draw around a 6cm square twice, as you see in the picture. Cut these squares out.

2 Cut the 6cm square in half diagonally to make two right-angled triangles.

3 Place the triangle on the top strip of the paper, as shown in the picture. Pencil along the diagonal line then cut along this to make a notch. Do this again in the three other places shown in the picture. Fold the cardboard into shape. Join the sides with sticky tape.

4 Thread the two mirrors through the notches.

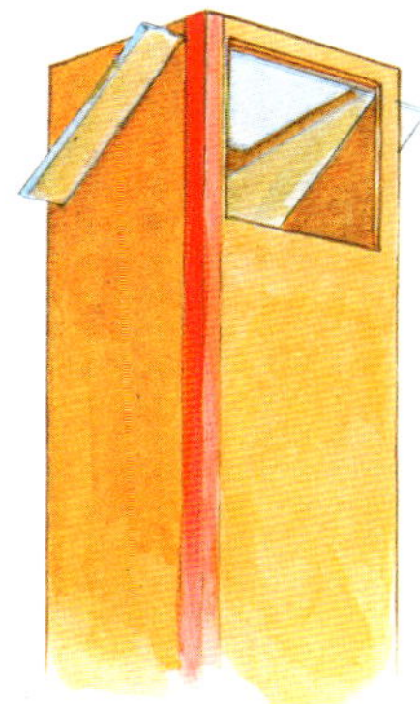

5 Get behind an obstacle (such as a wall, or a window sill) so that the periscope is sticking up above your head. Look through the square at the bottom.

What happens?

In the mirror inside the periscope you will see a reflected image of whatever is behind the obstacle.

Because...

.. the light which rebounds from the objects or people on the other side of the obstacle strikes the mirror at the top of the periscope. Because of the angle of this mirror, it is reflected in the bottom mirror. You can use your periscope to look at something without being seen – just like submarine crews who need to survey the sea before coming up to the surface!

Mirrors reflect light in an ordinate way and reproduce the images of things facing them.

Can light bend?

LIGHT BOUNCES BACK

You need:
- a see-through container with flat sides
- water
- a small quantity of milk
- a torch
- a piece of black card
- scissors
- sticky tape
- a book
- a darkened room

What to do

1 Fill the container with water and add a few drops of milk. (This makes the rays of light easier to see.)

2 Pierce a hole in the middle of the black card. Then fasten this around the lens of the torch with the sticky tape.

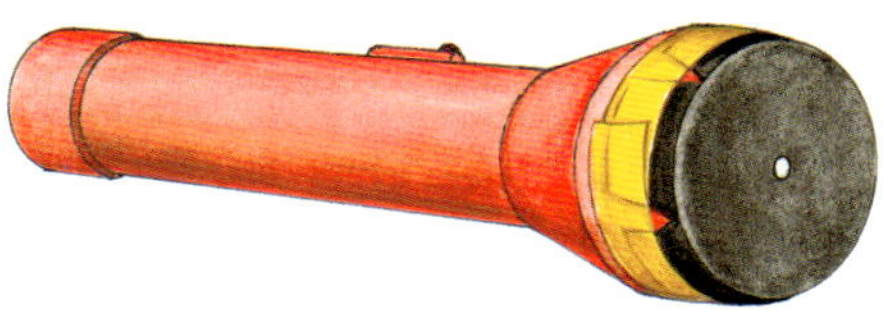

3 In a darkened room, switch on the torch and shine it as you see in the picture, so that the beam of light falls on the surface of the water. (You may find it helps to put the container on a book.)

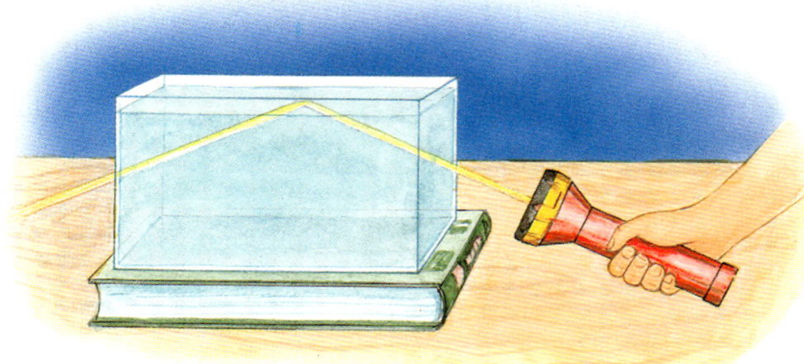

What happens?
When it strikes the surface of the water, the light bends and goes out of the container from the opposite side, so that the beam forms an angle.

Because...
... light enters the container along a straight path. The surface of the water works like a mirror, and reflects the light. This reflection alters the path of the light, which, in order to stay straight, changes direction.

The laser

The laser beam is a very intense and fine ray of light which carries an enormous amount of energy. To make a laser, the light is produced by special procedures and is then reflected back and forth between a pair of mirrors to increase the intensity. When it reaches the intensity required, the laser beam passes through one of the mirrors, which is only partly reflective. Because of its power, its precision and the fact that it can be controlled easily, the laser is used in numerous fields – cutting materials (from lengths of fabric to sheets of steel), joining metal parts together, making precise measurements, in surgical operations, creating special effects for open air spectaculars, the production and use of compact discs, code reading, producing and reading bar codes for products on sale in our shops and many other purposes.

A LUMINOUS JET

You need:
- a clear, soft plastic bottle
- a piece of thin, clear plastic tubing
- a bowl
- plasticine
- sticky tape
- a thick, dark cloth
- a darkened room
- water
- scissors

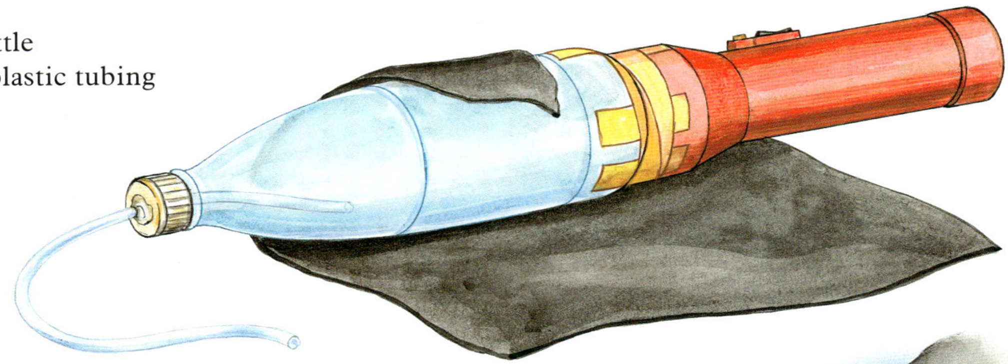

What to do

1 Fill the bottle with water.

2 Ask an adult to make a hole in the cap of the bottle with the scissors. Then thread the tube inside, keeping it firm with plasticine.

3 Fix the torch at the bottom of the bottle with the sticky tape. Switch on the torch. Wrap the whole thing in the cloth, leaving only the tubing uncovered.

4 In a dark room, place the bottle so that a jet of water can be poured smoothly through the tubing and into the bowl.

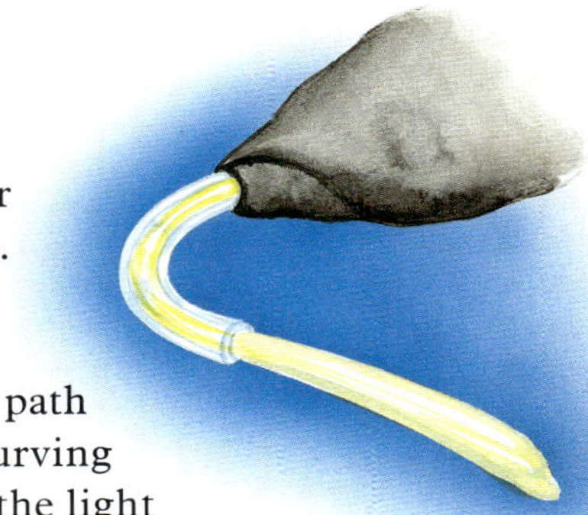

What happens?
A jet of luminous water comes out of the bottle.

Because...
... the light follows the path of water through the curving tube. Inside this tube, the light cannot bend, but is constantly reflected against the walls of the tubing, proceeding in a zig-zag direction because it is trapped inside. This phenomenon is called total internal reflection.

Fibre optics

Fibre optics are very thin transparent filaments through which the light enters at one end and escapes through the other. By the effect of total internal reflection, the light stays trapped on the inside and in this way becomes bent by the filament. Fibre optics are used to examine the human body. Because of their flexibility and their fine dimensions, they can reach many parts of the body (such as the stomach and the arteries) illuminating these parts and sending back an image for a doctor to see by looking into a lens outside the body. Fibre optics are also used for telephone and television communication and for the transmission of data in computer systems.

Light can pass through curved tubes. These tubes break up its path into little tracks which are always straight.

Refraction

You have probably noticed that when people up to their knees in water, their legs look short and fat. Perhaps you have also looked through a goldfish bowl at a particular angle and seen two fish instead of one. Or, going along in a car on a sweltering hot day, you may have noticed how the road looks steamy, even though it is perfectly dry. All these things are tricks of the light, because of the way in which it can break up. The next pages of experiments will show you how light, passing from the air to water and vice versa, changes speed and direction, producing strange visual effects. You will also discover how, by breaking the path of light, we can bring closer and enlarge images of objects which are at great distances, such as the Moon.

Why does water change the image of objects?

LIGHT BROKEN UP

You need:
- a glass
- water
- a little milk
- a drinking straw
- a torch
- a darkened room

What to do

1 Fill the glass with water. Add a little milk to make it cloudy.

2 In a darkened room, switch on the torch. Shine the beam of light from the top to the bottom, so that it shines crookedly on the surface of the water.

What happens?
When the beam of light enters the water, it changes direction.

3 Now fill the glass with clean water. Put in the straw.

What happens?
The straw seems to be broken at the point where it enters the water.

Because...
... when light passes from air to water, and usually from one transparent substance to another, it changes speed, which, in turn, causes a change in direction. We call this *refraction*. This can make an object appear to be in a different position to what it really is. That is why the part of the straw which is under water looks as if it has moved away from the part above water.

Misleading depths
Seas, lakes and rivers often appear less deep than they really are, because refraction makes the bottom seem nearer. You only have to try picking up an object from under the water to realize that it is always a little deeper than we think. Fishermen who use harpoons never aim at fish where their eyes see them, but at a point which seems lower in the water.

Mirages
Rays of light can also undergo a change as they pass from cold air to hot air and vice versa, because these have a different density. (Hot air is thinner than cold air.) Therefore the light passes through at different speeds. On very hot days, the air near the ground gets hot quickly, and so the rays which pass through this become crooked. That is why at a distance a street appears to be steamy on a hot day; what we see, in fact, is a reflected image of the sky. In the desert, this can cause mirages – imaginary images of things which are not really there.

Light from water makes us see different images, or changes the appearance of the real object by the effect of refraction.

How do lenses work?

ENLARGED BY WATER

You need:

- a round, glass jar
- paper with a pattern on it
- a drinking straw
- water

What to do

1 Fill the jar with water. Put the straw in it, keeping it up straight. Look carefully at the top of the water.

What happens?

The part of the straw in the water looks larger.

2 Take out the straw. Place the paper with the pattern behind the jar. Look at this from the same position as before.

What happens?

The drawing appears to be enlarged.

Because...

... in the passage from water to air, the rays of light become refracted (change direction). If the surface of separation (e.g. the jar or a glass) is curved, the refraction makes the object look bigger than it actually is.

RAYS WHICH MEET

You need:

- a shoe-box
- a glass
- water
- a torch
- a pencil
- a ruler
- scissors
- a darkened room

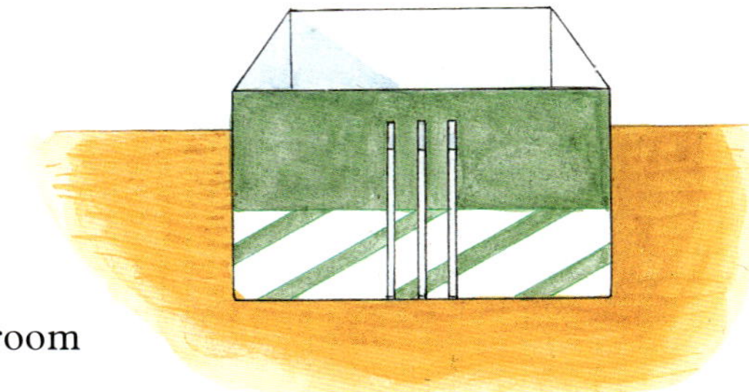

What to do

1 In a short side of the shoe-box, draw and cut three notches 1cm apart.

2 Fill the glass with water and place this in the centre of the box, in line with the notches.

3 In the darkened room, switch on the torch and shine it on to the notches.

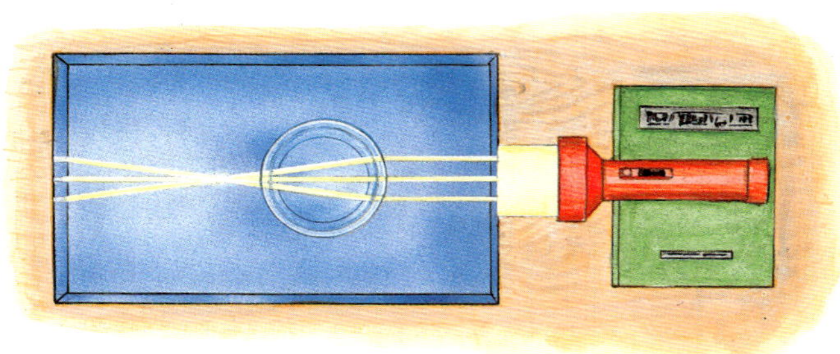

What happens?

Before meeting the glass of water, the rays of light are parallel. But after passing through the glass, they meet at a certain point (to obtain this effect, you may have to move the glass). At the point where the rays of light meet they are stronger.

Because...

... the curved surface of the glass and the water causes refraction of the rays of light, making them meet together and then cross over.

UNITING AND SEPARATING LIGHT

You need:
- the shoe-box used in the last experiment
- scissors
- a convex lens (with the surface curving outwards)
- a concave lens (with the surface curving inwards)
- a sheet of white paper
- a torch
- a darkened room

What to do

1 Cover the bottom of the shoe-box with the white paper.

2 With the scissors, make a notch at the bottom of the box in which you can put one of the lenses to look through.

3 Place the convex lens in the notch. In the dark, set the torch against the upright notches.

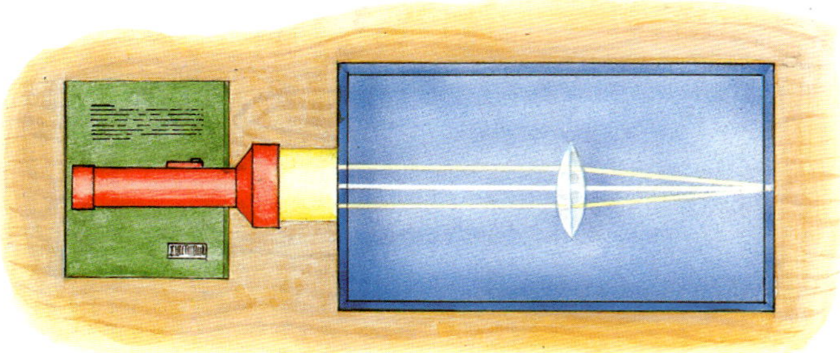

4 Repeat stage 3, using the concave lens.

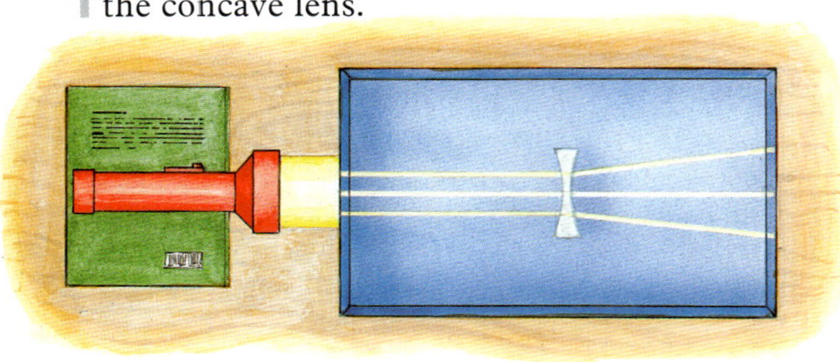

What happens?

The rays which pass through the convex lens change direction and meet at a point. The rays which pass through the concave lens spread out from each other.

Because...

... the different shape of the lenses cause a different angle of refraction. Convex lenses bring the rays of light closer together. These can be used to see objects bigger, or smaller, according to the distance of the object from the lens. The concave lens causes a separation of the beam of light. If this is put between the eye and the object, it will make the object appear smaller.

Fire

If a transparent convex surface is made in a dome shape (as in the bottom of a bottle), it is not only the rays of light which strike them but also heat. The concentration of rays from the Sun on a bottle thrown away among litter or dry leaves can cause a fire.

Spectacles

As you will see in the next pages, inside the human eye, there is lens called the crystalline lens. This enables people to see images both near and at a distance. If the crystalline lens does not work properly, vision can be corrected by the use of external lenses – spectacles or contact lenses enable short-sighted people to see better at a distance, and long-sighted people to see closer. They can also make images clearer for people whose eyes cannot focus properly.

Lenses have curved surfaces, so that the light can make objects appear bigger or smaller.

How does a telescope bring an image closer?

THE MOON AT HOME

You need:
- a concave mirror (such as a shaving mirror)
- a plain mirror
- a magnifying glass
- a window

This experiment must be done at night when the Moon can be seen through the window.

What to do

1 Place the shaving mirror in front of the window, turned towards the Moon.

2 Stand in front of the window and slowly turn the plain mirror towards you, so that you can see the image of the Moon reflected in the shaving mirror. Look through the magnifying glass at the image of the Moon which appears in the plain mirror.

What happens?
In the plain mirror, the Moon appears to be nearer and you can make the image larger with the magnifying glass.

Because...
... the concave mirror reflects and brings nearer the image of the Moon. The plain mirror, not being curved, reflects the image exactly and bounces it back through the magnifying glass. This makes the image larger. Telescopes work in the same way, by using reflection.

Who invented the telescope?

The first instruments to bring distant objects nearer and enlarge them were invented in Holland in 1608 by an optician, Hans Lippershey. A year later, Galileo Galilei came to know about this, and decided to try making a telescope to study the night sky. The first of Galileo's telescope was made of two tubes which slid into each other, with a lens at each end. The larger, convex lens was the *objective* which collected the light and the smaller, concave lens the *ocular* through which Galileo made his observations. Using this refractor telescope which made enlargements of objects up to 30 times, Galileo observed and studied the Moon, the planets and the stars and made important discoveries about the Inner Solar System. In 1668 Isaac Newton invented the reflective telescope, adding mirrors to the lenses to produce clearer images. The largest telescopes used for astronomical observation are all reflective.
Later in 1758, achromatic lenses were invented by John Dolland. These were developed so that colours could be seen more distinctly.

The telescope of the Observatory at Brera a Merate, Italy.

A SIMPLE TELESCOPE

You need:
- two magnifying glasses
- two cardboard tubes of different diameters
- sticky tape

What to do

1 Slide one tube into the other. Fix a magnifying glass at one end with sticky tape.

2 Look at the Moon through the tubes, with your eye against the taped magnifying glass and holding the second glass at the other end. Make the tube longer and shorter and move the second glass until you get a clear image.

What happens?
Through the taped magnifying glass, you can obtain a closer image of the Moon, but upside down.

Because...
... the lens at the end make the rays of light from the Moon converge and create the image inside the tube. The lens nearest the eye enlarges this image and makes the Moon appear closer. Refractor telescopes work in the same way, but these are much larger in order to show images which are not upside down.

Telescopes and microscopes work by a combination of lenses and mirrors, enabling us to see images which are closer and bigger. The picture to the left shows a modern microscope used for the analysis of blood; to the right, a microscope of the 20th century is equipped for the study of minerals.

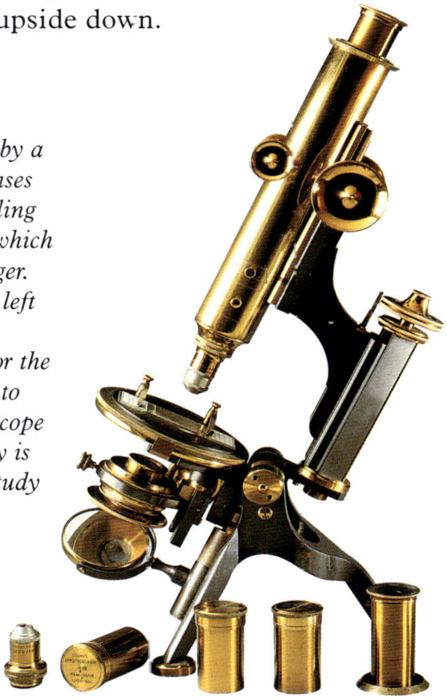

Telescopes make distant objects appear nearer, using a combination of lenses and mirrors.

Colours

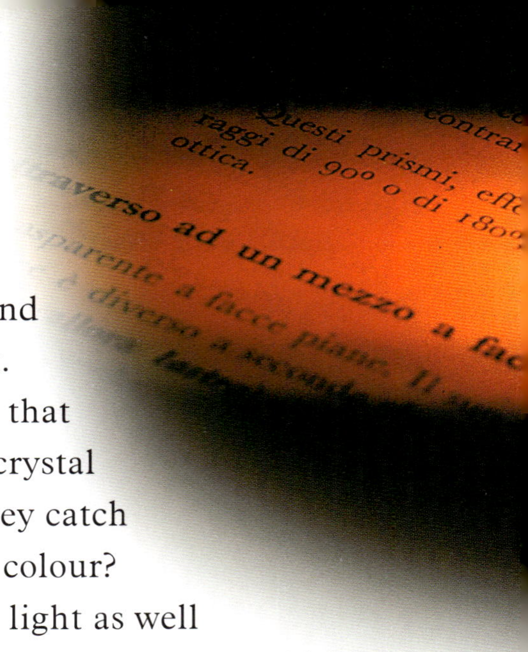

When we come out of the dark into the light, we could say that instead of seeing things in black and grey, we see colours. Without light, colours do not exist. But how can light enable us to see them? And how is it that two colours mixed together make a third? Why do the crystal drops of a chandelier cast rainbows on the wall when they catch the light? Why is it that the sky is not always the same colour? To answer these questions we must find out more about light as well as colour, and discover the colours which we can see and those which are hidden.

What colour is light?

COLOURED SPINNING TOP

You need:
- a piece of white card
- a short pencil with a sharp point
- a protractor
- felt tipped pens
- geometry compass
- scissors

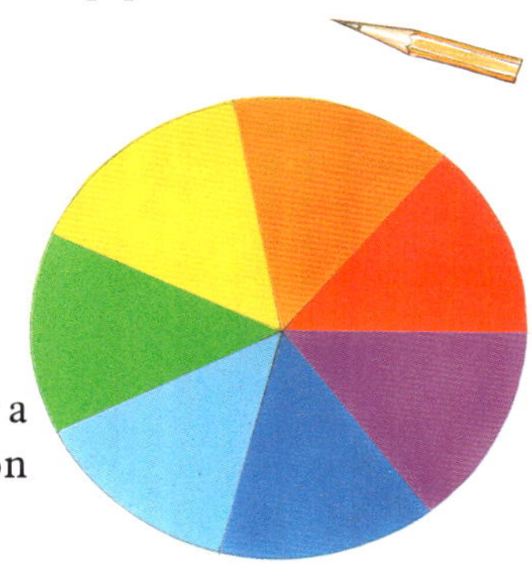

What to do

1 Set the compass at 5cm radius to draw a 10cm diameter circle on the card. Cut out.

2 Using the protractor, divide the cardboard circle into 7 equal sections, with each section at about 51°.

3 Colour the sections in this order; red, orange, yellow, green, sky blue, indigo and violet.

4 Thread the pencil through the centre of the circle with the point at the bottom.

5 Spin the circle, as if it were a spinning top.

What happens?
While the top is spinning, the colours cannot be picked out. The circle seems almost white.

Because...
... with the fast rotation, all the seven colours which you have used become mixed together, resulting in a whitish colour.

Newton's prism

In the second half of the 17th century, Isaac Newton discovered that light, when it passes through a prism (a triangular shaped solid piece of glass) becomes split up into rays of different colours which are always in the same order, and at the same angle to each other. He called this group of colours the colour spectrum.

THE COLOURS OF THE RAINBOW

You need:

- a torch
- a shallow rectangular container
- a plain mirror
- piece of white card
- water

What to do

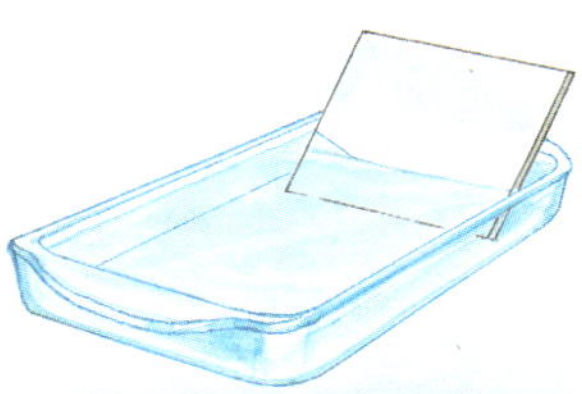

1 Fill the container with water.

2 Put the mirror in the water, and slowly lean it at an angle against a short side of the container.

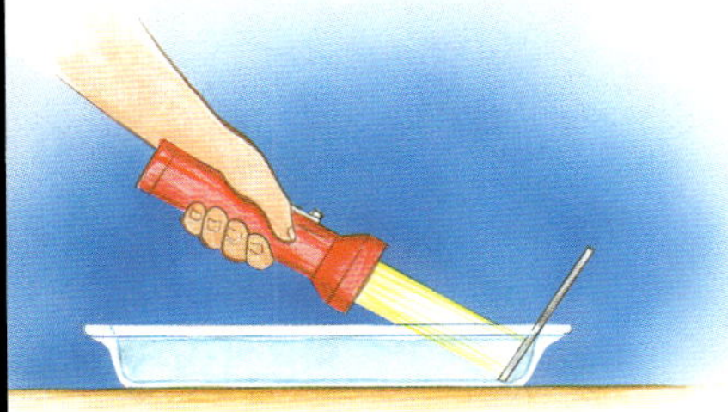

3 Shine the torch on the water so that the beam lights up the part of the mirror which is under the water.

4 Place the white card in front of the mirror to catch the reflected light.

What happens?

The white card catches a reflection with the colours of the rainbow.

Because...

... the beam of light reflected on the mirror, as it escapes from the water, becomes refracted. But the colours which comprise the white light are not refracted at the same angle, and so they fall at different points and become visible.

How a rainbow forms

The tiny drops of water suspended in the air after rain work as tiny prisms. As each one is struck by the light, they reflect the light and refract it, breaking it up into the seven colours of the spectrum.

Light appears to be white, but it is made up of the seven colours of the rainbow, or the colour spectrum.

How are colours formed?

COLOUR MIXING

You need:
- two torches
- two pieces of see-through plastic (one red, one green)
- two elastic bands
- a piece of white card
- green, red, yellow and blue paints
- a paint-brush
- a plate

What to do

1 Use the elastic bands to fix a piece of plastic to each torch.

2 Switch on the torches. Shine them on the white card, overlapping the two beams of light.

What happens?
The place where the two beams overlap appears yellow.

3 Mix an equal quantity of red and green paint on the plate with the brush.

4 Wash out the brush. Then do the same with the yellow and blue paint.

What happens?
Mixing the red and green paint makes a colour rather like maroon. The yellow and blue paints make green.

Because...
... from the primary colours of sunlight – green, red and blue – which you mixed two at a time, originates all other colours, (secondary colours). The pigments of primary colours (used in paint, varnishes, inks, etc.) are magenta red, cyan blue (greenish blue) and yellow. From the three primary colours of light together, we can obtain white light; and from all these, together with the three primary colour pigments, we obtain a very dark colour which is almost black.

Towards the end of the 19th century, two artists called Signac and Seurat invented the technique of pointillism. Instead of mixing the colours on their palettes, they covered their canvasses with tiny little dots of different colours which, seen from a distance, seem to be fused into one colour. You can also try this, perhaps by drawing a meadow with yellow and blue dots close together. From the distance they will appear green.

How do we see colours?

We can see things around us only if they are illuminated by light rays. But the light which strikes an object is partly absorbed, so it is only partly reflected towards our eyes. The colour of an object depends on the colour of the light which it reflects. An apple appears red because it reflects only the red colour and absorbs all the other colours. White objects reflect the light completely, whilst black objects absorb almost all the light.

COLOURS IN INK

You need:

- a bottle of coloured ink, or felt-tipped pens of different colours (including black)
- a large, flat dish
- water
- strips of white toilet paper, 20cm long and 2-3cm wide.

What to do

1 Let one or two drops of ink fall on each strip, at about 2cm from the bottom. Or make a blot with one of the felt-tipped pens.

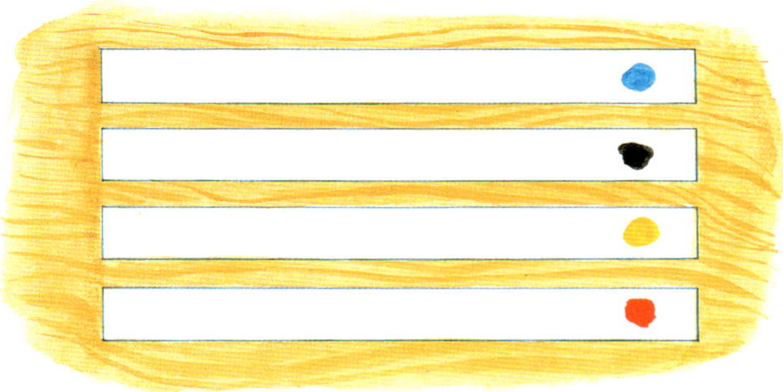

2 Pour a little water into the dish, and dip the end of each strip (one at a time) into the water. Wait until the water reaches the inky patch.

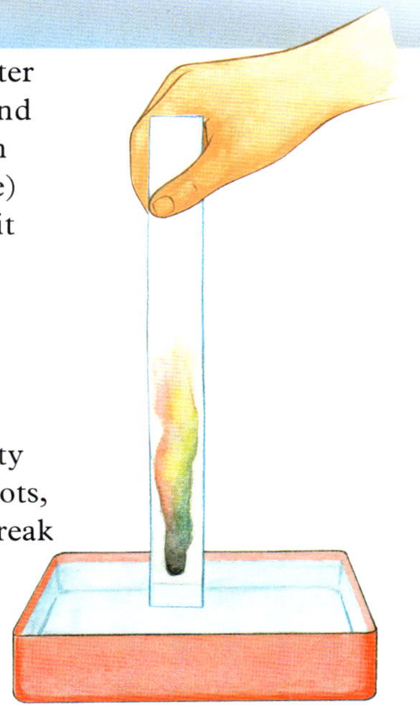

What happens?
The water gets dirty and some of the blots, including black, break up into different colours.

Because...
... the water dissolves (that means it breaks up) the pigment which, according to the colour, moves through the water at a different speed. This means that the colours separate and each one begins to reflect its own colour. This experiment will enable you to distinguish which of the inks and felt-tipped pens are made up of the most colours, and which ones are composed of only one colour.

Colour on television, colour on paper

The images we see on television are composed of tiny little lines of the three primary colours of light (red, green and blue). The eye 'mixes' them and sees clear images in all the colours. For printing books and magazines we use the primary pigment colours (yellow, magenta red and cyan blue) as well as black to make the images more definite. Until recently, each page had to go through the printing machine once for each colour. Now one-stage, multi-colour printing is widespread.

By mixing two primary colours together, we obtain other colours, which are called secondary colours.

Can we colour white light?

A RED FILTER

You need:
- a piece of white paper
- felt-tipped pens
- a piece of see-through red plastic

What to do

1 With the felt-tipped pens, make blots of different colours on the paper.

2 Look at all the colours together through the red plastic.

What happens?
The piece of paper appears to be completely red. You will be able to pick out only the brightest blots.

Because...
... the plastic acts as a filter. It lets through only the red light, and absorbs all the other colours. In the same way, a coloured filter placed in front of a spotlight or torch blocks out all the colours of white light except its own. So the light which is allowed to pass through seems to be the same colour.

Stained glass windows

Like filters, stained glass lets through only its own colour, stopping us from seeing the others. That is why, when light from the Sun filters through stained glass windows, we see coloured reflections on the walls and on the floor.

When light is coloured, the colour acts as a filter, blocking out all the colours of the spectrum except its own.

Why does the sky change colour?

AN ARTIFICIAL SUNRISE

You need:
- a large see-through vase
- water
- milk
- a torch

What to do

1 Fill the vase with water. Add a few drops of milk.

2 Switch on the torch and shine it down into the water.

What happens?
The water looks bluish.

3 Point the torch on the outside of the vase. Go to the other side and look at the light through the water.

What happens?
The water takes on a colour which is rather pink, whilst the part which is illuminated appears yellowy-orange.

Because...
... changing the position of the beam of light, the water, darkened by the milk, causes a refraction of the colours of light. In the same way, the atmosphere reflects the rays of the Sun, according to its position in relation to the Earth.

The colours of the Sun and the sky

When the Sun is high it appears yellow, and the sky, if it is a calm day, appears blue, because the atmosphere filters out all the other colours. When the Sun at dawn is low, it looks red and the sky is pink, red and yellow. With the luminous rays of light coming at this angle, the colours of the spectrum become merged into the atmosphere.

The sky changes colour because the atmosphere spreads the light in a different way according to the position of the Sun.

Why does the colour black attract heat?

LIGHT AND HEAT

You need:
- a piece of thick aluminium foil
- an all-surface black marker pen
- scissors
- a ruler
- pencil
- sticky tape
- thread
- large, clear glass jar
- piece of strong card, larger than the opening of the jar

What to do

1 Cut two strips of aluminium foil each 10cm x 2.5cm.

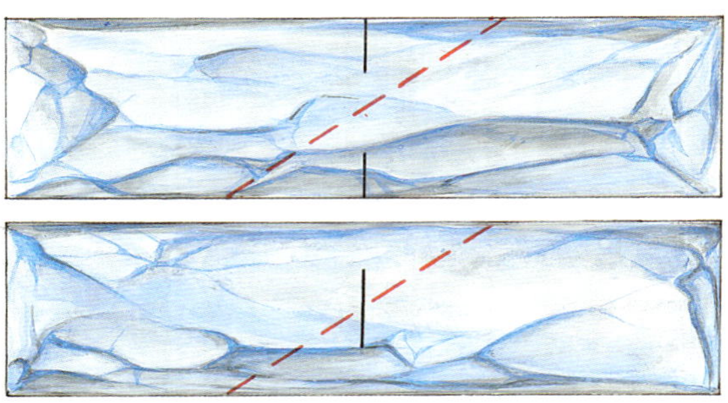

2 With the scissors, cut notches (shown as black lines in the picture).

3 Colour one side of each strip black. Then fold as shown in the picture so that the black side is inside the fold.

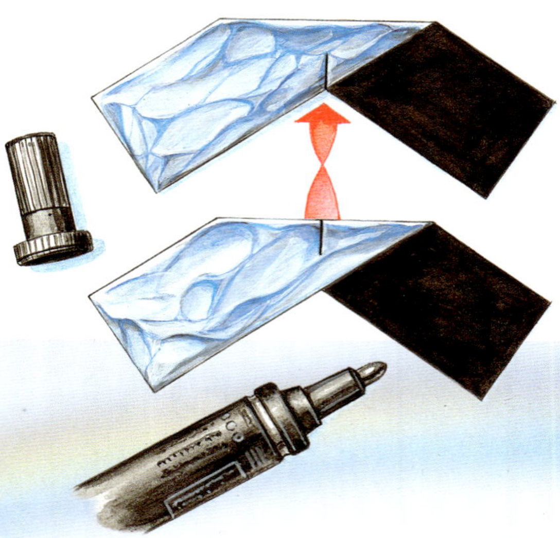

4 Place one strip underneath the other and fasten with sticky tape. Thread cotton through the card, as shown in the picture.

5 Hang the strips inside the jar, with the card as a cover. Then put the whole thing in direct sunlight.

What happens?
When the jar has warmed up, the 'sails' begin to turn slowly.

Because...
... the black side of the sails absorb more light than the silver, which reflects the light. So the black sails gets even hotter. As they warm the air around them, this warm air spreads out and pushes against the sails, making them turn.

TRAP THE HEAT

You need:
- two glass containers
- water
- a piece of black material
- a thermometer

What to do

1 Fill the two containers with water.

2 Cover one of them with the black cloth.

3 Put the two containers in direct sunlight and check the temperature each half hour.

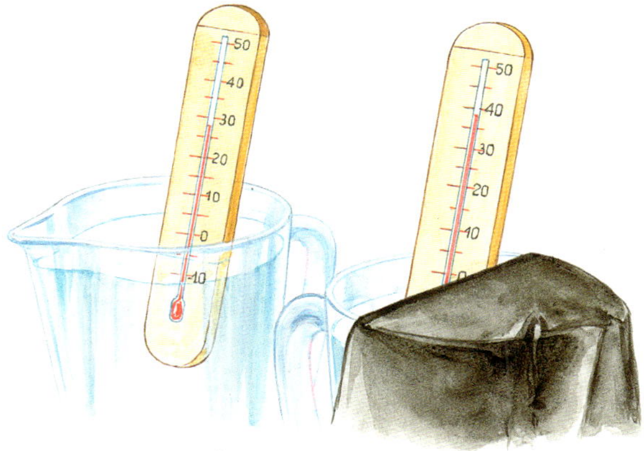

What happens?

The temperature of the water in the jar covered by the black cloth increases more quickly.

Because...

... the black cloth almost completely absorbs the light, whilst the surface of the water merely reflects it. The light absorbed by the black cloth is transformed into heat. This warms up both the air around it and the water underneath it, more than it would in the open air. That is why wearing black clothes when it is sunny makes us feel hotter than if we were wearing clear colours or white.

White houses

In very hot countries, houses are painted white to reflect the light. This prevents the intense heat of the Sun from entering the inside of the building.

Black objects completely absorb sunlight. Some of this absorption is converted into heat.

Capturing an image

For centuries people have searched for ways to record the images of things which they saw around them. Stone Age artists made wall paintings, sculptors built statues, artists painted pictures and frescos. Today it is nothing unusual for us to capture images and to keep them to look at (things like photographs, cinema films, television and video cassettes). But none of this would be possible if scientists and inventors had not discovered and understood how the human eye works and tried to reproduce the function of the eye by mechanical means. From simple boxes in which short-lived images are formed, right up to modern methods of technology which can preserve images how, when and where required, the function of the human eye is always at the beginning of the story.

How does the human eye see?

HOW THE EYE WORKS

You need:
- clear glass bowl (like a goldfish bowl)
- a table lamp
- a piece of card which is black on both sides
- a piece of white card
- scissors
- water
- a darkened room

What to do

1 Fill the bowl with water.

2 With the scissors make a small hole at the centre of the black card. Place this against the glass bowl.

3 Place the white card opposite so that it faces the bowl.

4 Darken the room and switch on the table lamp. Line this up in front of the black card, so that the beam of light is the same height as the hole.

What happens?

On the white card there appears an image of the lamp, but upside down.

Because...

... the light from the table lamp enters through the hole of the black card and becomes refracted through the bowl of water, which works like a lens. When the refracted light shines on the white card it reproduces an image of the lamp, but upside down.

How our eyes work

The pupil in our eye works like the hole in the card. It lets in the luminous light reflected by objects. On the inside of the eye, the light rays meet the crystalline lens (represented in the experiment by the bowl full of water) which works as a convex lens and brings the rays together to pass through it. These rays then strike the retina at the back of the eye. This is a sort of screen on which the image is projected, but smaller and upside down. (In the experiment, the retina is represented by the white card.)
Why are images projected upside down?

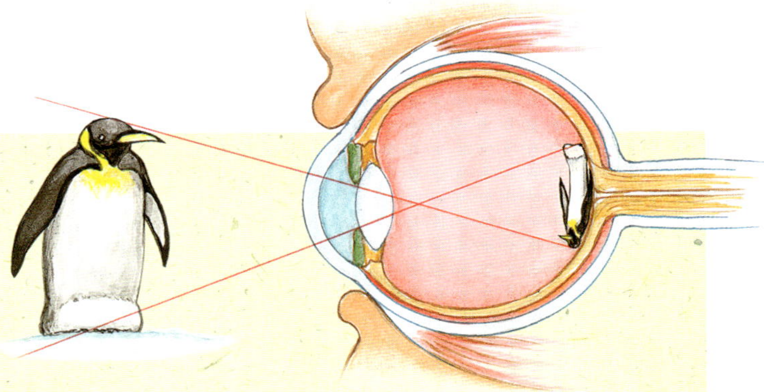

Because the rays of light which enter through the pupil travel in a straight line. As they converge through the crystalline lens, they cross over, changing their positions. But our brain 'straightens them up' through the impulses of the optic nerve at the back of the eye so that we see the image correctly.

The images of illuminated objects become projected on to the inside of the eye through the pupil.

How does a camera work?

IMAGES IN A BOX

You need:

- a square shaped box without a cover
- a cardboard tube
- a magnifying glass
- a piece of tracing paper
- scissors
- sticky tape
- black paint
- a paint brush

What to do

1 Paint the box black and allow to dry.

2 Draw around the tube on to the base of the box with a pencil. Cut inside the pencil line with scissors. Push the tube into the box.

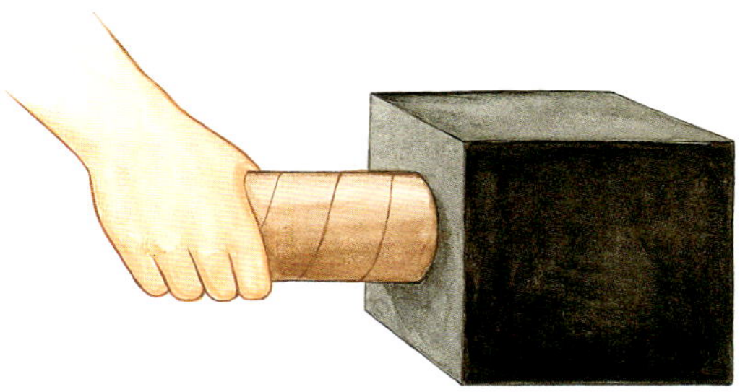

3 Use the sticky tape to fix the piece of tracing paper over the opening of the box, in place of a cover.

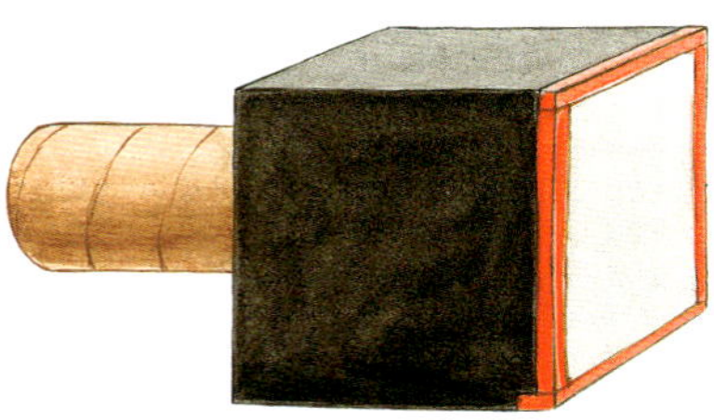

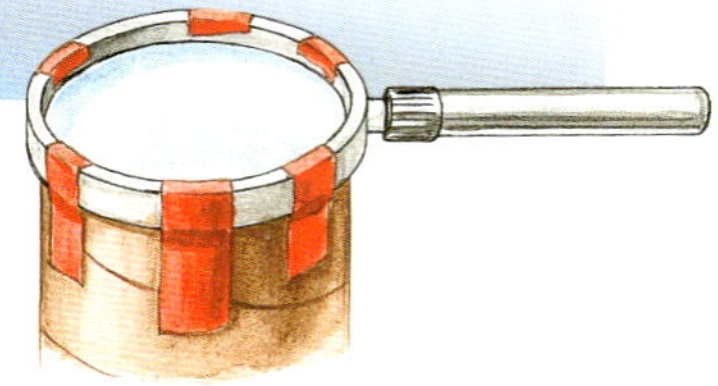

4 Fix the magnifying glass with sticky tape at the opening of the cardboard tube.

5 Aim the whole thing towards an object which is in a good light. Keep the end of the tube with the lens pointed at the object, and the part with the tracing paper towards you.

What happens?

On the tracing paper you see an image of the object, but small and upside down. (You will be able to make the image clearer by moving the tube.)

Because...

... the magnifying glass, which is convex, makes the rays of light converge on the inside of the box. The rays cross each other and form an upside down image on the tracing paper. Thousands of years ago, before it was discovered that eyes do not give out light, boxes similar to this one were invented, in which the light reflected by an object entered simply through a hole, without a lens. The image of the object reproduced on a sheet of paper was then observed with much wonder.

Photographic equipment

In photographic machines, the light enters through the *objective*. This is a lens which gathers in the light, and can be more or less convex in order to give a narrower or wider image of the object being photographed. The light passes through the opening for a short time (the time to 'click' the shutter!) and this makes an impression on the photographic film, which is inside, at the back of the camera. The film is covered in a substance which can record images. These images can be revealed only when the film is immersed in developing fluid to obtain a negative, which will enable a print to be made on paper. Ask an adult to show you the inside of a camera. Make sure that this does not have any film inside, otherwise this will be ruined by the tiniest amount of light getting inside.

Through the camera lens, the image of objects in the light is projected and impressed on photographic film.

Fact-Finder

Day and night

The Earth rotates on its own axis. This movement of rotation lasts 24 hours (one day) and determines the alternation of the day (hours of light) and the night (hours of darkness) in different parts of the Earth's surface. The length of the day and the night vary during the year, because, as the Earth travels around the Sun during the course of one year, the position of the Earth's axis changes in relation to the Sun. In Spring and Autumn, when the axis is perpendicular to the rays of the Sun, the day and the night last more or less the same time. At the beginning of the summer, when the North Pole is inclined towards the Sun, in the Boreal Hemisphere (the part of the globe north of the Equator) the day lasts far longer than the night; whilst in the Austral Hemisphere (south of the Equator) the night is much longer than the day. When the South Pole is nearer to the Sun, at the beginning of the winter, in the Austral Hemisphere the day lasts longer than that in the Boreal Hemisphere, where the night lasts longer than the day. At each extremity of the axis, that is at the North and at the South Pole, these phenomena are greater.

Space is dark

When the light from the Sun penetrates into a semi-darkened room, you may see tiny little particles moving about in its rays. These particles are called motes, tiny particles of dust. Just as the sunlight illuminates these particles clearly enough to be seen, so light spreads through the air during the hours of daylight, and we see everything which is lit up by the Sun. Models of the Solar System show the planets wrapped in darkness, because in space there is no atmosphere to reflect and spread the rays of the Sun. The planets break up the darkness only when their surfaces reflect light from the Sun. The Moon, Earth's only satellite, also reflects light from the Sun.

The ability of the Archerfish

Malay people call this the 'blowpipe fish'. Although the Archerfish is only 20cm long, it has an amazing ability. Without coming up to the surface of the water, it can send jets of water from its mouth on to the insects which live near the riverbanks. Even though they may be up to 1.5m above water, these insects still become easy prey for the Archerfish. What is even more extraordinary is that the Archerfish, as it takes aim, has to allow for refraction of the light, which makes insects seem to appear in a different place!

Curved mirrors

The curve of a mirror distorts an image because it changes the angle of reflection of the luminous rays of light. Try to look at yourself in a shining spoon, first, on the inside (concave) and then on the outside (convex). Draw the spoon away from yourself, then bring it closer. You will see your reflection changing until it turns upside down. Because of this characteristic, curved mirrors can be used for particular purposes. Convex makes images smaller, but gathers together a greater number of light rays. So a convex car mirror gives the driver a wider vision of the road behind. Concave mirrors enlarge the image, so these are useful for tasks like applying make-up or for shaving.

Magnetism

Can a magnet attract anything? What makes a needle move on a compass? Can an object be magnetized? How is an electromagnet made?

You will find the answers to these and many other questions by doing the experiments in the following pages, under the following sections:

The Magnet • Magnetic Poles • Magnetic Force
Magnetism and Electricity

Magnets

The power of magnets to attract steel objects and to attach themselves to metal surfaces has fascinated people for hundreds of years. To understand this power, we must first study the structure and the characteristics of a magnet. In the following pages we put large and small magnets to the test and discover how to interrupt and obstruct their force, as well as using magnets to make toys and games. All the experiments are safe to do, but an adult must be on hand to use some of the tools required.

Can magnets attract anything?

WHAT CAN RESIST ATTRACTION?

You need:
- things made of different materials: iron, wood, glass, plastic, steel, fabric, paper
- different surfaces: the door of a refrigerator and a wardrobe, a wall, a window pane....
- a magnet tied to a thread

What to do

1 Divide the objects into two groups: metal and non-metal.

2 Hold the magnet close to the objects in the first group, one at a time.

3 Now do the same with the objects in the second group.

4 Hold the magnet close to the surface of the refrigerator, the wardrobe, the wall and the window.

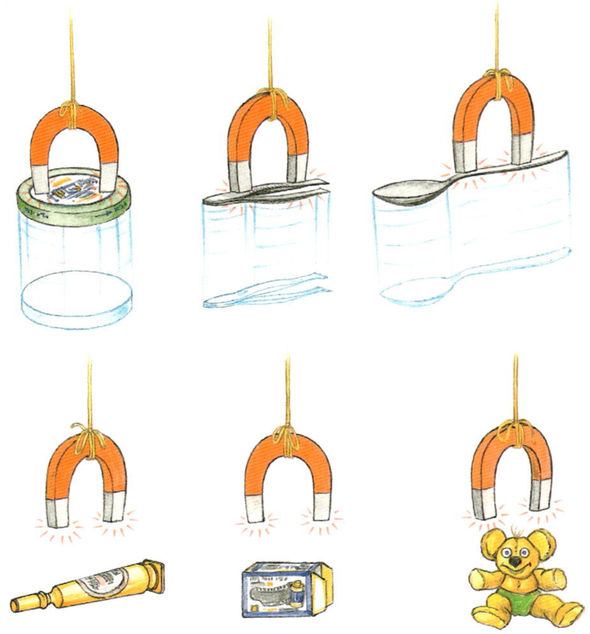

What happens?
Some metal objects attach themselves to the magnet. Others do not. The non-metal objects are not attracted. The magnet is attracted to some surfaces, but not to others.

Because...
... magnets are pieces of steel or iron which have a special ability to attract objects made from steel, iron, nickel, cobalt, chrome, or materials which contain a small amount of any of these metals. Wood, glass, plastic, paper and fabrics are not drawn to the force of the magnet. The force of attraction between the magnet and a large-size steel surface makes the magnet move towards the surface, because the magnet weighs less than the surface.

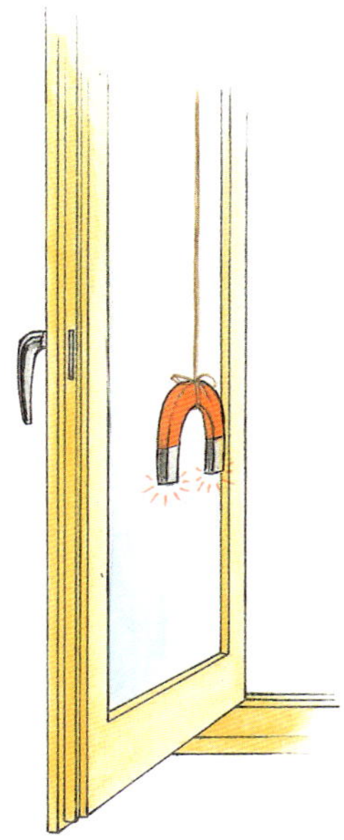

The discovery of magnetism

More than 2000 years ago, the Ancient Greeks discovered a mineral which was able to attract steel. This mineral is magnetite (magnetic iron ore). Magnetite gets its name from the ancient city of Magnesia (today called Manisa in Turkey) where it was found.
The fragments of magnetite are called natural magnetite. Nowadays, magnets can be made from pieces of iron or steel, by using a special process called magnetization.

Magnets exert their power of attraction on objects of iron, steel and other metals.

Can magnets work through substances?

UNDERWATER MAGNETISM

You need:
- a magnet
- a jug
- a paper-clip
- water

What to do

1 Pour water into the jug and drop in the paper-clip. Then invite a friend to take the paper-clip out, but without putting a hand in the water.

2 Place the magnet on the outside of the jug, on the side of the paper-clip. When this moves towards the magnet, draw the magnet slowly up towards the top.

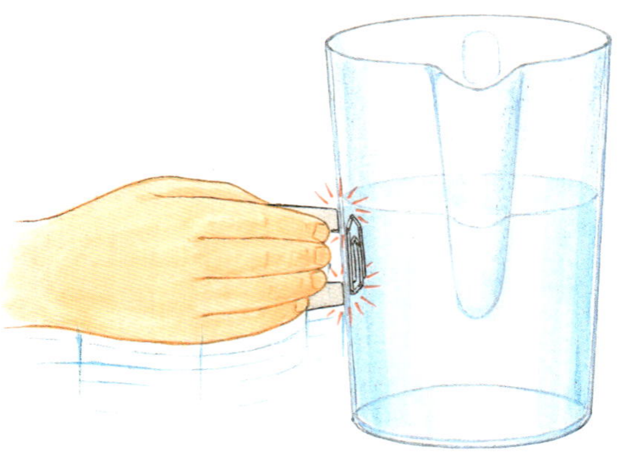

What happens?
The paper-clip follows the movement of the magnet until it is above the level of the water. In this way, it is possible to take it out without getting your hand wet!

Because...
... the force of the magnet also works through the glass of water. If the sides of the jug were iron or steel, the paper-clip would still be drawn to the magnet, but with a lesser intensity, because part of the magnetic force would be 'absorbed' by the sides of the jug.

Magnets under water
Because they can also exert their power underwater, magnets are widely used during the construction and the repair of underwater installations. For example, engineers use magnets to hold instruments and equipment in a safe place, and for holding parts of the installation in position during work.

A SET COURSE

You need:
- card
- scissors
- sticky tape
- felt-tipped pens
- a large piece of strong cardboard
- two little sticks
- two magnets
- two cubes of steel
- four thick books
- a table

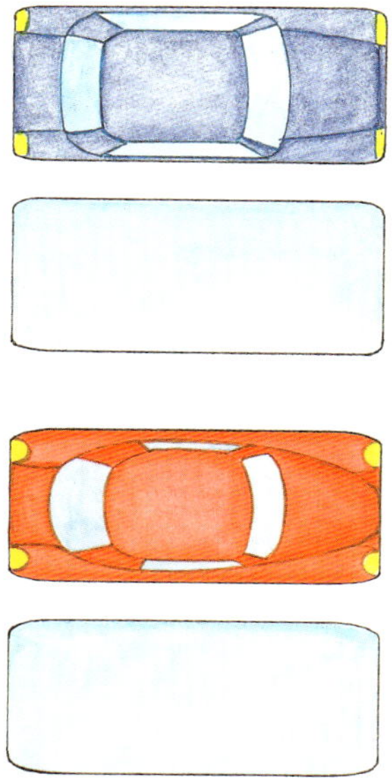

What to do

1 Draw four rectangles with rounded corners and cut out. Draw the outline of the top view of a car on two shapes. Colour these in.

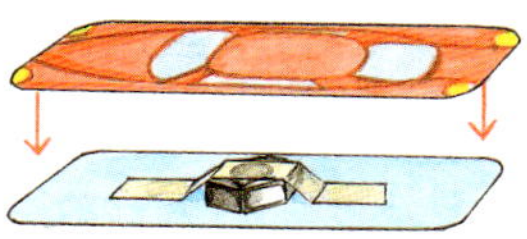

2 Fix the cube of steel between two car shapes with the sticky tape.

3 Draw two courses on the cardboard, each course with a start and finish. Colour in. Then place the cardboard on the books, as shown in the picture.

4 Put the two cardboard cars at the start.

5 Fasten a magnet to each stick with the sticky tape.

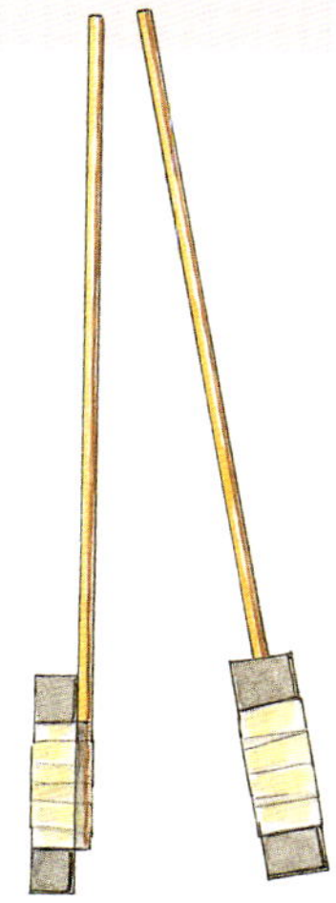

6 Position the stick magnets underneath the cardboard, under the two cars, so that you can move them along the course with the stick magnets. Then ask a friend to have a race with you.

What happens?

The cars move along the course following the magnets which are under the cardboard.

Because...

... the force of the magnet passes through the cardboard and attracts the cubes of steel taped inside the cars. So they go along, following the movement of the magnets.

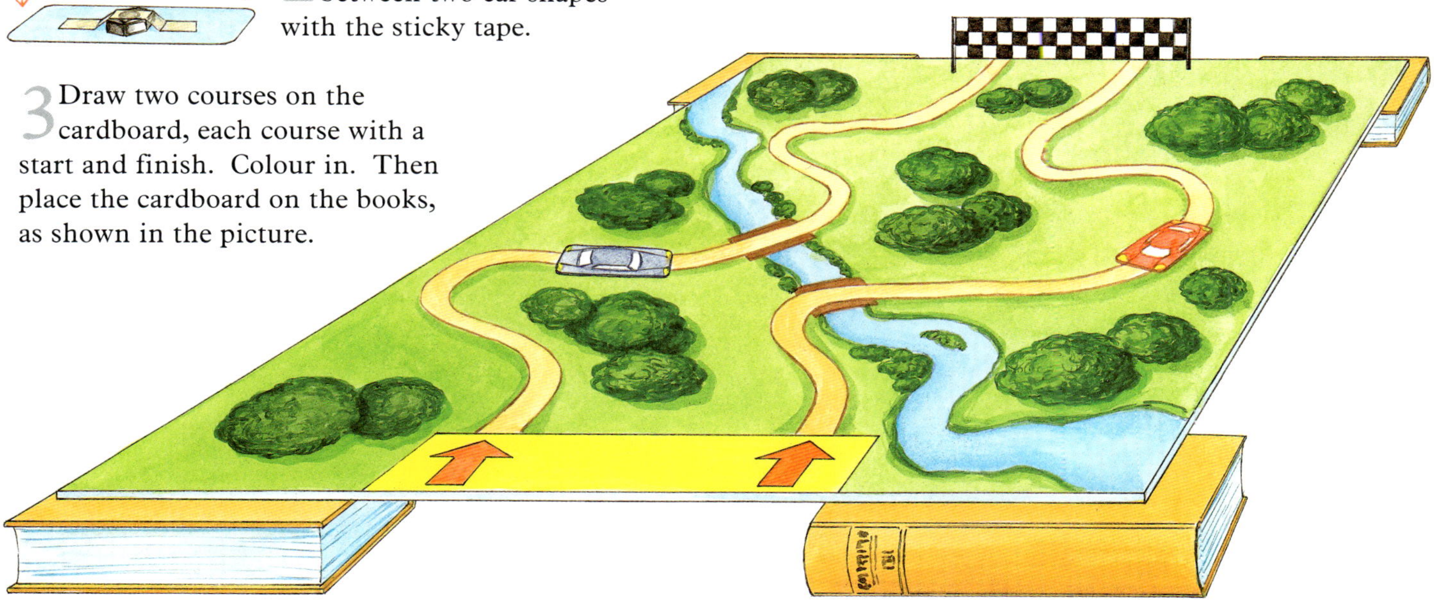

Magnetic force can pass through objects and substances.

Can magnets work at a distance?

MAGNETIC REGATTA

You need:

- two sticks, about 40cm long
- two magnets
- two pieces of string about 30cm long
- needles
- coloured card
- scissors
- six corks
- toothpicks
- sticky tape
- a large bowl
- water

What to do

1 To make a 'fishing rod', tie one end of a string to the end of a stick, and the other end around a magnet. Make a second fishing rod in the same way.

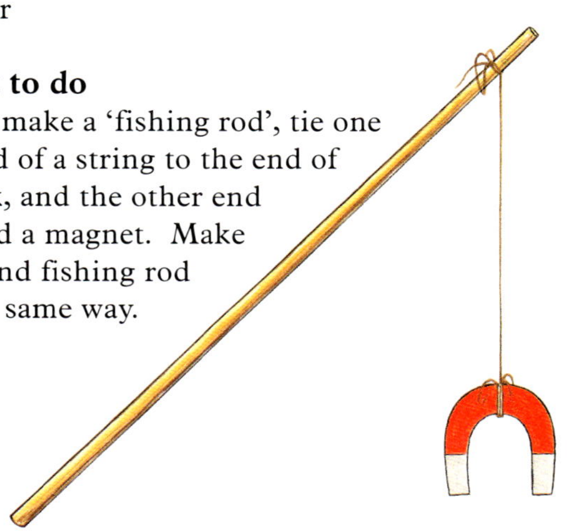

2 To make a fishing boat, first take three corks and link them together with a toothpick, as shown in the picture.

3 Stick the two needles into the centre cork to make the ship's masts. For the sails, cut squares from the card. Fasten to the needles with sticky tape.

2 Fill the bowl with water and launch the boats. Hold your fishing rod above one of the boats and invite a friend to hold the other fishing rod.

What happens?

The movement of the fishing rods above the bowl make the boats move, without them being touched.

Because...

... the force of the magnet draws the needles, even at a distance, and this guides the movement of the boats.

COMPARE THE FORCE

You need:
- three magnets of different sizes
- some objects of iron or steel (coins, for example)
- a table
- a ruler

What to do

1 Place the things on the table about 10cm apart.

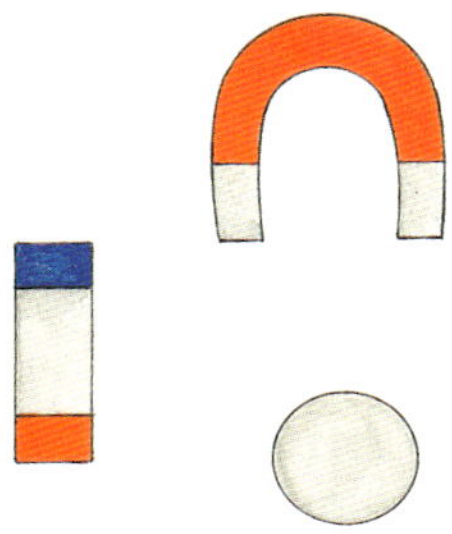

2 Place some coins on the table in the same way. These should be facing the magnet, but some distance from it.

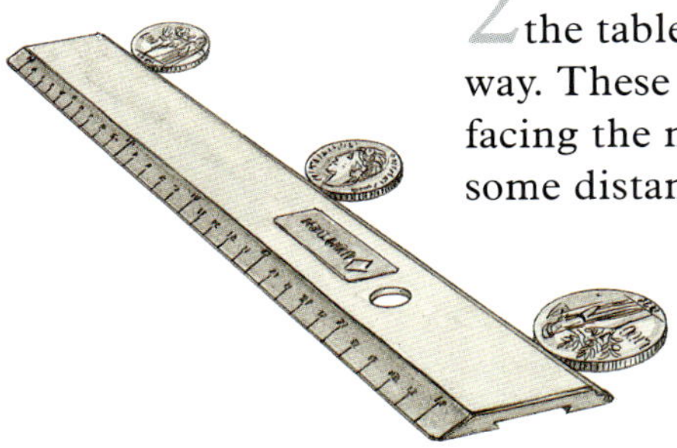

3 Using the ruler, gradually push the coins closer and closer to the magnets.

What happens?
Some of the coins are attracted by the magnets almost at once, others only when they are a short distance away.

Because...
... magnets can exert their force at a distance from things. The larger the magnet, the stronger its force and the greater the distance at which it can attract objects.

Stir with a magnet

Because they can exert their force at a distance and through substances, magnets can be used for medical research. In chemical laboratories, it is often necessary to mix delicate substances in tiny quantities, without these coming into contact with anything which is not perfectly sterile. This is done by a tiny metal plate with a sterile covering being placed in the bottom of a test-tube, and a magnet underneath the test-tube. When the substances have been put in the test-tube, the magnet is set to turn at a regular pace. The magnet turns the plate inside the test-tube and so mixes the substances. (These pieces of equipment are called 'agitators'.)

A magnet can even exert its force at a considerable distance, according to its power.

What can block out the force of a magnet?

TRAP THE MAGNETIC FORCE

You need:
- some sheets of newspaper
- pieces of aluminium foil
- bits of material
- some foam rubber
- a large magnet
- something made of iron

What to do

1 Wrap the magnet in a sheet of newspaper. Then try to attract the iron object.

2 Do the same thing with the other materials.

3 Now wrap each magnet in a second layer of the same material. Add more layers, until the force of the magnet weakens and then stops.

What happens?
The magnet attracts the object through one thin layer of material. But as the thickness of layers increases, it can no longer exert its force.

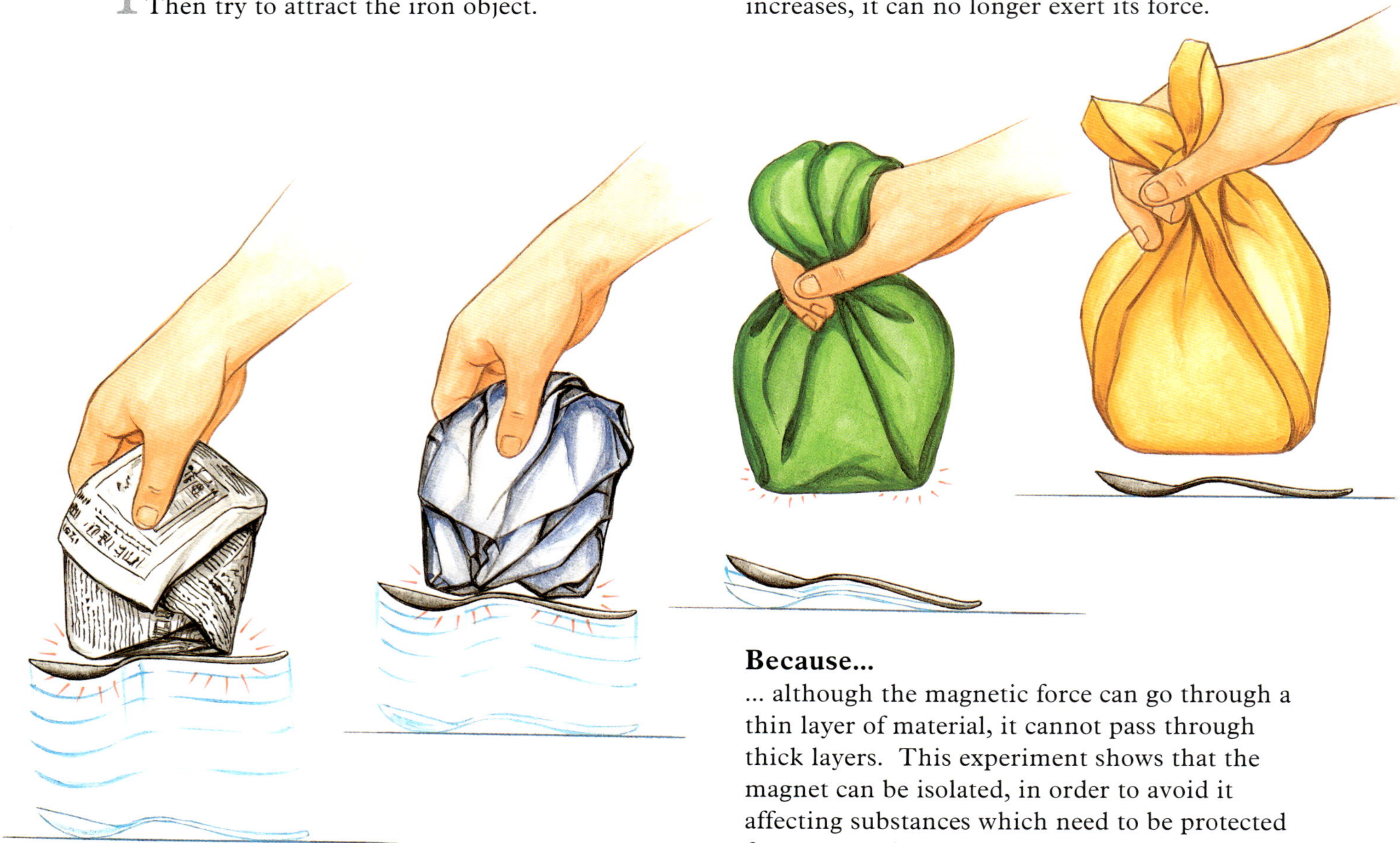

Because...
... although the magnetic force can go through a thin layer of material, it cannot pass through thick layers. This experiment shows that the magnet can be isolated, in order to avoid it affecting substances which need to be protected from magnetic attraction.

The force of a magnet can be neutralized by a thick layer of non-magnetic material.

What does the power of a magnet depend on?

A TEST OF POWER

You need:
- magnets of different shapes (horse-shoe, bar, round) and different sizes
- things made of iron or steel (paper-clips, coins, nails)
- cardboard boxes

What to do

1 Sort the things into boxes.

2 Hold the magnet over each box in turn, and count how many of the same objects are drawn to it.

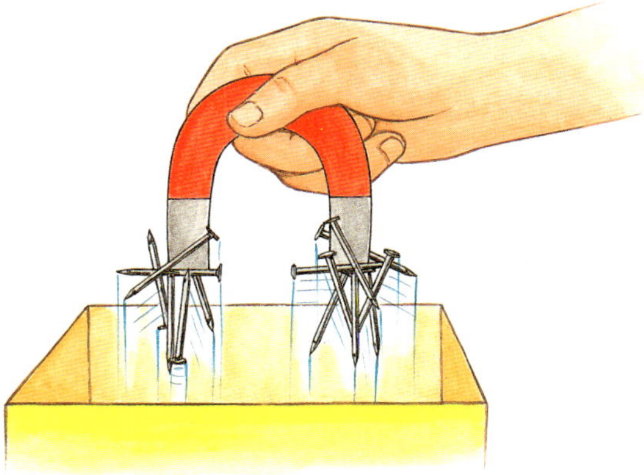

What happens?
Some magnets attract more objects than others.

Because...
... the shape of a magnet influences its power. An iron horse-shoe magnet is more powerful than a bar magnet, which, in turn, is more powerful than a round magnet. With magnets of the same shape, the larger the magnet, the more powerful it is.

Tiny magnets on tape

The tape used in a cassette player is magnetic tape. It is covered in metal oxide which can easily be magnetized. Patterns of varying magnetic fields on the tape pass the recording head in the machine. The recording head is made of a magnet worked by electricity. This puts the magnetization of the tape in a certain order so that, as the tape passes the playback head, the magnetic patterns become 'translated' into electronic signals which are transformed into sound through a loudspeaker.

The strength of a magnet is linked to its shape and its size.

The Magnetic Poles

Have you ever tried to beat the invisible strength of two magnets which are attracted to each other? It is almost impossible to do! In the next pages you can find out why this is so, and discover that the largest magnet of all is right under your feet... This is the Earth, which, just like any other magnet, has its own magnetic poles. These poles determine the positioning of all compass needles, as well as being the cause of the spectacular aurora borealis.

Do all parts of a magnet have the same force?

LINES OF POWER

You need:

- iron filings (obtainable from a workshop, or by filing a piece of iron)
- a bar magnet
- a horse-shoe magnet
- two postcards

What to do

1 Place one postcard on the bar magnet.

2 Gradually sprinkle the iron filings on the card. Give the card a few taps with your finger.

3 Now do the same with the horse-shoe magnet.

What happens?

Most of the iron filings are centred around the outside of the magnet. A lesser amount is scattered around.

Because...

... the magnetic force of a magnet is concentrated at the poles, meaning the ends of the magnet. Away from the poles, the magnetism is not so strong.

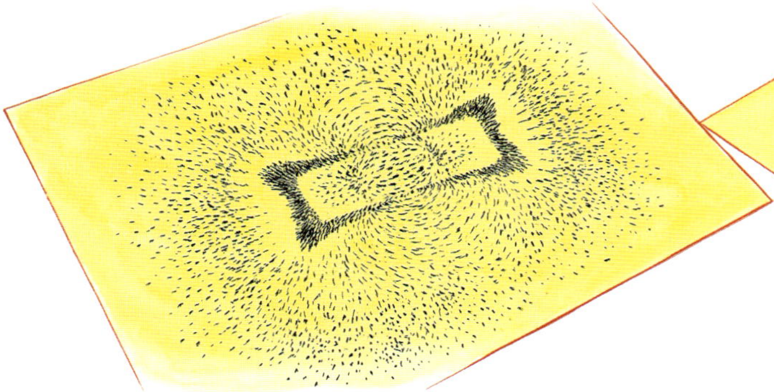

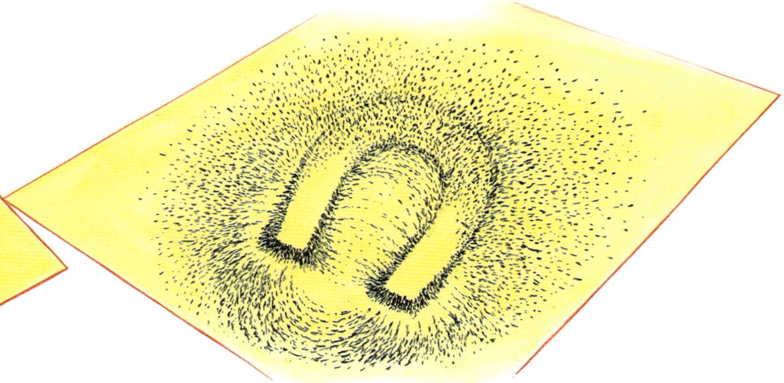

Magnetic fields

Iron filings placed around a magnet arrange themselves according to the lines of force which show us the area in which magnetism is active. This area is called a magnetic field. The objects attracted by the magnet are drawn inside this magnetic field. The magnetic forces are distributed around the magnet in a set way. With the filings in the last experiment, we saw this only in a horizontal plane. The same force also works on a vertical plane.

The magnetism exerted by a magnet is more intense at its ends, which we call the magnetic poles.

Why do two magnets sometimes repel (push apart)?

FLOATING MAGNETS

You need:
- two bar magnets
- sticky tape in red, blue and transparent
- a compass
- two cardboard boxes of the same size
- scissors
- two pencils
- string

What to do

1 Tie a magnet on to a piece of string, as shown in the picture. Hold it over the compass until it stops spinning. Then compare the position of the magnet with the needle of the compass. Put a little piece of red sticky tape on the pole indicated by the needle, and blue sticky tape on the opposite pole. Now do the same with the other magnet.

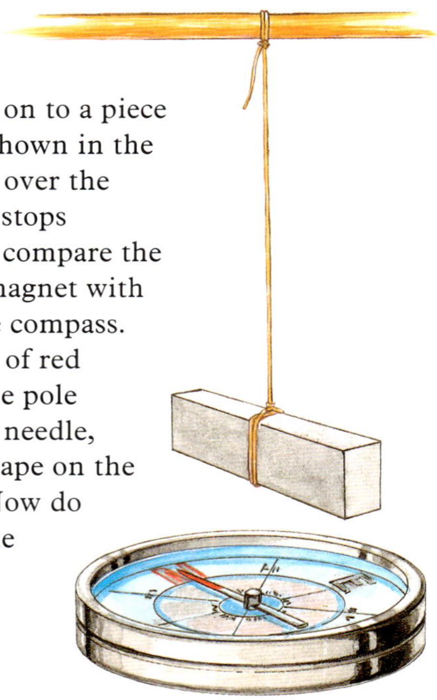

2 Bring the two poles of the same colour close together. Then do the same with poles of a different colour.

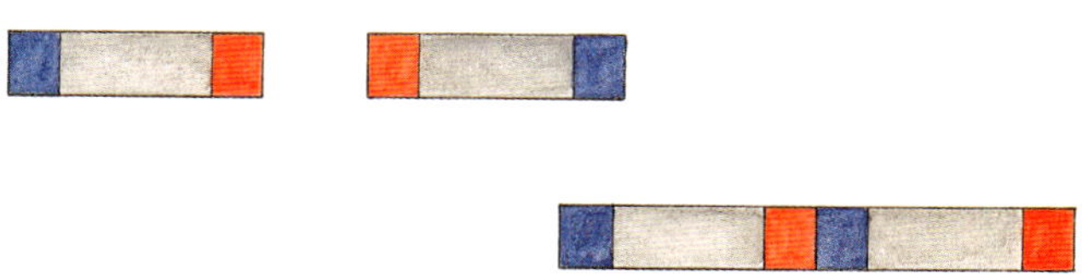

What happens?

The poles of the same colour are not attracted. Poles of the opposite colour are attracted.

3 Tape a magnet inside each box. Close the box. On the outside, put a piece of blue or red sticky tape to match with the two poles of the magnet inside.

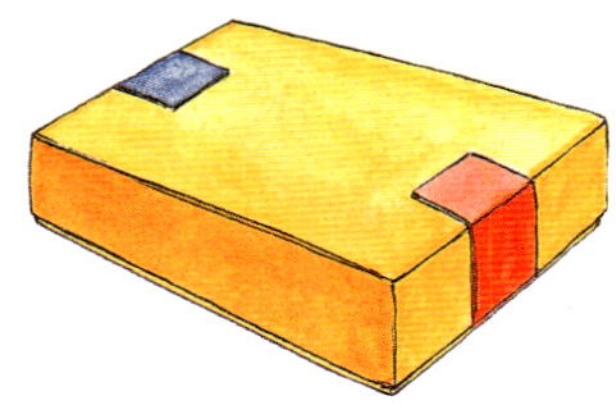

4 Place the two pencils on one of the boxes. Put the second box on top of the pencils, matching the marks of the same colours at the ends.

5 Wrap the clear sticky tape around the two boxes. Then take out the two pencils. Press down the upper box.

What happens?

The upper box seems to float above the one underneath.

Because...

... the two poles of each magnet are charged with a different magnetism (negative and positive). The charge of opposite poles attract. The charge of the same poles repel (push apart). That is why, because the same poles corresponded, each box pushed the other away. And after you managed to beat this force of repulsion between them, once you released the pressure of your hand, the upper box returned to its original position.

PUSH AT A DISTANCE

You need:
- two bar magnets with opposite poles (see last experiment)
- a toy lorry
- sticky tape

What to do

1 Fix the bar magnet on the lorry with the sticky tape.

2 Use the other magnet to draw the lorry towards it.

What happens?

When you bring the same pole closer, you push the lorry away. When you bring a different pole closer to the lorry, you bring it towards you.

Because...

... the movement of the lorry is determined by the magnetic force which draws in two directions – towards the magnet which you have in your hand (two different poles attract each other) and in the opposite direction (two poles of the same repel each other). You can use this experiment to play games with your friends.

Trains without wheels

Some high speed trains do not have wheels. Instead, there is a system of magnets near the rails, roughly where the wheels would be. These magnets are worked by electricity, so that the same magnetic poles are pulled towards the other. So, as the magnets repel, the train 'floats' above the rails. This means the trains move without any friction. Because of this, they can reach considerable speeds.

The opposite poles of two magnets attract each other. Two of the same poles repel each other.

What makes the needle of a compass move?

TO FIND NORTH

You need:
- a bowl
- water
- a bar magnet
- a flat polystyrene tray (smaller than the bowl; it must be able to move on the surface of the water without hitting the sides of the bowl)
- coloured sticky tape

Check that there are no items of steel or iron within reach.

What to do

1 Fill the bowl with water and place on the surface of the water a polystyrene tray with the magnet taped at the centre.

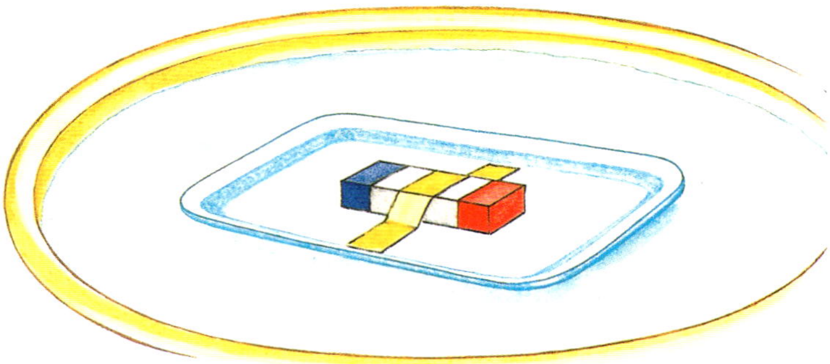

2 Twirl the tray around. Wait until it stops.

3 Put two pieces of sticky tape in the edge of the bowl according to the two poles of the magnet.

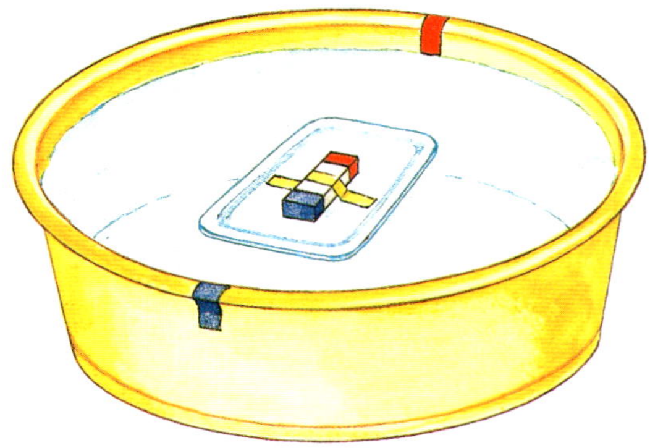

4 Now twirl the tray once again.

What happens?
When the tray stops, the poles of the magnet match the two marks once again.

Because...
... the magnetic force exerted by the Earth is so strong that it makes all movable magnets point one of their poles towards the north pole, the other towards the south pole.

Earth's magnetism

The Earth acts like a great big magnet. It produces a magnetic field which makes compass needles and magnets point in the direction of its magnetic poles. It is believed that this phenomenon is due both to the composition of the internal nucleus of the Earth, which is made of steel and nickel, and the rotation of the compass needle brought about by the rotation of the Earth.

The lines which mark out the Earth's magnetic field go from one pole to the other. The needle of a compass moves following these lines. The magnetic north pole, which points towards the tip of the south pole of the compass needle, is not the same as the geographical North Pole, which we see on the map. The magnetic north pole is on the island of Bathurst in Canada 1900 kilometres from the geographical North Pole. The magnetic south pole is located at a point in the sea, 2600 kilometres from the geographical South Pole. These magnetic poles are not fixed. They change their position, although these changes take place over thousands of years.

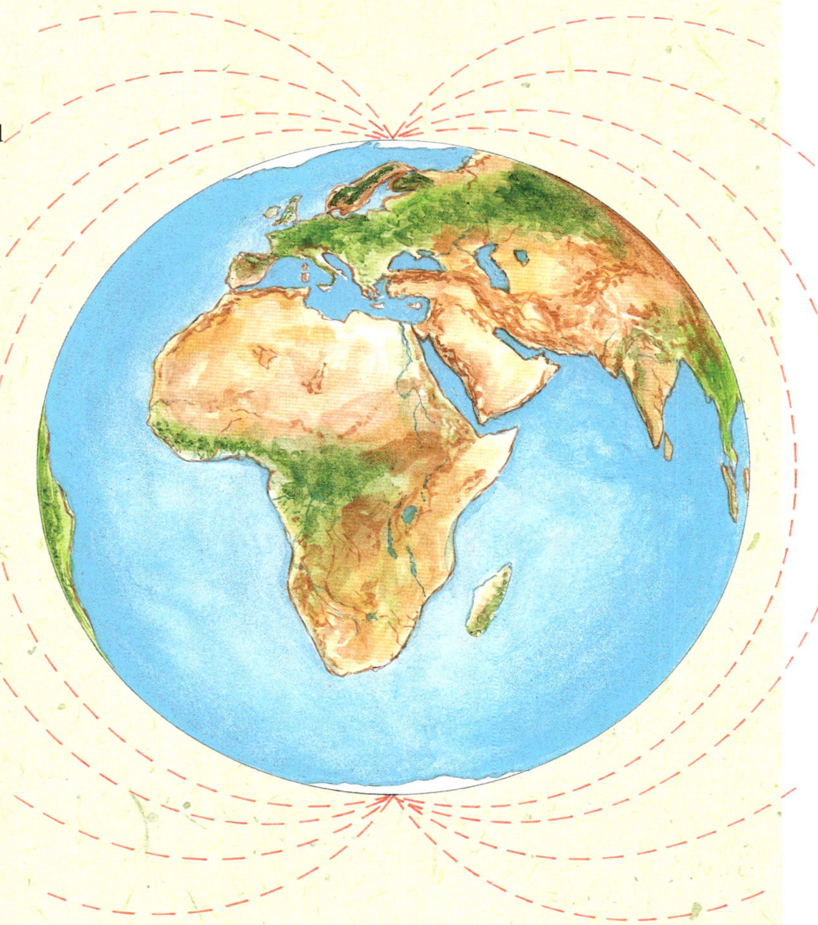

The compass

The first to make use of the Earth's magnetism to find their way around were the Chinese. They floated a little table with a bar of magnetite on it on water and watched how it moved. The first compasses began to be used in Europe in 1200, perhaps introduced by the Arabs.

There are different types of compass, but the best known is the magnetic compass. The magnetic needle is fixed at the centre of the face on a pivot, so that it can rotate. The needle positions itself in the north/south direction by the effect of the Earth's magnetic field, and so indicates the four cardinal points, (north, south, east and west), with mid-way directions (northeast, southwest, etc.) in between. The cardinal points and midway directions are shown on the face of the compass, with the coloured tip of the needle always pointing north.

Earth acts like an enormous magnet. It attracts any magnetic needle which is free to move.

Magnetic Force

Now we must discover something more about the mysterious force generated by magnets. In this section you will be able to experiment with a magnetic object which in turn can become capable of attracting other objects; then discover how it is possible to give a needle or a nail a permanent magnetic force, and how we can make it lose this force. You will see what happens when a magnet is broken in half, and finally how we can play at beating the force of gravity with the magnetic force.

Can something be made magnetic?

MAKE A MAGNET

You need:
- a bar magnet
- two large needles

What to do

1 Using the end of the magnet, stroke each needle along its entire length 40 times, each time in the same direction.

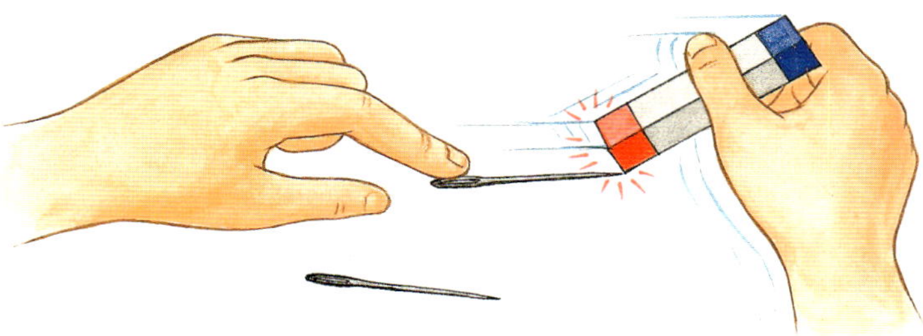

2 Push one needle close to the other, first pushing with the point, then with the eye of the needle.

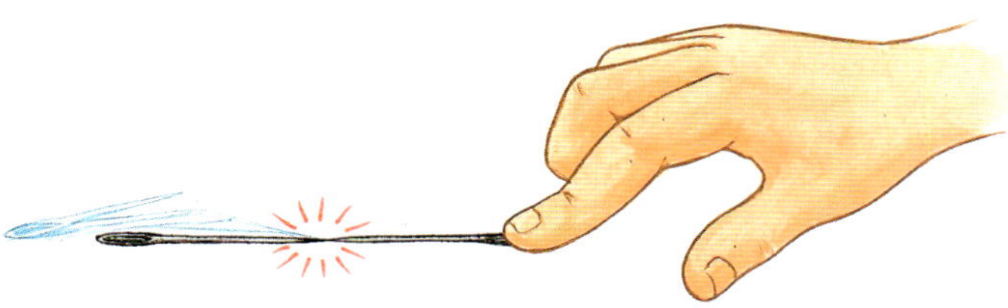

What happens?
The needles either attract or repel, according to the end which you push forward.

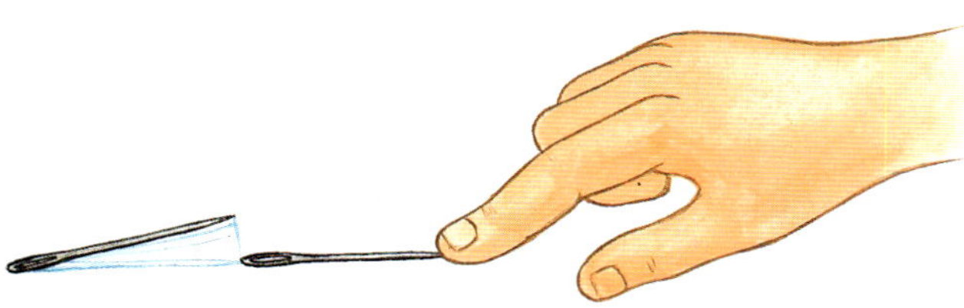

Because...
... the rubbing of the magnet on the needles has created a permanent magnetization. The needles are, in fact, acting like two magnets and they attract or repel according to the poles which you bring closer.

Making magnets

People have not only learned to use natural magnets, but also to make artificial magnets from iron or other special metals. The materials used to make artificial magnets are subjected to heat and then left to cool in moulds in the presence of a strong magnetic field. Once cooled and hardened, the material will have acquired magnetic properties.

Watches and magnets

Bringing a magnet near a steel watch with a hairspring is dangerous. The force of the magnet is likely to magnetize the steel parts permanently. This means that the parts will no longer be able to move correctly and the watch will not work.

An object made of iron or steel can be magnetized by stroking it with the end of a magnet.

Can a magnet lose its force?

TO ATTRACT OR NOT TO ATTRACT

You need:
- some needles
- a magnet
- a hard surface

What to do

1 Stroke the needle along its entire length using one end of the magnet. Stroke in the same direction for 40 times.

2 Bring the magnetized needle near to the other needles.

What happens?
As in the last experiment, the magnetized needle attracts the others.

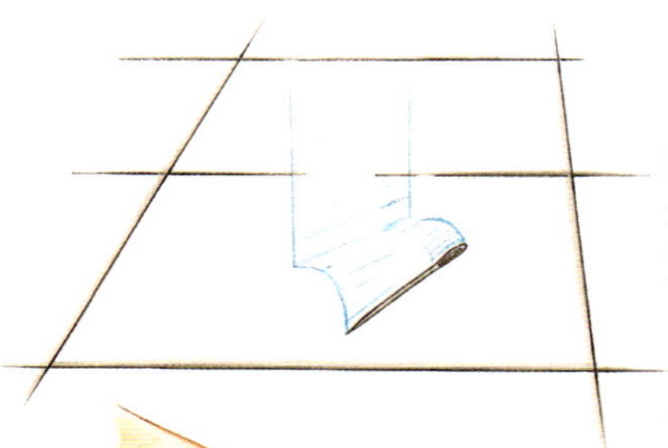

3 Now let the magnetized needle drop repeatedly on the hard surface.

4 Bring this needle close to the others once again.

What happens?
The magnetized needle no longer attracts the others.

Because...
... the needle has lost its magnetic force as a result of being dropped on the hard surface. With each drop, the particles which comprise the needle are shaken around in the opposite direction to the strokes of the magnet. This puts the particles in a muddle. The result is a loss of the magnetic power.

How an object is magnetized

Metal objects on the inside are subdivided into tiny little sectors called domains. Normally these are positioned in a different way to each other and their magnetic force is cancelled out. The stroking of a magnet brings them all into the same direction and makes it so that the object becomes a magnet. But if a magnet is then dropped repeatedly, the domains become disarranged, and the magnetic force ceases.

When magnets are dropped or subjected to knocks, they can become de-magnetized.

Can a magnet have only one pole?

DIVIDE UP THE MAGNETIC FORCE

You need:

- a big needle
- a bar magnet
- pliers
- pins

What to do

1 Magnetize the needle, as explained in the last few experiments.

2 Bring the magnet close to the two ends of the needle in turn. One end of the needle will be attracted. The other end will be repelled.

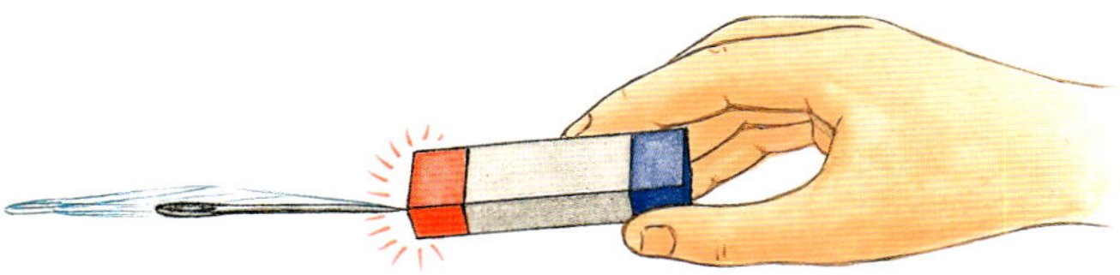

3 Ask an adult to break a needle in half with the pliers.

4 Try again to bring the magnet near to the two pieces of the needle.

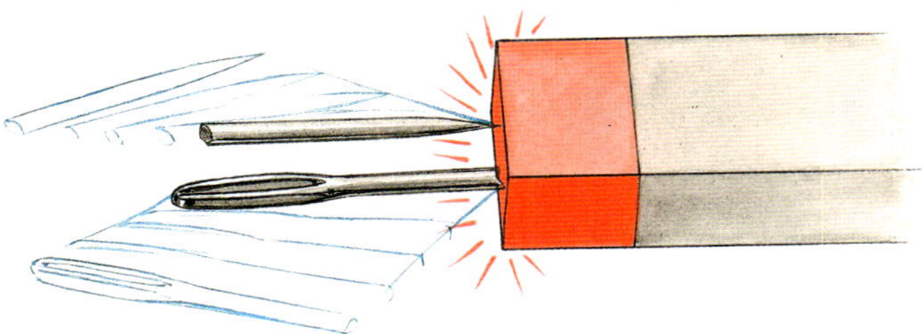

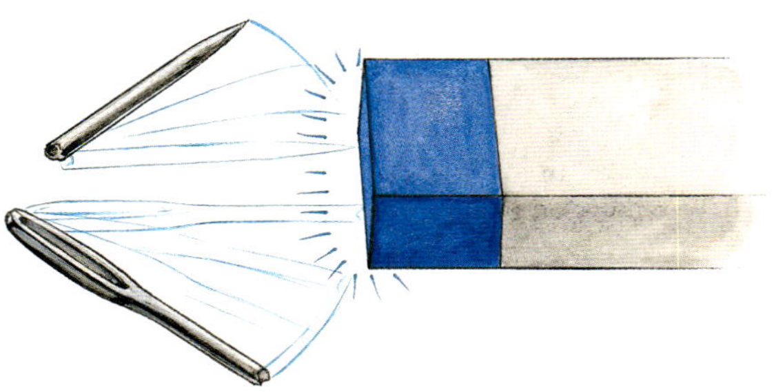

What happens?

The two parts of the needle both act like small magnets, each with a north and a south pole.

5 Divide each piece of the needle in half once again. Bring the magnet close to each piece, and the pins.

What happens?

All the pieces of the needle are attracted or repelled by the two poles of the magnet and they are able to magnetize the pins. So the pieces of the needle are now small magnets, each with two poles.

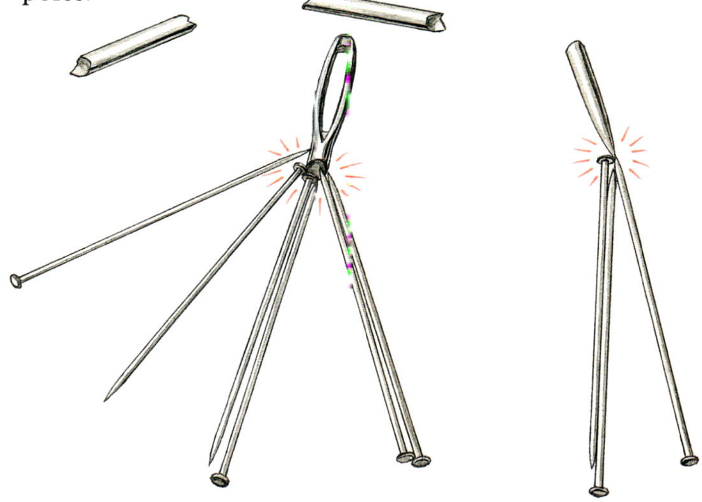

Because...

... magnets are made up of countless tiny, little magnets called magnetic elements, each one with a positive pole and a negative pole. Also, if we divide the magnet into tiny, little pieces, each piece will still keep two distinct poles.

From this experiment, you will see that magnetism is present in each atom (the tiniest part) of a magnet.

In magnets, the negative and positive charges are always at the two opposite ends.

Can magnetism be transmitted?

THE MAGNETIC CHAIN

You need:

- a magnet
- two nails

What to do

1 Pick up one nail with the magnet. Then draw this nail towards the second one.

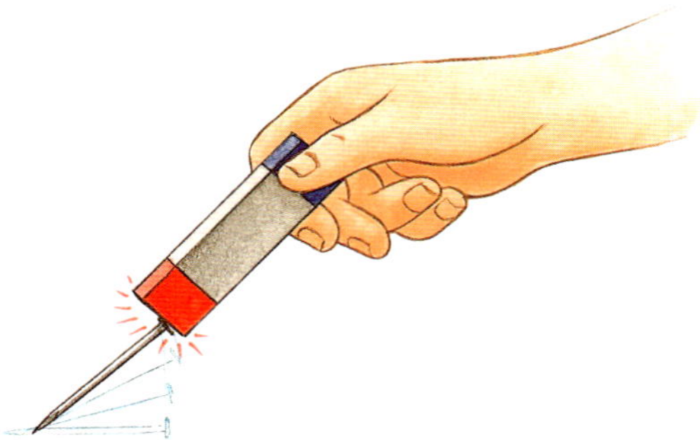

What happens?
The first nail attracts the second one.

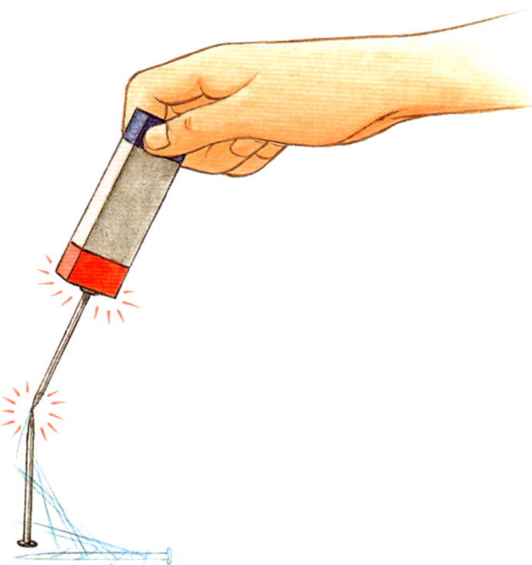

2 Take the first nail off the magnet, but keep the magnet close by.

What happens?
Once again, the first nail attracts the second. This time, the two remain linked.

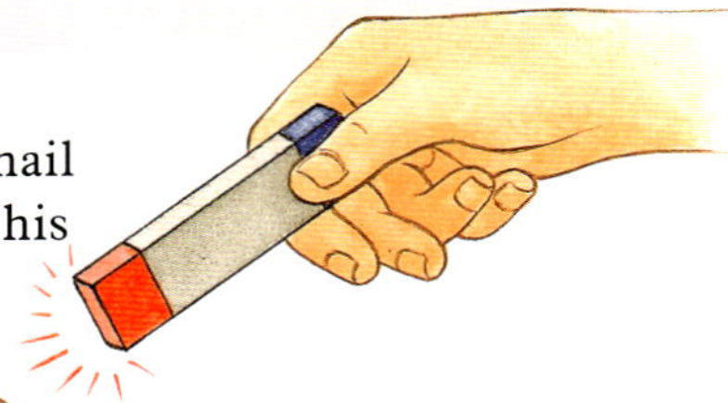

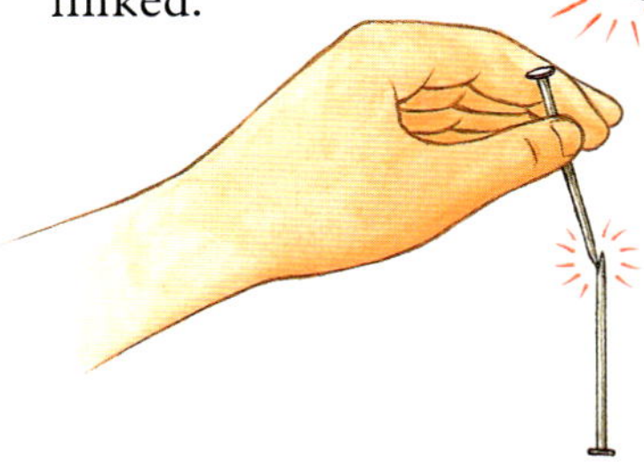

3 Draw the magnet away.

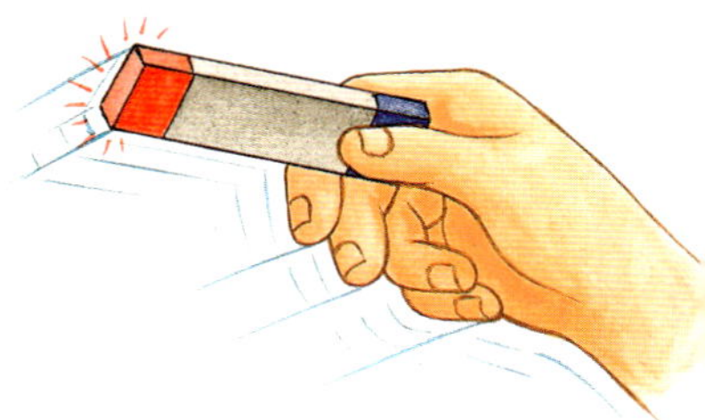

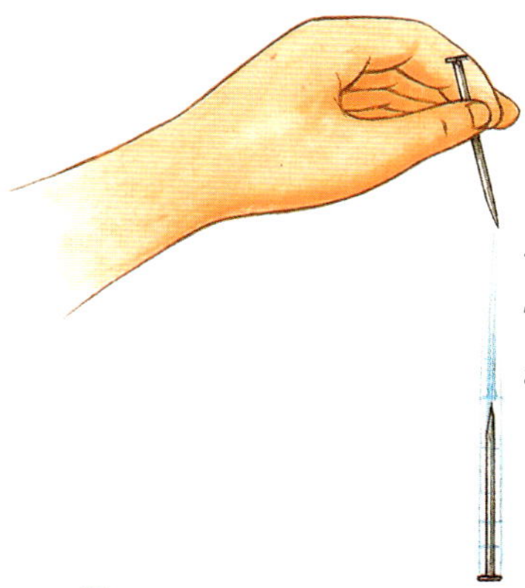

What happens?
The two nails separate and the second one falls.

Because...
... on contact with the magnet, the first nail is magnetized and works like a magnet on the second nail. The magnetic force of the magnet is also exerted nearby, and so this force is transmitted to the two nails in both parts of the experiment. This transmission is then broken by the magnet being drawn away.

EXCHANGE OF MAGNETISM

You need:
- a nail
- a bar magnet
- a steel ball (like the ones found inside a ball-bearing)

What to do

1 Bring the magnet close to the steel ball. Touch the ball with your finger to test the force by which it is drawn to the magnet.

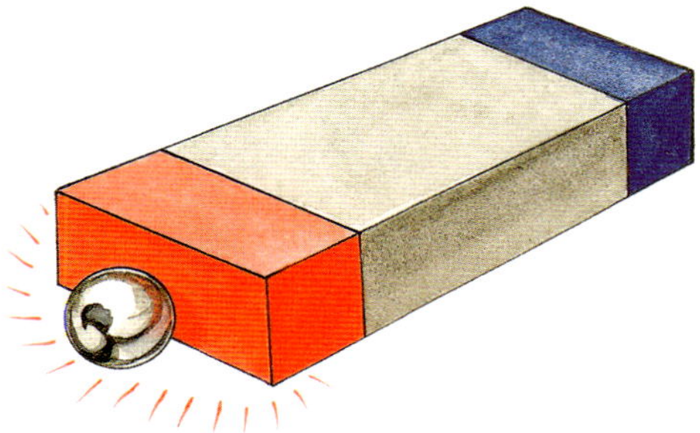

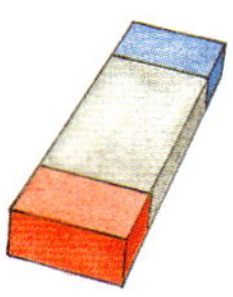

2 Take the nail, place it on the ball, then draw it away.

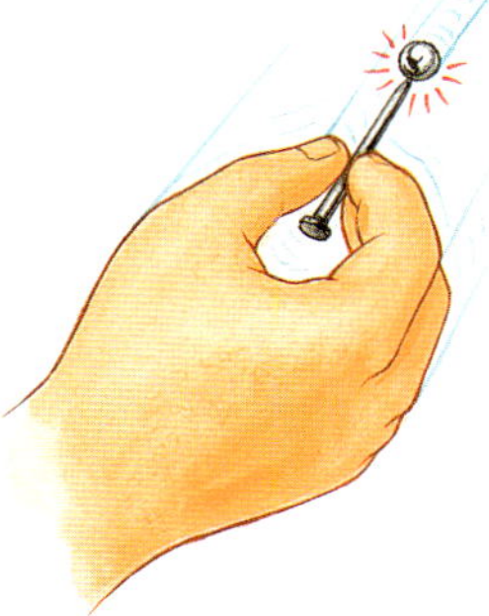

What happens?
The ball attaches itself to the nail.

Because...
... the magnetic force of the magnet passes through the nail, giving it the same magnetic force.

Magnetic Induction

In the picture below, a card has been sprinkled with iron filings, so that you can see magnetization by induction (that is magnetic force drawing but without contact) of a key which is near a magnet. Around the key, which is made of iron, a second magnetic field has been formed. Iron, like cobalt, nickel and steel, is a ferromagnetic material. The domains of ferromagnetic materials are composed of magnetic elements in the same way, and these become subjected to a magnetic field which goes in one direction, transforming the object into a magnet. But other substances, like air or water, have a low level of magnetism. So, when these substances are subjected to a magnetic field, they do not yield to change, nor do they force any increase or weakening of the magnetic field itself. Substances which are weakly pulled towards a strong magnet are called paramagnetic. Those weakly repelled by a magnet are called diamagnetic.

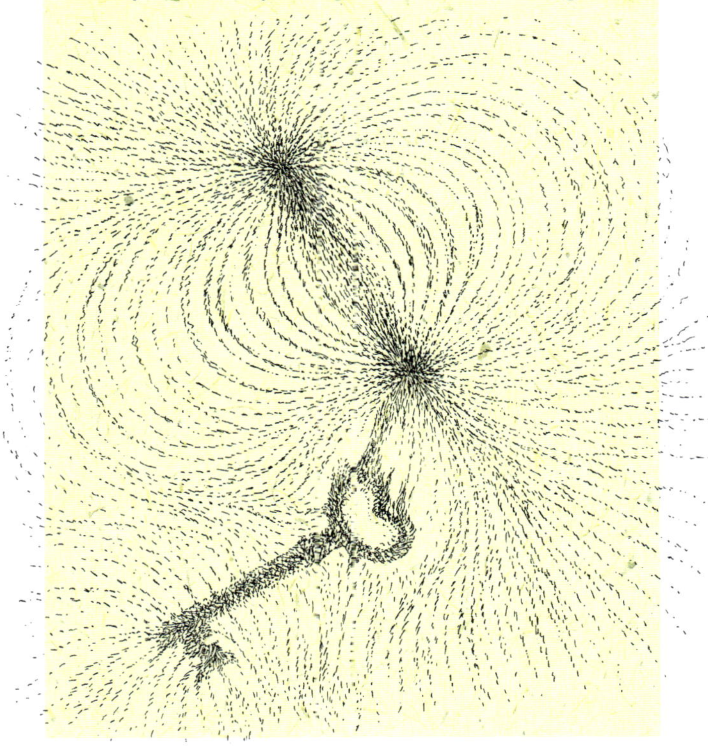

Magnetism can be transmitted temporarily by contact or by induction.

Can magnetic force hinder gravity?

THE KITE

You need:
- a magnet tied to a thread
- a paper-clip
- coloured card
- scissors
- sticky tape
- thread
- a pencil
- a table

What to do

1 Draw a kite shape on the coloured card and cut out. Fix a paper-clip in the centre with sticky tape.

2 Cut a piece of string about 30cm long. Tie one end to the paper-clip, then thread through the card. Fix the other end to the table with sticky tape.

3 Bring the magnet closer to the kite from above.

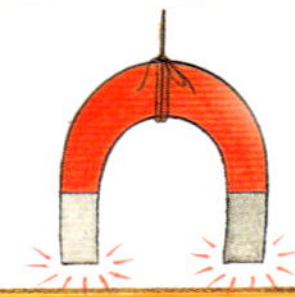

What happens?
The kite rises and follows the movements of the magnet.

Because...
... the magnetic force of the magnet is stronger than the force of gravity which pulls the kite towards the table.

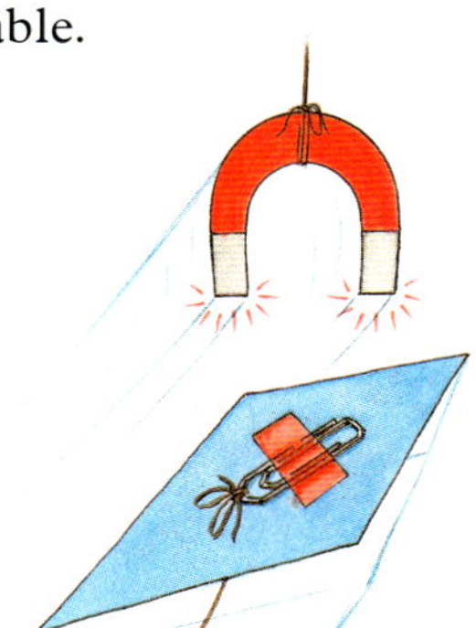

LET'S GO FISHING!

You need:
- scraps of coloured plastic
- paper-clips
- a little stick
- thread
- a horse-shoe magnet
- a little bowl
- water
- scissors

What to do

1 Cut the plastic into some little fish shapes.

2 Put a paper-clip at the 'mouth' of each fish.

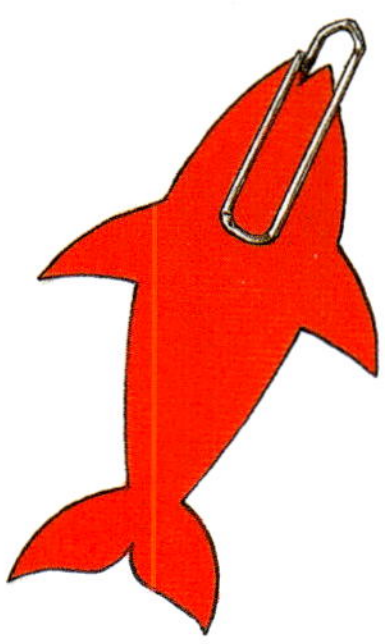

3 Tie the magnet on to the stick with the string. This will be your fishing rod.

4 Fill the bowl with water and put the fish in it.

5 Lower the magnet into the water without touching the fish.

What happens?

The fish rise up towards the magnet, as if they are swallowing the bait!

Because...

... the magnet exerts a force greater than the gravity which pulls the fish towards the bottom of the bowl.

Scrap iron for recycling

When buildings or large items of machinery have been demolished, giant magnets are used to separate and lift out large quantities of scrap iron and steel from other metals for recycling. These magnets are worked by electricity (electromagnets).

The force of magnetism can overcome the force of gravity.

Magnetism and Electricity

At one time it was believed that magnetism and electricity were two separate phenomena. But at the beginning of the 18th century, the Dutch physicist Hans Oersted and the French scientist André Ampère, proved that there were close links between the two. Today, modern technology makes good use of electromagnetism in the development of turbines, engines, drills, toys, video and tape recorders, telephones, medical equipment and lots more. An electricity generator, for instance, can be turned on or off to cut the flow of electricity in an emergency or a particular situation. In the next pages you too will discover how it is possible to generate magnetism by electricity, and learn how to build a little electromagnetic motor.

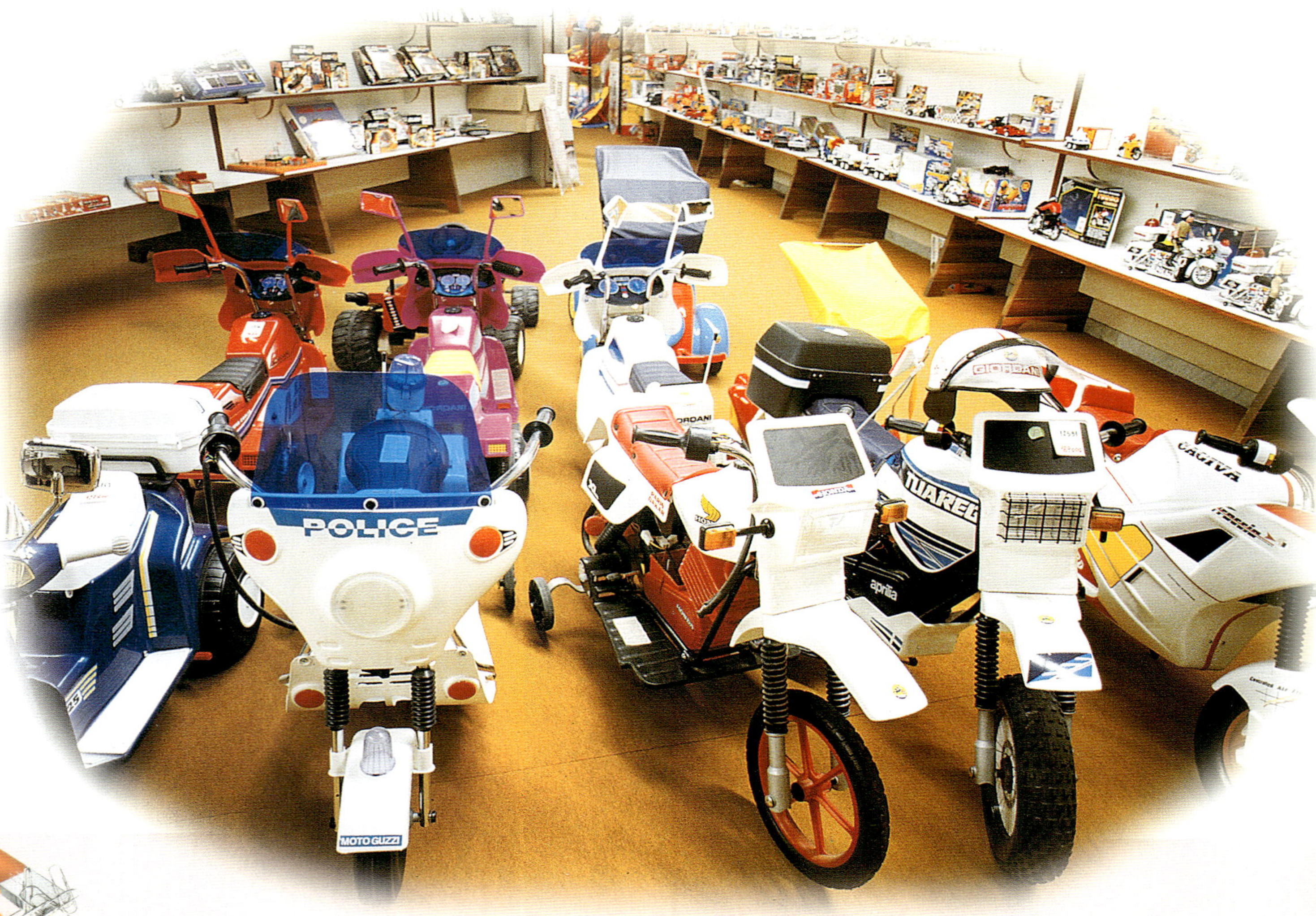

Is magnetic force produced only by magnets?

ELECTROMAGNETIC CURRENT

You need:
- a 4.5 volt battery
- copper wire
- a piece of card
- scissors
- iron filings

What to do

1 Ask an adult to make two holes in the cardboard at least 10cm apart.

2 Ask an adult to cut a piece of copper wire about 30cm long. Thread this through the holes in the card. Then wind the ends around the battery contacts.

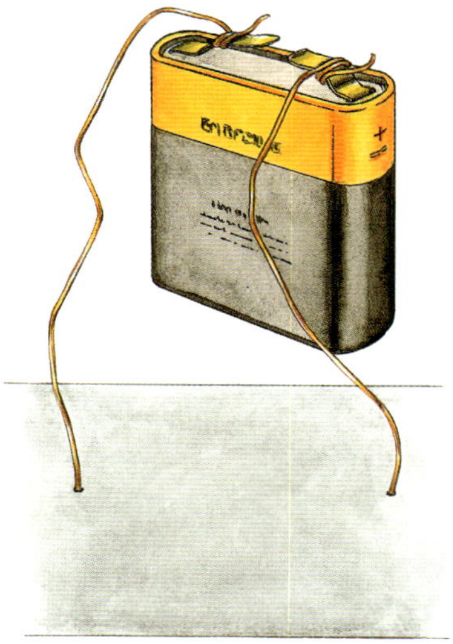

3 Sprinkle the card with iron filings.

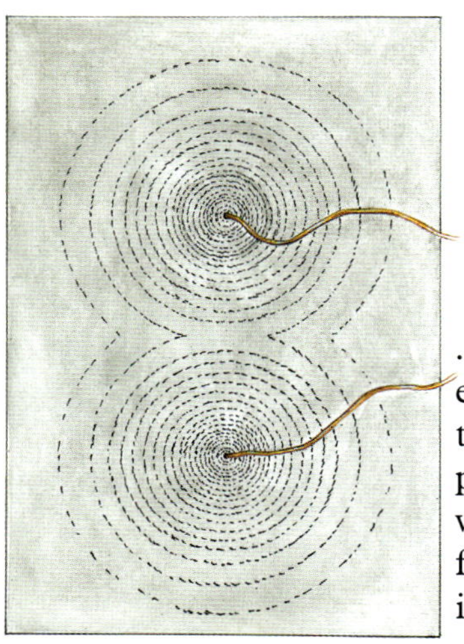

What happens?
The iron filings arrange themselves around the copper wire in concentric circles.

Because...
... the current of electricity generated by the battery and which passes through the copper wire, produces a magnetic field, which attracts the iron filings.

4 Detach one end of the wire from a battery contact.

5 Move the card to displace the iron filings.

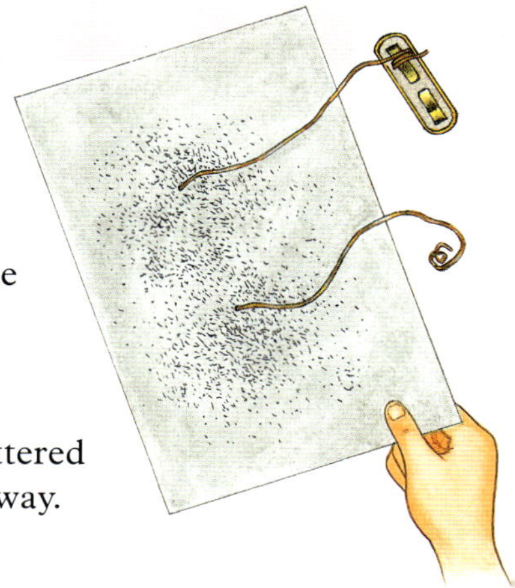

What happens?
The iron filings remain scattered on the card in a haphazard way.

Because...
... the magnetic field generated by the electricity is broken when the flow of electric current is interrupted.

Fundamental forces

Electricity and magnetism are two different aspects of a unique phenomenon, electromagnetism. It is the electromagnetic force which keeps atoms together in a molecule and stops solids from falling apart. So you can see how important a force it is, once you remember that everything around us is made up of molecules! The electromagnetic force is one of the four fundamental forces. The other three are – the force of gravity, the weak nuclear force and the strong nuclear force.
The most intense fundamental force is the strong nuclear force, which keeps the protons and neutrons within the nucleus (central part) of an atom. Second in intensity is the electromagnetic force, which keeps the atoms in a molecule together. Third in the list of fundamental forces is the weak nuclear force, which keeps together the elementary particles which form the components of the nucleus. The force of gravity comes last on the list – although this force is still strong enough to exert its pull on everything across the whole Universe!

Electrical current can also generate a magnetic field.

How is an electro-magnet made?

MAGNETISM ON DEMAND

You need:
- a 4.5 volt battery
- a little piece of wood
- two metal drawing pins
- a metal paper-clip
- copper wire
- a large iron nail
- sticky tape
- a box of pins
- scissors

What to do

1 First, make a switch. Push the two drawing pins in the wood 2cm apart. Open up the paper-clip and thread one end under the wire.

2 Ask an adult to cut a piece of copper wire about 15cm long. Wind one end around the battery contact. Fix the other end under the drawing pin on the switch.

3 Cut another piece of copper wire about 60-70cm long. Wind the centre of the wire around the nail, about 10 times.

4 Wind one end of the same wire around the other battery contact. Slip the other end under the second drawing pin.

5 Turn on the switch by making a connection between the two drawing pins with the paper-clip.

6 Bring the point of the nail near to the pins in the box.

What happens?
The pins are not drawn by the nail.

7 Disconnect the switch. Wrap the wire around the nail as many times as possible and as tightly and as close as you can. (It may help to keep the wire firm with sticky tape.) Re-connect the wire to the battery and to the switch.

8 Turn on the switch. Try to attract the pins once again with the point of the nail.

What happens?
The nail attracts the pins.

Because...
... the more wire which is around the nail, the greater the intensity of the magnetic field which is generated. The nail is now just like a proper magnet.

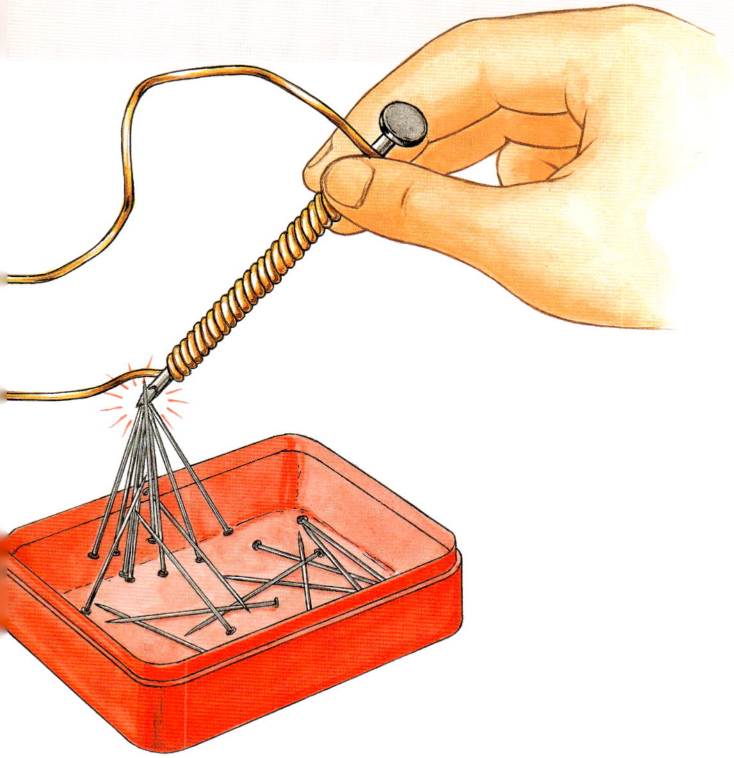

9 Turn off the switch by moving the paper-clip.

What happens?
The pins fall into the box.

Because...
... when the flow of electricity generated by the battery is interrupted, the magnetic field goes, and the iron nail is de-magnetized. But if the nail were made of steel, its magnetic power would remain, even in the absence of an electric current.

The invention of the telegraph

The telegraph invented by Samuel Morse in 1837, was one of the most revolutionary inventions based on electromagnetism. Morse had the idea of an electric current making an electromagnet work intermittently on a piece of soft iron to which a writing point was attached. If the current failed for a short time, the point would stamp a dot on a moving strip of paper. If the flow of electricity current lasted longer, the point would impress slightly longer. Morse worked out a code alphabet (Morse Code) with letters are represented by dots and dashes. His telegraph made it possible to communicate across a greater distance than could be seen – unlike light signals, smoke signals or flag signalling, which each depended on the sender and the receiver being at a certain place at a certain time. And so the story of long distance communication began.

An electro-magnet is a metal object which acquires magnetic properties by the passage of a current of electricity.

Can electromagnetic force power a motor?

A SIMPLE MOTOR

You need:
- two bar magnets with marked poles
- a cotton reel
- a few metres of copper wire
- three pieces of electric cable
- a wooden skewer-type toothpick
- two metal drawing pins
- a small piece of wood
- a paper-clip
- two elastic bands
- four large corks
- two iron washers
- a 9 volt battery
- sticky tape

What to do

1 Wind the copper wire a number of times around the cotton reel from the bottom to the top. Wind as tight and as closely as you can, leaving the two ends of the wire free. Keep the wire around the reel with elastic bands.

2 Thread the toothpick through the holes in the cotton reel, taking care not to pierce the copper wire if you possibly can. Thread a washer at either end of the stick. Thread an end of the wire through each washer.

3 With the sticky tape, fix the magnets to two corks and place them with the opposite poles facing each other. Place the other two corks crossways between the two magnets. Put the stick on top of these corks and fasten down with sticky tape.

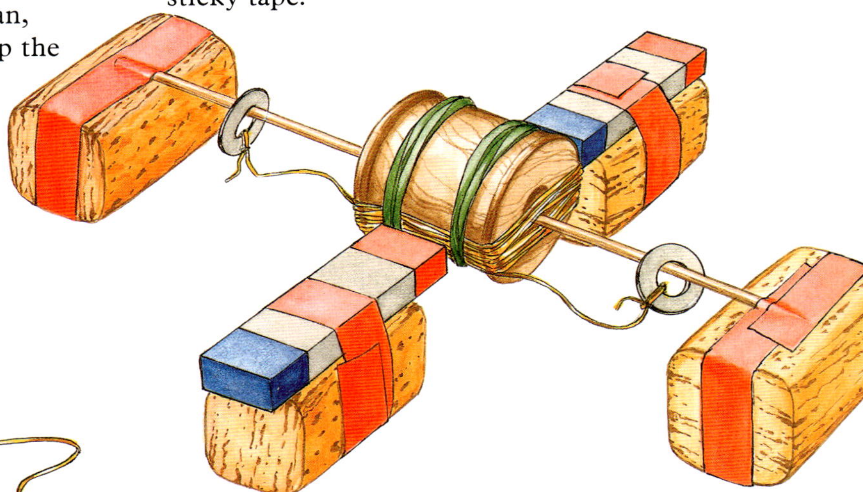

4 Stick the two drawing pins in the wood about 2cm apart. Open up the paper-clip, and thread one end under the drawing pin so that the clip can be turned to connect up with both pins. This will be your switch.

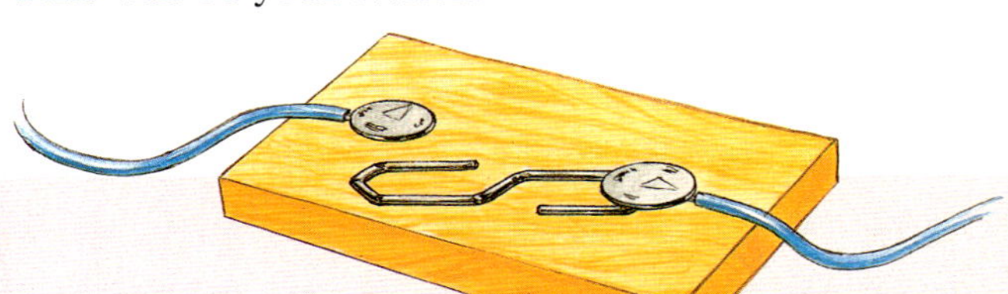

5 Peel off a little of the plastic covering from the ends of the three pieces of electric cable. Then make this circuit: one wire between a battery contact and the washer; one from the other washer to the drawing pin on the wood; and one from the other drawing pin to the second battery contact.

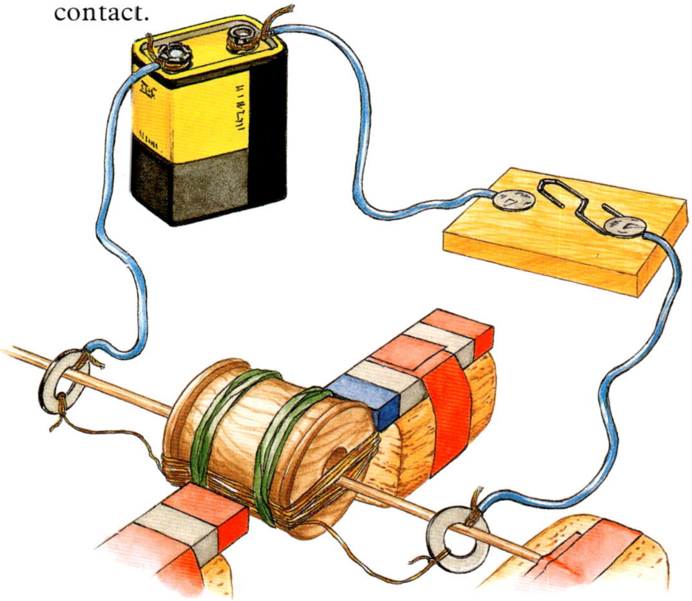

6 Turn on the switch by putting the paper-clip on the drawing pin (so that the current of electricity can flow through).

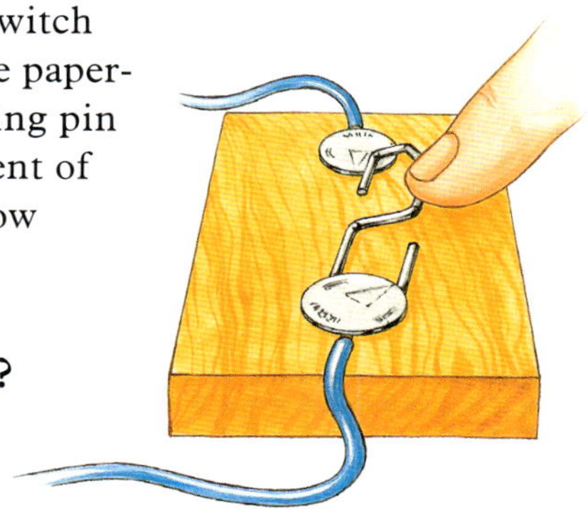

What happens?
The cotton reel moves jerkily.

Because...
... the two magnets generate a magnetic field which comes from the positive pole of one magnet to the negative pole of the other. When we activate the flow of an electric current, a second magnetic field is created around the copper wire. The two fields alternately attract and repel, making movements of winding the wire on the reel towards the top and then towards the bottom.

The electricity of magnetism

The connections between electricity and magnetism allows not only the activation of magnetic fields to enable the flow of an electrical current, but also the other way round – that is, electricity activated by a magnet.
This is what happens with the dynamo of a bicycle. This uses the mechanical energy of a moving wheel to produce the electrical energy necessary for a lamp to shine. The movement of the wheel is transmitted through the rotating head of the dynamo. This, in turn, causes a magnet at the centre of a thick spring to move. An electric current is created in the wire, due to the magnetic field generated by the magnet. This electric current is transmitted to the lamp, which in turn lights up. The brightness of the lamp depends on the speed of the bicycle.

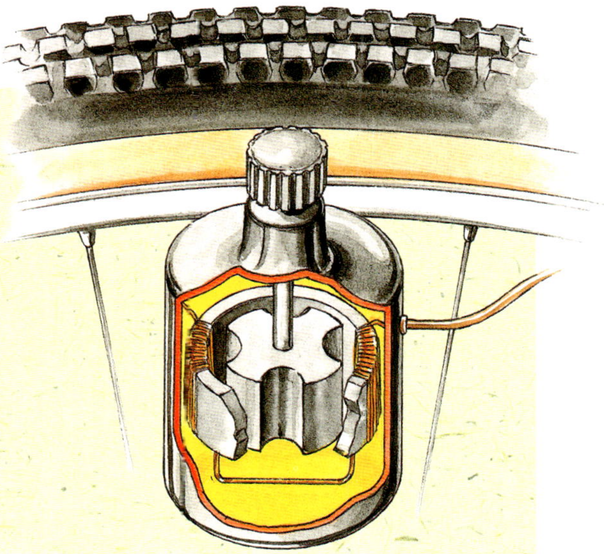

Electrical motors work due to the combination of electricity and magnetism.

Has an electromagnet two poles, like an ordinary magnet?

ALTERNATING FLOW

You need:
- a large iron nail
- a bar magnet with two poles marked
- a 4.5 volt battery
- copper wire
- a needle
- a piece of cork
- sticky tape
- a bowl
- water
- coloured paint

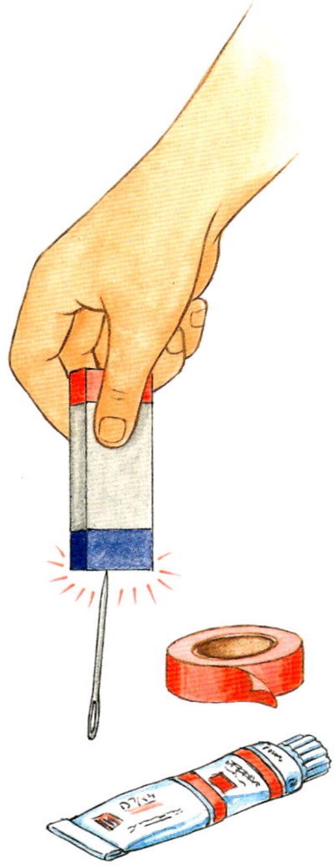

What to do

1 Magnetize the needle by stroking it 40 times along its length in the same direction with the end of the magnet. Watch the attraction between the needle and the magnet, especially at the north pole of the needle. Paint the north pole of the needle red.

2 Fix the needle to the cork with the sticky tape. Fill the bowl with water. Place the cork on the surface of the water.

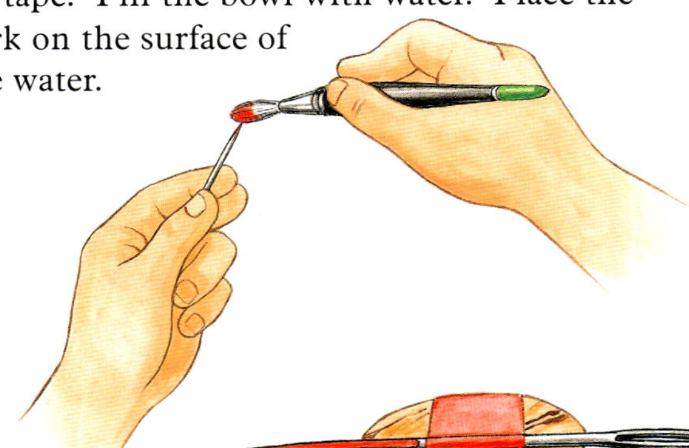

3 Make an electromagnet as explained in the last experiment. Wind the middle of copper wire around the nail then connect the ends of the wire to the battery contacts.

4 Draw the nail towards one end of the needle, and then the other end.

What happens?

One end of the needle becomes attracted by the nail. This is the coloured tip. From this, we know that the point of the needle is the south pole and the eye is the north pole.

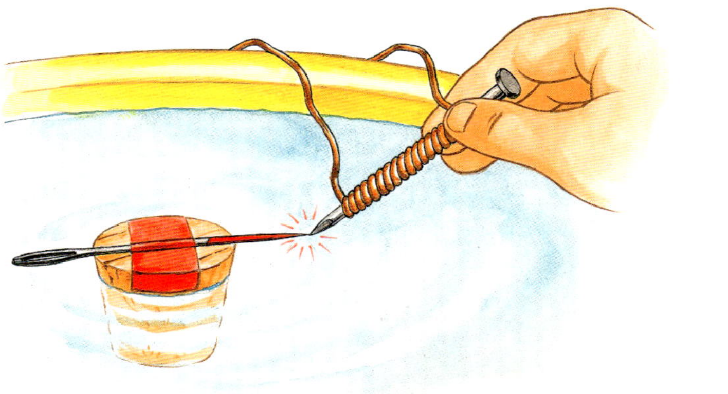

5 Detach the copper wire of the electromagnet and from the battery contacts. Then re-attach each end on the opposite battery contact.

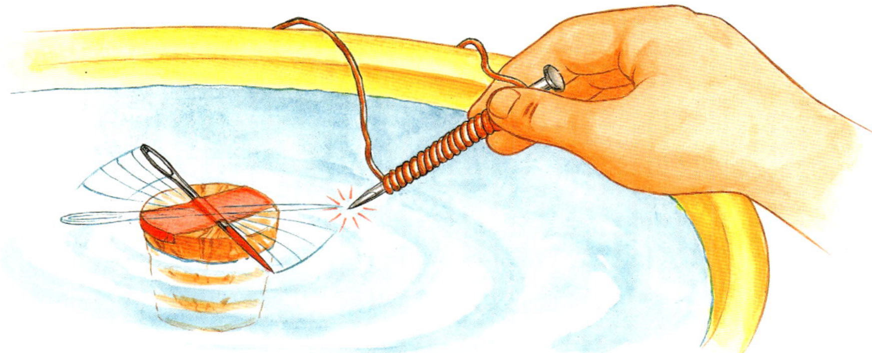

6 Bring the point of the nail near to the end of the needle. At first, the needle will be attracted.

What happens?
The needle begins to spin.

Because...
... in an electromagnet, the magnetic field is positive or negative, according to the direction in which the current flows. When you changed over the position of the wires, you changed the direction of the electrical flow. As a result of this, you also changed the polarity of the nail.

Electromagnetic toys

Most moving toys have a little electric motor inside which transforms the electrical energy of the battery into mechanical energy. In these toys there are two electromagnets, one fixed and the other mounted on a rotating axle. The flow of the electrical current creates magnetic fields in which the negative pole of the rotating electromagnet moves as it tries to reach the positive pole of the fixed magnet, thus completing the means of rotating. The movement of the motor reverses the direction of the current and therefore also the polarity of the magnetic fields which these generate: so the rotating electromagnet continually completes the circuit in search of the opposite polarity. This means that the rotation of the magnet is transformed into energy to make the toy move.

The electromagnet has two poles, but these are not fixed. They change according to the direction of the electrical current.

Fact-Finder

The magnetosphere

This is the name for the volume of space which extends about 500km above the Earth and in which the electrical particles charged by the Sun become trapped by the action of the Earth's magnetic field. On the outside of this layer is the magnetopause, the region in which the Earth's magnetic field prevents further electrical particles becoming trapped.

Inverted poles

At present, a compass needle is attracted to the north pole. If Earth's magnetic poles were inverted, the needle would point south. We call this magnetic inversion. Some polar reversals took place over 500 thousand years ago (magnetic epochs), others over four or five thousand years ago (magnetic events), one reversal lasting about a thousand years. Each time, iron minerals were deposited in rocks. As these cooled and solidified, they became magnetized according to the direction of the magnetic field existing at that time. This is how scientists know that polar reversal has occurred, and when it happened.

Orientation in flight

There have been many theories to explain how migrating birds can safely find their way across vast distances. One theory suggested is that birds know how to use the Earth's magnetic field.

Polar Aurorae

Polar Aurorae are trails of coloured light which appear in the night sky near the Earth's magnetic poles. In the Arctic these are called aurora borealis and aurora australis in the Antarctic. At about 100km above Earth, high speed, charged particles from the Sun called the solar wind, are drawn by the Earth's magnetic field towards the north and south magnetic poles. These particles bombard the gases in the Earth's atmosphere, making the gases burst into light.

Measure the magnetism

We call the instrument which is used to measure the intensity of magnetic fields a magnetometer. The most widely used is the Hall Effect Sensor, which measures the intensity of a magnetic field parallel to the surface of the Earth. This device has no moving parts and it is related to the transistor. The presence of a magnetic field changes the direction that a flow of electrons takes through the device, which can be measured as an electrical signal.

Electricity

What is lightning? Where does a current of electricity come from? How does a lamp light up?
You will find the answers to these questions and many more by doing the experiments in the next section, under the following headings:

Static Electricity • The Electric Current
Circuits and Switches • The Effects of Electrical Current

Static Electricity

The word electricity comes from the word 'electron', the name which the Ancient Greeks gave to the mineral amber. They discovered that after amber was stroked on sheepskin, it was able to attract lightweight objects, such as feathers and splinters of wood. At the end of the seventeenth century it was also found that glass could 'electrify', although in a different way. Since then, scientists have tried to discover all the secrets of electricity, tracing back to the origin of an atom. You too will be able to discover the effects of static electricity and to understand what causes the little shocks which you feel on your hands, your clothes and your hair, and how lightning strikes during a thunderstorm. All the experiments are safe to do, but an adult must be on hand to use some of the tools required.

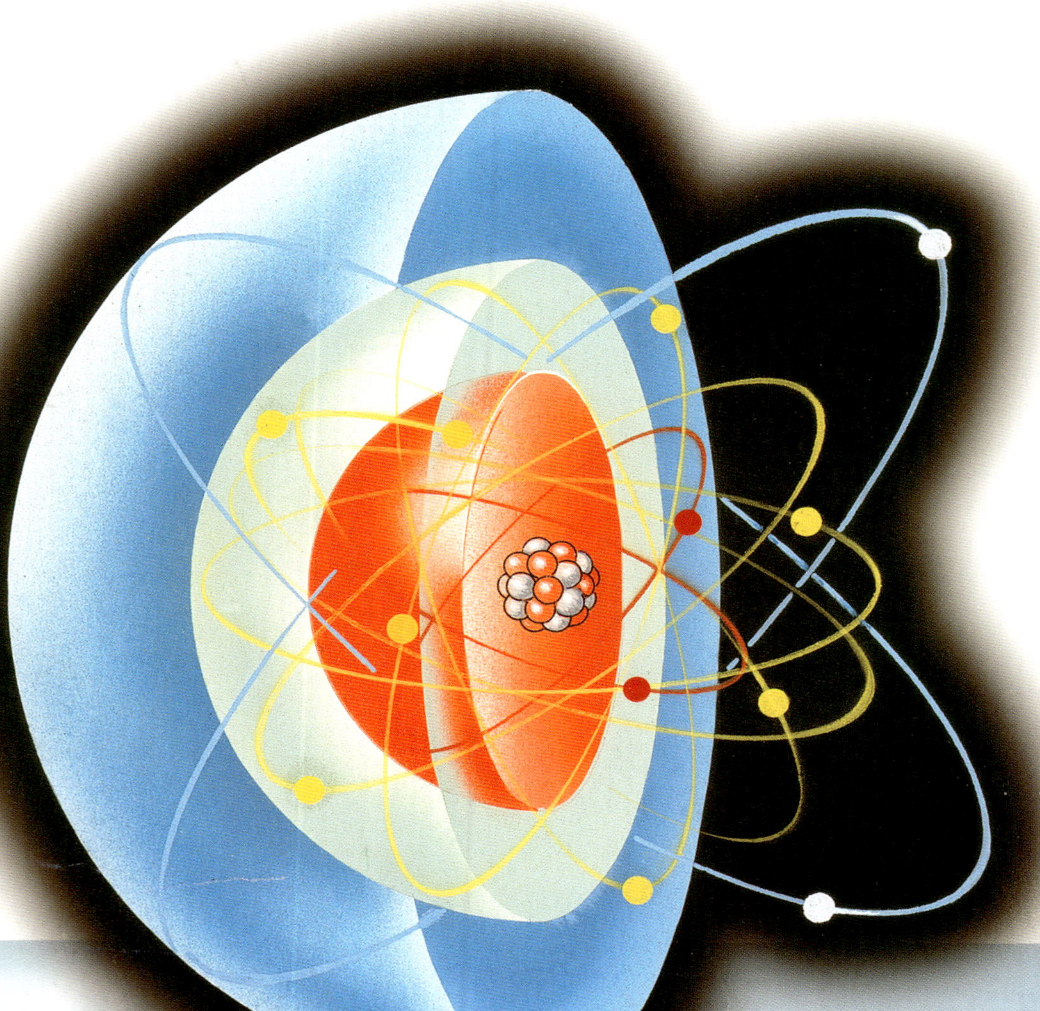

How can something be electrified?

SPECIAL POWERS

You need:
- a balloon
- some pieces of thin paper
- a wall
- a tap
- a piece of woollen material

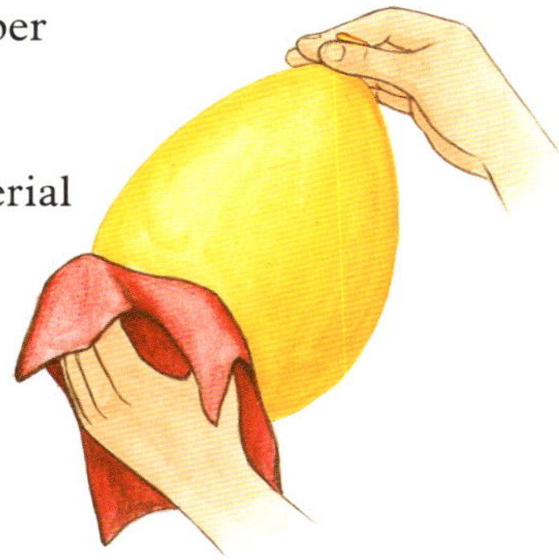

What to do

1 Blow up the balloon. Stroke it vigorously with the piece of material.

2 Hold the balloon close to the pieces of paper, without touching them.

What happens?
The pieces of paper jump up and stick to the balloon.

3 Stroke the balloon again with the cloth. Hold the balloon close to the wall.

What happens?
The balloon sticks to the wall.

4 Turn on the tap. Stroke the balloon again and hold it near the stream of water.

What happens?
The jet of water curves and follows the movement of the balloon.

Because...
... when you stroked the balloon with the woollen material, it became electrified, with the power to attract things, almost like a magnet. You can also try holding the balloon near your hair, and see how the hairs rise up, as if by magic.

The passage of electrons

All matter is made up of tiny particles called *atoms*. Atoms contain even smaller particles, called *protons* and *neutrons*, which each have an electrical charge. Protons have a *positive charge* (indicated by a + [plus] sign). Neutrons have a *negative charge* (indicated by a – [minus] sign. Signs of the opposite charge attract. Charges of the same sign repel each other. Atoms contain an equal number of electrons and protons, so that each positive charge is balanced by a negative charge. Some atoms have *neutrons*, particles without any electrical charge. Protons and neutrons remain still and these constitute the *nucleus* of an atom. Electrons move continually around the nucleus. When we stroke the balloon with the cloth, some electrons of the atoms of the wool enter the atoms of the balloon. So because the atoms of the balloon now have a greater number of electrons, the balloon becomes electrified.

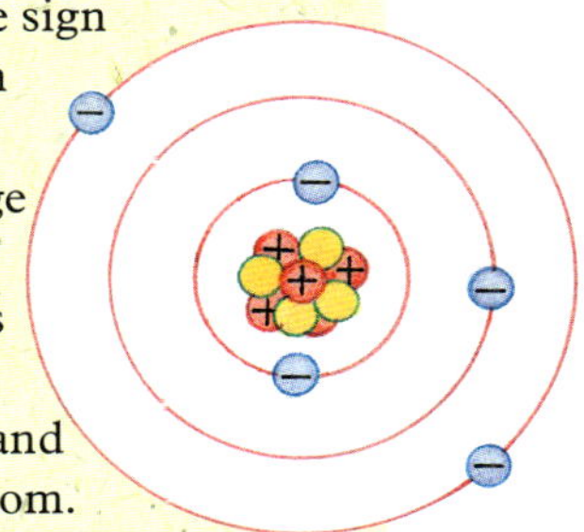

A thing becomes electrified because the amount of electrons in its atoms is either increased or diminished.

Why do some electrified objects attract and others repel?

BALLOON TEST

You need:
- two balloons
- thread
- a woollen cloth
- a piece of paper

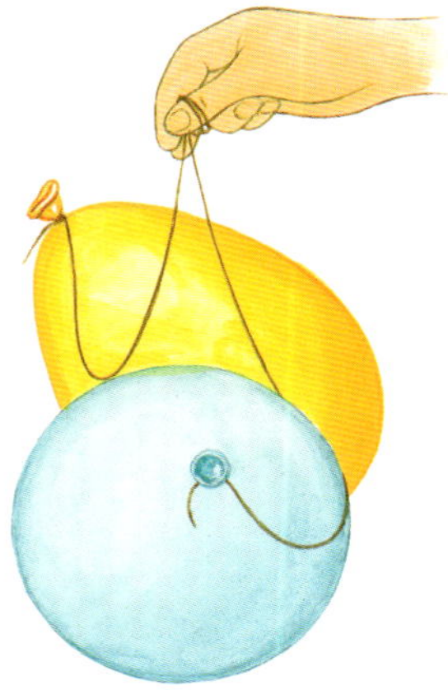

What to do

1 Blow up the balloons. Tie the ends with each end of the thread.

2 Stroke both balloons with a woollen cloth.

3 Lift the thread at the centre, and let the balloons hang down towards the floor.

What happens?
The two balloons draw away from each other.

4 Now put a piece of paper between the two balloons.

What happens?
The two balloons draw close together.

Because...
... objects of the same material acquire the same electrical charge. And electrical charges of the same type repel. The balloons, which both have a negative charge, draw away. The paper, which is not electrified, has the same number of negative and positive charges. It is the positive charges which attract the negative charges of the balloon.

MOVING STRAWS

You need:
- 4 plastic drinking straws
- a glass rod
- a woollen cloth
- table

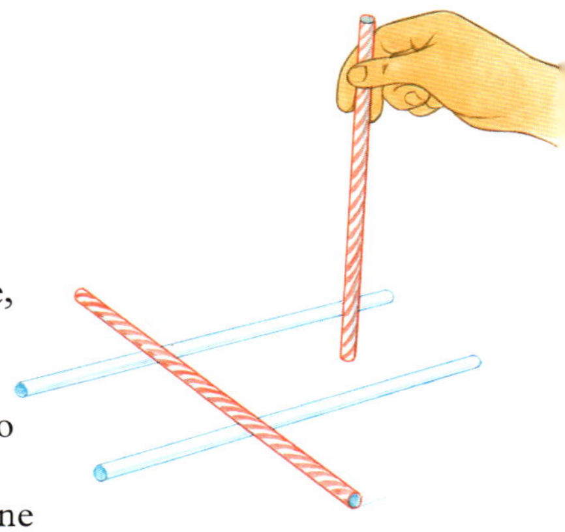

What to do

1 Put two straws parallel on the table, 5cm apart.

2 Stroke the other two straws with the woollen cloth. Place one across the first two straws. Bring the fourth straw near to the others, first from the left, then from the right. Take care not to touch the other straws.

What happens?
The drinking straw placed on the first two straws rolls forward and then back, as if it is being pushed by the electrified straw.

3 Stroke the glass rod with the woollen cloth. Repeat the experiment.

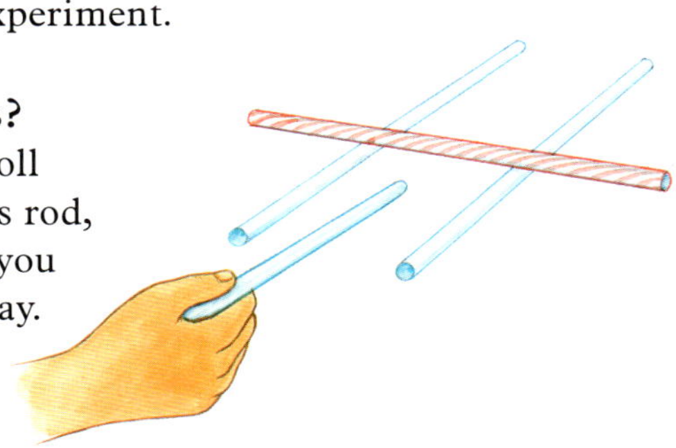

What happens?
The straw will roll towards the glass rod, and follow it as you draw the rod away.

Because...
... the plastic has a negative charge, whilst stroking the glass rod with the cloth gives it a positive charge. The two plastic straws, having the same charge, repel. The glass and the plastic, having opposite charges, attract each other.

A MAGIC STICK

You need:
- a drinking straw
- a square piece of thin paper
- a toothpick
- a woollen cloth
- an eraser
- scissors

What to do

1 Fold the piece of paper into four, and cut as shown in the picture. When you unfold the paper, you will have a star shape.

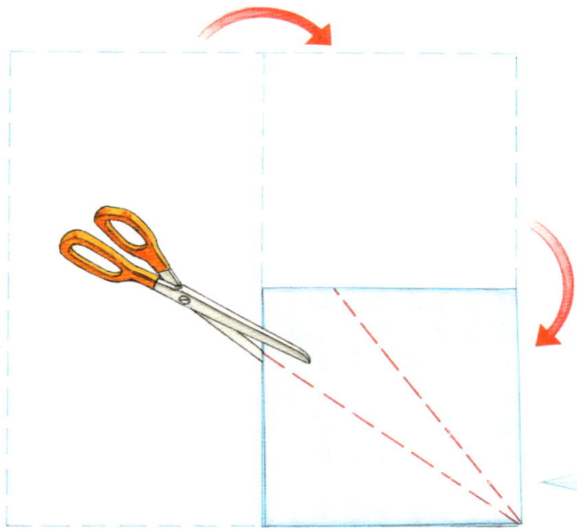

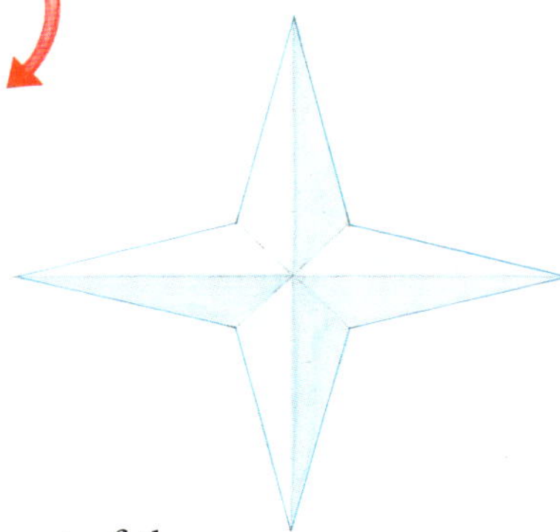

2 Stick the toothpick in the eraser. Place the centre of the paper star on the point of the toothpick.

What happens?
The star follows the movement of the drinking straw.

3 Stroke the drinking straw with the woollen cloth. Then move the straw around the top of the star, as if drawing circles around it.

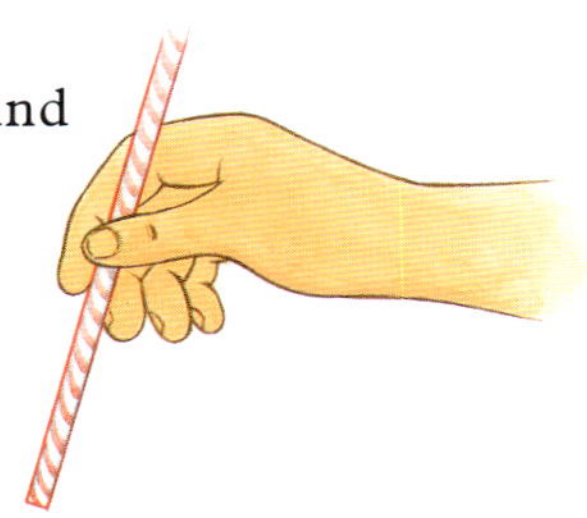

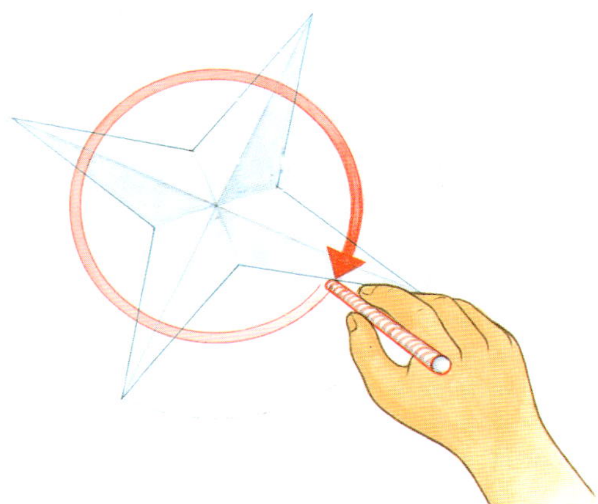

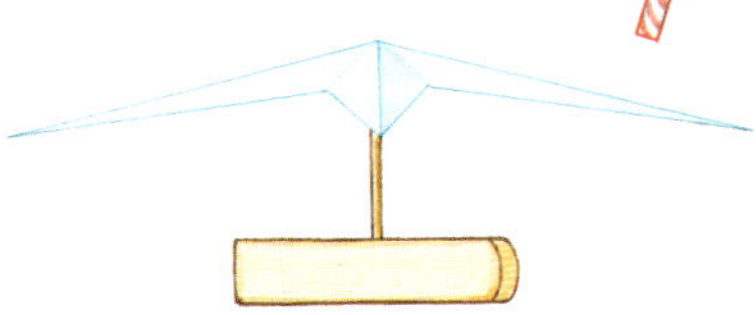

Because...
... stroking with the woollen cloth has given the straw a negative electrical charge. So the straw can attract the opposite (positive) charge of the paper. That is why the star follows the movement of the straw.

Electrical charges can be positive or negative. Charges of the same type repel. Opposite charges attract.

How is the type of electrical charge revealed in an object?

REVEAL THE CHARGE

You need:
- objects of different materials (plastic, metal, wood, paper) to test
- plastic pen
- a glass rod
- thread
- a cotton cloth
- a silk cloth
- a woollen cloth
- a piece of fur

What to do

1 Using the thread, hang the plastic pen and the glass rod from sticks. Keep them a good distance from each other.

2 Stroke the pen and the rod with the cloth.

3 Stroke each test object with a cloth and bring each one near to the pen in turn. Then hold each object near to the glass rod.

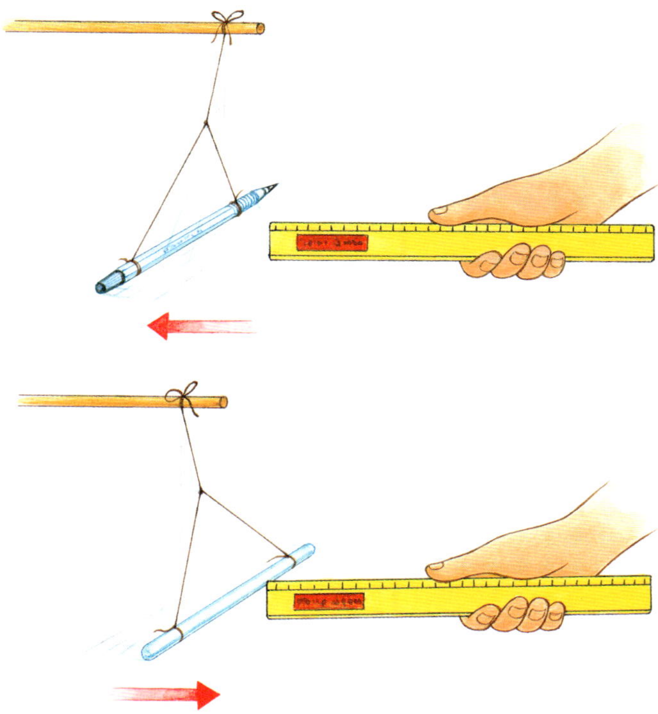

What happens?
Each object is electrified by stroking with the cloth. This causes the object to repel from one of the charged objects (the pen or the rod) and to attract the other.

Because...
... the plastic pen has a negative charge. The glass rod has a positive charge. From this, we know that the objects which attract the plastic pen and repel the glass rod have a positive charge. Those which cause the opposite effect have a negative charge.

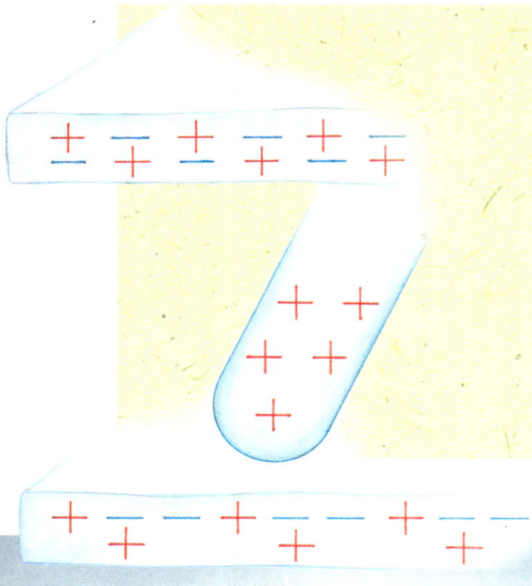

Induction and contact

Sometimes an object has a neutral electrical charge, which means it has no charge at all. In a neutral object the charge distributes itself evenly at first (top diagram). Then it separates, because the electrified object attracts an opposite charge (bottom diagram). When the two objects are separated, the charge of the neutral object once again distributes itself evenly. The neutral object immediately has a temporary electrification by induction.

If we touch the neutral object with an electrified object with, let us say, a positive charge, it will attract the neutral object and neutralize its negative charge. So the positive charge would then be present in both objects. But, such electrification by contact does not last.

BUILD AN ELECTROSCOPE

You need:

- a glass jar
- a cork which fits tightly enough to act as a seal
- a length of iron wire
- a strip of tinfoil
- a glass rod and a plastic rod
- a woollen cloth

Once the experiment has been set up, take care not to touch the iron wire with your hand, otherwise the electrical charge will be lost.

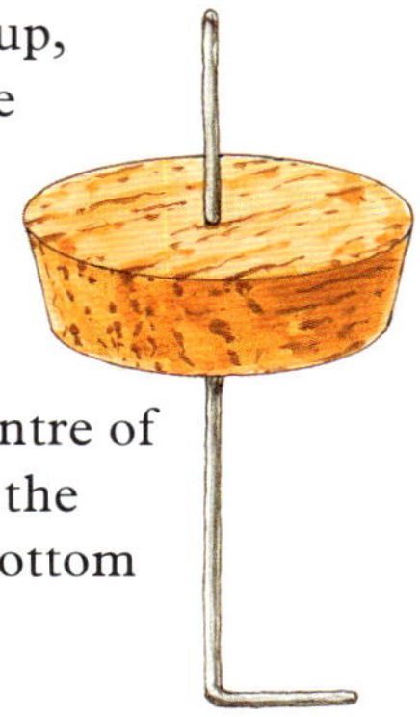

What to do

1 Thread the wire through the centre of the cork, so that it sticks out at the top and at the bottom. Bend the bottom end, as shown in the picture.

2 Fold the strip of tinfoil in half. Hang the tinfoil on the bottom end of the wire. Place the cork in the top of the jar.

3 Stroke the plastic rod with the woollen cloth. Then touch the top end of the wire with the plastic rod.

What happens?
The two 'fins' of the tinfoil spread apart.

4 Now electrify the glass rod by stroking it with the woollen cloth. Touch the top wire with the glass rod.

What happens?
The tinfoil 'fins' close together.

Because...
... the contact between the plastic rod and the wire causes the negative charge of the plastic to be transmitted through the wire to the two halves of the tinfoil. As these acquire the negative charge, they repel. When you bring the glass rod closer, the positive charge of the rod neutralizes the negative charge and the two halves close again. The same thing happens by touching the wire first with the glass rod and then bringing the plastic rod near (both are electrified).
The instrument you have made is an *electroscope*, used to detect a positive or negative charge. You can repeat the experiment, charging your electroscope each time with a negative charge (by contact with the plastic) or a positive charge (by contact with the glass). Then test objects of different materials which have been electrified by stroking. When the tinfoil fins close together, the object is something with a positive charge. When they open, it is something with a negative charge.

When does the electrical charge end?

By doing these experiments, you will find that electrification of an object is exhausted after a time. This happens because more electrons are attracted by atoms in the air, or in whatever supports the electrified object (such as a hand, or a shelf) and this changes the balance between the charges.

The charges which are equal to that of the glass are positive. Those which are equal to the plastic are negative.

What is lightning?

ARTIFICIAL LIGHTNING

You need:

- a large, flat baking dish
- a large handful of plasticene
- a sheet of plastic
- a coin
- a dark room

What to do

1 Soften the plasticene and stick it down in the centre of the dish. The plasticene must be stuck down firmly enough for you to be able to lift the baking dish with it.

2 Place the baking dish on the sheet of plastic. Then, using the plasticene, stroke the dish vigorously around the plastic for about a minute.

3 Still using the plasticene, lift up the baking dish. Take care not to touch the baking dish with your hands.

4 In the dark room, bring a coin close to the corner of the dish.

What happens?

The contact between the coin and the dish produces a spark.

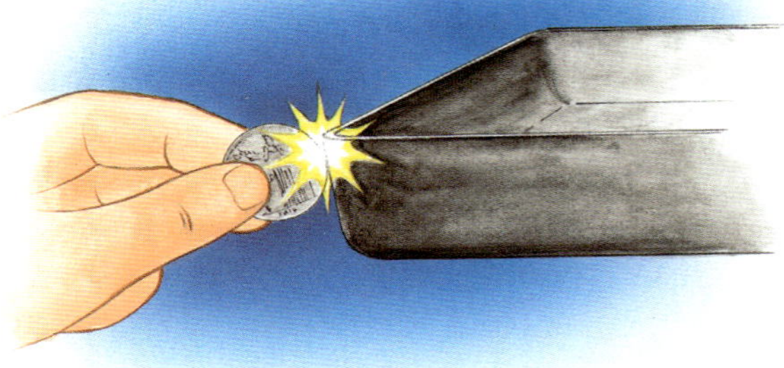

Because...

... having been stroked on the plastic, the baking dish is electrified with a negative charge. When you brought the coin closer, the excess charges were quickly transferred through the air, from the sheet to the coin, and to your body (you will have felt a slight shock). The passage in the air was shown by the spark. This experiment reproduces in miniature a flash of lightning in a storm.

Electricity in the sky

During a storm, the lower parts of the clouds, having been rubbed by the masses of air, become charged with negative electricity. This causes the attraction of the positive charges on the Earth's surface (on trees, houses and large structures, for example) opposite this accumulation of negative electricity in the clouds. When the negative charge of the clouds is too high up, lightning strikes – a short transfer of electrical charge from the clouds to the ground or between one cloud and another. Lightning is seen as a flash of light, and heard as thunder – because of a build-up of heat, the air expands suddenly, causing a loud rumble.

The Invention of the Lightning Conductor

The lightning conductor was invented by the American Benjamin Franklin in 1752. He believed that lightning was an enormous electrical charge and was convinced that a metal point would attract this charge. To prove his theory, Franklin built a kite with an iron tip, and threaded a key on the end of the string of the kite. He tried out his kite during a violent storm. This experiment showed that the metal point attracted the electrical charge which was transmitted through the wet string and into the key. In fact, when Franklin touched the key, it gave him an electric shock! Following this experiment, Franklin built the first lightning conductor, a metal pole with a very high point which he put in his garden. During storms, there were lots of sparks to be seen around this point. This metal pole attracted the greater part of the electrical charge from the clouds before it reached the ground, avoiding damage to houses and other structures.
Modern lightning conductors have a metal thread leading to the ground, which enables electrical charges to descend and disperse safely in the soil.

Lightning is an electrical charge from a highly electrified cloud to the Earth.

The Electric Current

Another quality of electricity is its ability to move, to run along pre-set courses called circuits. But how can electricity move from one object to another? What is the unbroken path of a circuit? And from what materials is a circuit made? Can electricity flow through anything? Why do we call a force which we use to switch on a light a current? By using simple batteries in the next set of experiments, you will be able to work safely to understand how it is possible to 'tame' such a powerful and dangerous force as electricity so that we can use it every day.

How is an electric current generated?

A PATH CALLED A CIRCUIT

You need:

- a 4.5 battery
- two pieces of insulated (plastic-covered) electric cable
- a small light bulb
- wire-cutters

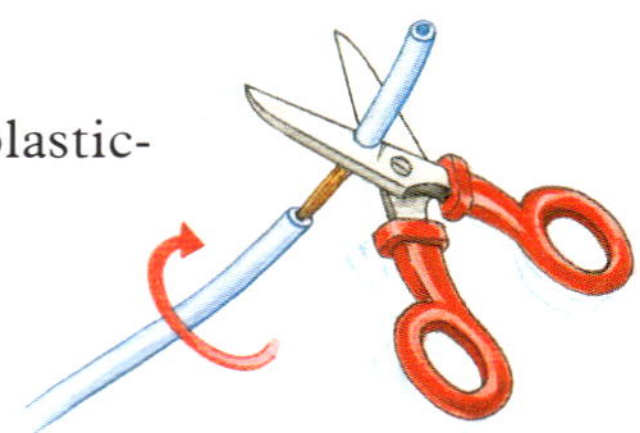

What to do

1 Use the wire-cutters to peel off the plastic from both ends of the wires. (Ask an adult to do this for you.) Be careful not to cut into the small wires inside.

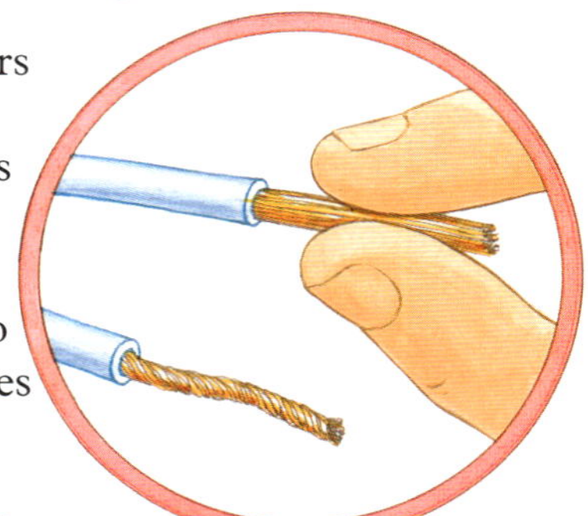

Wind the uncovered end of each piece of wire around a battery contact, as shown.

3 Take the two free ends of wire and place them on the bulb. One wire must touch the bottom of the metal screw and the other against the side.

What happens?

The bulb lights up.

Because...

... what you saw transformed into the light energy of the bulb was the electrical current. This is a flow of electrical charge conducted from the battery through the wires and into the bulb, along a set course called a circuit.

When does electricity move?

The electrical current is generated when electrons in excess of an electrified object are free to move towards an object which is less charged. This difference in charge between one thing and another is called potential difference. The battery is able to maintain a certain difference in potential between one end of the circuit and the other.

A CONTINUOUS COURSE

You need:

- a 4.5 volt battery
- three pieces of insulated electric cable
- a small bulb
- wire-cutters
- a bulb-holder

What to do

1 Ask an adult to peel away the plastic from the ends of the pieces of wire, using the wire-cutters. (Be careful not to cut the copper wires inside!)

2 Put the bulb in the bulb-holder, so that you do not have to hold the bulb in your hand.

3 Connect the battery, the two wires and the bulb-holder, as in the picture.

4 Alternately bring into contact and then draw apart the two free ends of the electric cable.

What happens?

When the wires touch, the bulb lights up. When they are apart, it remains unlit.

Because...

... the circuit (the course through which the electricity flows from the battery) must be unbroken (closed) for it to work. If a circuit is broken (open), the current of electricity cannot flow through it.

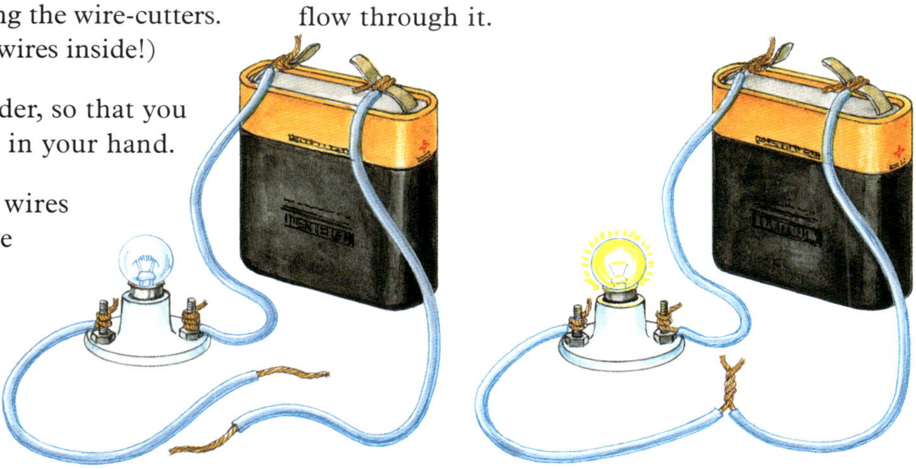

When electrical charges move in a circuit between two objects, these objects will have a certain difference in potential.

Can electricity flow through all substances?

CONDUCTORS OF ELECTRICITY

You need:
- a 4.5 volt battery
- a 5 volt bulb in a bulb-holder
- three pieces of insulated electric cable (with the ends uncovered, as in the last two experiments)
- two metal brackets
- two screws
- a tablet of wood
- some objects to put to the test: a nail, a strip of rubber, a toothpick, a strip of tinfoil, a glass rod, a leather shoe-lace, a drinking straw

What to do

1 Screw the two brackets to the wood, about 2cm apart.

2 Place the bulb-holder alongside the brackets and connect the battery, the bulb-holder and the two brackets with the three pieces of electric cable, as shown in the picture.

3 Place each object, one at a time, on the brackets.

What happens?
The nail and the tinfoil make the bulb light up. The other objects do not.

Because...
... the bulb lights up only when an object made of metal is placed on the metal brackets. The metal object closes the circuit and so allows the current to flow. Rubber, plastic, wood, glass and leather are insulators, which means that these materials trap the electrical charge, and do not let it escape. These insulating materials are used as protection from electricity. Electric cable, for example, is covered with plastic so that it can be touched on the outside without the handler getting an electric shock.

Insulators and conductors

In substances which conduct electricity, there are electrons which are free to move because they are not closely attracted to their atoms. Such electrons are able to transport electricity from one place to another. On the other hand, the electrons of insulators are strongly attracted to their atoms, so they do not conduct electricity because they cannot move about. The aptitude of an object to conduct electricity is indicated by the term resistance. The less resistance which an object 'puts up' against the flow of the electricity, the greater its capacity to conduct the current.

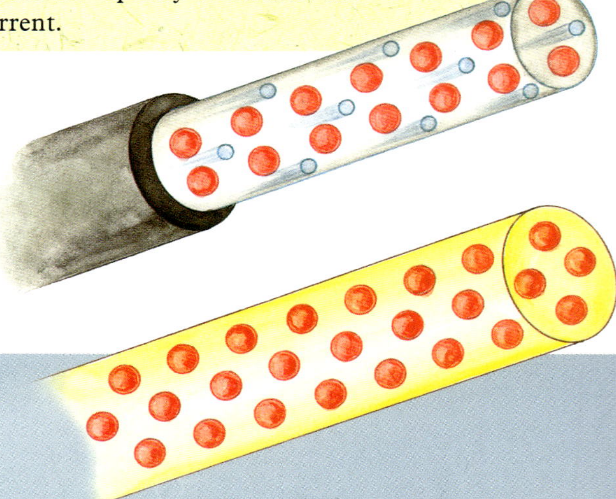

WINNING CONNECTIONS

You need:
- a piece of strong cardboard
- a sheet of paper
- ten treasury tags
- electric cable
- wire-cutters
- a 4.5 volt battery
- a small bulb with bulb-holder
- glue
- a pencil
- scissors

What to do

1 Cut 10 rectangles from the paper. On these write the names of 5 countries and their 5 capital cities. Then paste them on the cardboard, so that the countries and the capital cities are mixed up.

2 Make 10 holes in the cardboard against each name. Thread a treasury tag through each hole.

3 Ask an adult to cut 5 pieces of electric cable and strip the ends with wire-cutters. On the back of the cardboard, use the wire to connect each nation with its correct capital city. (Wind the wire around the metal 'fins' of each treasury tag.)

4 With another piece of electric cable, connect a battery contact with one side of the bulb-holder. Take another two pieces of wire. Connect one to the other battery contact and the second to the free side of the bulb-holder. The other two ends of these wires will be left free.

5 Invite a friend to try matching up the right nation with the right capital city, using the free ends of the wires.

What happens?

If the connection is correct, the bulb will light up. If the connection is wrong, the bulb remains unlit.

Because...

... the ends of the treasury tags are made of brass, a metal conductor of electricity. If the player's wires touches two treasury tags which are connected at the back, the circuit closes and the electricity which flows through lights up the bulb. If the wires are placed next to a nation and a capital city which are not correct, then the circuit remains open and the bulb does not light up.

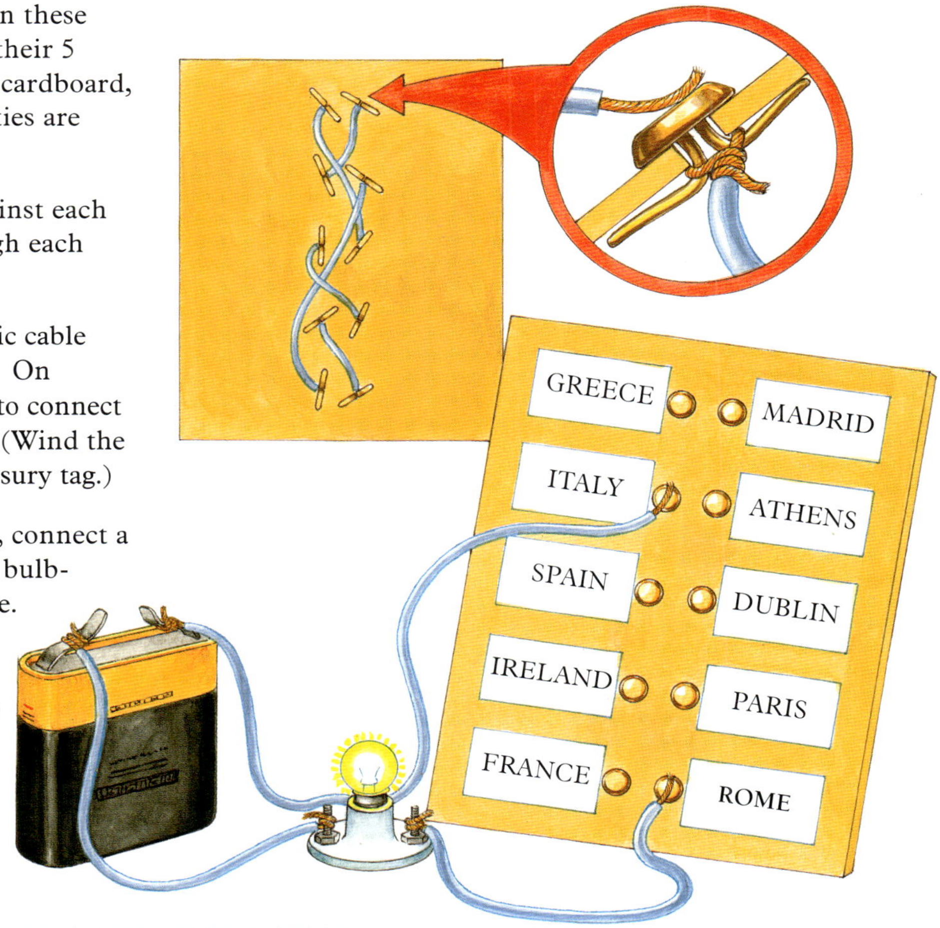

Some materials are conductors of electricity. These allow the passage of current. Others are insulators. These stop the flow.

Can water conduct electricity?

DIFFERENT REACTIONS

You need:
- a glass or plastic container
- two small terminals (clamps)
- electric cable
- a 4.5 volt battery
- a bulb
- distilled water (from a garage or hardware shop)
- salt
- wire-cutters

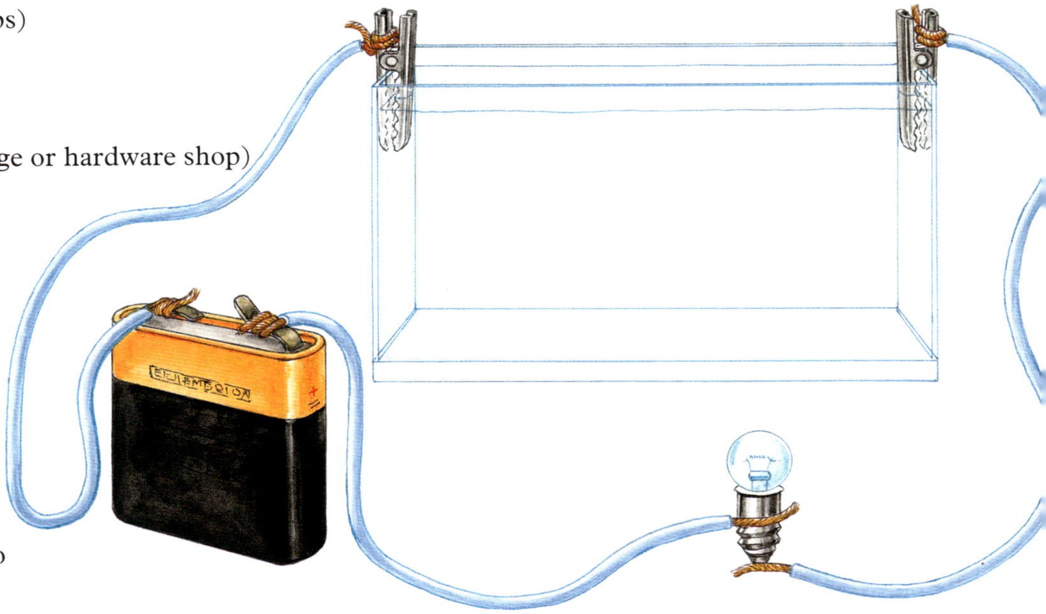

What to do

1 Fill the container with distilled water.

2 Ask an adult to cut 3 pieces of cable. Strip the ends. Connect one end of 2 wires to the battery contacts, and one free end to a terminal. Connect one end of the third wire to the second terminal.

3 Place a terminal on each side of the container, so that these touch the water.

4 Connect the free ends of the wire to the bulb, one wire touching the bottom of the metal screw, the other touching the side of the screw.

What happens?
The bulb does not light up.

5 Add a few handfuls of salt to the water. Re-connect the wires to the bulb.

What happens?
The bulb lights up.

Because...
... the distilled water is an insulator which means that it prevents the flow of the electrical charge. But if you add salt to the water, it becomes a conductor. When the salt dissolves, the particles in it, being electrically-charged, start to become attracted to the terminals connected to the battery. This creates a sort of connection which closes the circuit and so allows the electricity to pass through.

Dangers of electricity

You must NEVER touch switches or electrical equipment which is switched on if you have wet hands, or if you are standing with bare feet on a wet surface. The water in our homes is not distilled and is therefore a good conductor of electricity. So if an electric current is flowing through the water, it can give you a very serious electric shock.

Pure water is an insulator, but water containing salt is a good conductor of electricity.

Why is the position of the battery important?

PAY ATTENTION TO THE SIGNS

You need:

- two 1.5 volt batteries
- a small bulb
- two pieces of electric cable with the ends uncovered
- a ruler
- sticky tape

What to do

1 Stick the two batteries along the length of the ruler with the sticky tape. Follow a positive pole (marked with a plus [+] sign) with a negative pole (marked at the opposite end with a minus [–] sign).

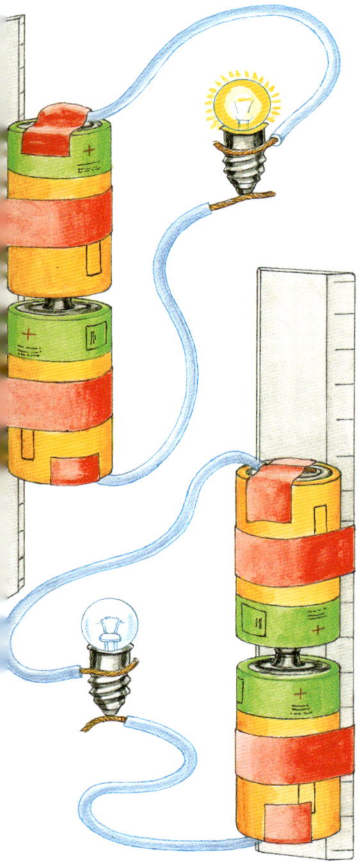

2 Use the sticky tape to stick the ends of the two wires to the opposite heads of the batteries. Bring the two batteries together. Then touch the bulb with the free ends of the wires, as shown.

What happens?
The bulb lights up.

3 Now reverse the position of the batteries, so that the two positive poles touch.

4 Re-connect the wires to the two ends of the 'double' battery. Touch the bulb again.

What happens?
The bulb does not light up.

Because...

... when they generate an electrical current, the electrons flow continually from the negative pole to the positive pole of the battery. The same thing happens if two batteries are connected to each other, because the electrons still escape from the negative pole on the one hand and go towards the positive pole on the other.
If the electrons escape from both the negative poles, they go one against the other and so the current does not flow. This is why an electric torch or toy will not work if a battery is inserted with the poles in the wrong positions.

The Invention of Alessandro Volta

The first electrical battery was built by the Italian scientist Alessandro Volta towards the end of the 18th century. It consisted of a series of zinc and copper discs, separated from each other by discs of material soaked in a solution of water and sulphuric acid. The discs were piled vertically, one on top of the other. By connecting the first disc of zinc and the last disc of copper with copper wire, Volta obtained a continuous passage of electrical current, due to the chemical reaction between the zinc and the acid solution. The current was broken only when the acid was used up.
Volta also discovered that a flow of current was created each time two different conductors were installed, with a suitable contact between them.

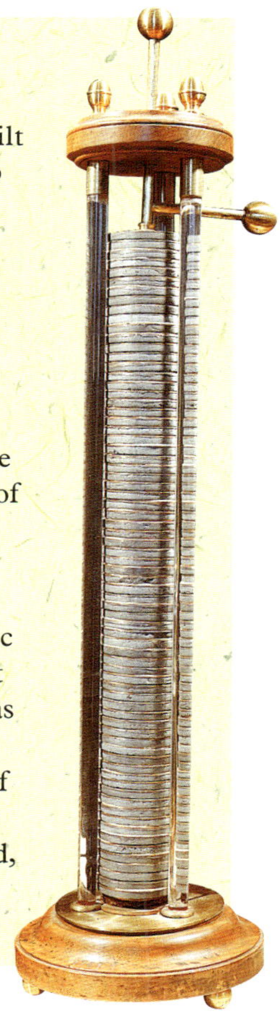

The flow of current generated by batteries can happen only between poles of the opposite sign.

Circuits and Switches

Switching the television on and off, then the computer, the hair-dryer, all the lights at home... how many switches must we use each day? What is needed behind all those toggles and buttons which we click? The switch is an extremely simple device, but one which it is impossible to do without! The switch is a small bridge which joins up a circuit which has been temporarily broken and allows us to use items of electrical equipment whenever we need them. Follow the experiments in the next section, and you can also try making your own switches.

Can a circuit light up more than one bulb?

DIFFERENT CIRCUITS

You need:

- two 4.5 volt batteries
- 4 bulbs, each with a bulb-holder
- electric cable
- wire-cutters (remember that each time you cut a piece of wire, you must strip the plastic off both ends; ask an adult to do this)

What to do

1 Connect one bulb to one of the batteries. Note the brightness of the light which it gives.

2 Connect two bulbs to the same battery, as shown in the picture.

What happens?

The two bulbs give out a light which is not so bright.

Because...

... the two bulbs 'share' the same energy, which passed first from one and then to the other. What you have built is called a series circuit. If you touch one of the two bulbs, the circuit will be broken and the other bulb will go out.

3 Connect a bulb-holder to the contacts of the second battery. Then connect another bulb to the first, as shown in the picture.

What happens?
The two bulbs give out the same light as the bulb on its own.

Because...
... each bulb is on a precise circuit which is fed directly from the battery. This type of circuit is called a parallel circuit. If one of the bulbs burns out or becomes detached, the other continues to shine because its own circuit is not broken.

A short circuit

If it is not kept under control, an electrical current can cause damage and lead to danger. One of the most common faults is the short circuit. If you were to take a short length of the insulating plastic coating off each of the wires which connect the battery to the bulb and put these in contact with each other, you would see them giving off sparks, and the bulb would go out. In this way, the current does not complete all the circuit, but returns directly to the battery without passing through the bulb, completing a circuit which is shorter. Not meeting any resistance on this circuit, the current becomes more intense (stronger) and so produces a lot of heat. In electrical installations, a short circuit can cause fires or seriously damage the installation. To avoid this, as you will soon see, we use 'safety valves' called fuses. When there is an 'overload' of current in the circuit, or the current is too strong, the wire in a fuse will break and this also breaks the circuit.

One circuit can power more than one bulb continuously, whether connected in series or in parallel.

Why do we need switches?

A DEVICE FOR LIGHT

You need:
- a tablet of wood
- two small drawing pins
- a metal paper-clip
- three pieces of insulated electric cable with the plastic stripped off the ends (ask an adult to do this)
- a bulb with a bulb-holder
- a 4.5 volt battery

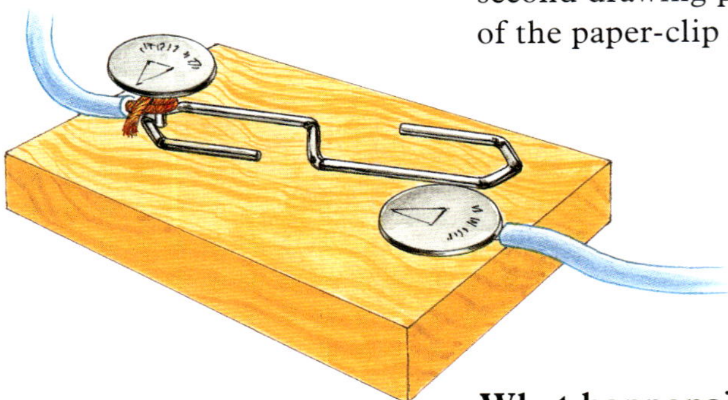

What to do

1 Stick the two drawing pins in the wooden tablet, about 3-4cm apart from each other.

2 Place the wire under each drawing pin. Connect the free end of one wire to a battery contact and the free end of the other wire to the bulb-holder. Connect the third wire from the bulb-holder to the other battery contact, as shown.

3 Open up the paper-clip and thread it under one of the drawing pins.

4 Move the other end of the paper-clip and bring it into contact with the second drawing pin. Then push the end of the paper-clip away.

What happens?
When the paper-clip touches both drawing pins, the bulb lights up. When the paper-clip is drawn away, the contact is broken and the bulb remains unlit.

Because...
... the paper-clip is made of metal, which is a conductor of electricity. So when this touches the two drawing pins, the circuit closes and allows the passage of the electrical current. When the paper-clip is drawn away from the drawing pins, the circuit is open, and the passage of the current is interrupted.

MESSAGE IN CODE

You need:

- two tablets of wood
- two bulbs, each with a bulb-holder
- eight pieces of electric cable, with the plastic stripped off the ends. (Ask an adult to do this.)
- four drawing pins
- two metal paper-clips
- two 4.5 volt batteries
- paper
- a pen

What to do

1 Make two electrical circuits exactly the same as for the last experiment. Connect the two bulbs with wires which are long enough to be taken into two different rooms.

2 With a friend, work out a code along the same lines as the Morse Code, with each letter of the alphabet corresponding to a long or a short flash of light.

3 Send your friend a short message from one room to the other. When he or she has the switch 'open', then you can 'operate' yours. For each short flash, press the paper-clip on the drawing pin quickly. For each long flash, keep the paper-clip on the drawing pin a little longer.

What happens?

Your friend will receive your message in the form of light signals. You can then send an answer in the same way.

Because...

... with each pressure of the paper-clip on the drawing pin, the circuit closes and the bulb lights up. The longer the contact, the longer the light.

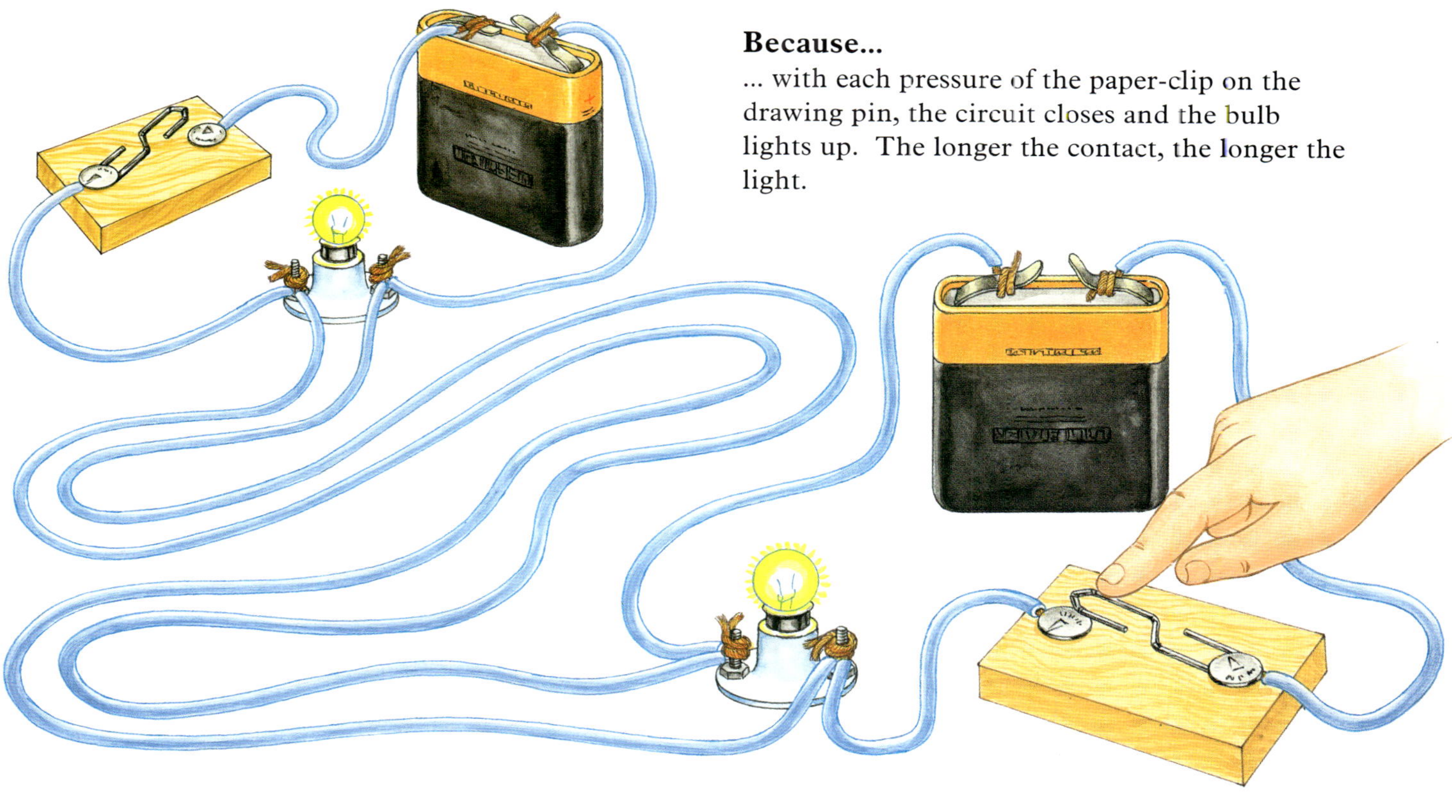

A switch either closes or opens an electrical circuit, as needed.

What is a current gate?

A TWO-WAY SWITCH

You need:
- electric cable
- six drawing pins
- two paper-clips
- a 4.5 volt battery
- two small tablets of wood
- a bulb and a bulb-holder

What to do

1 Push three drawing pins into each tablet of wood, as you see in the picture.

2 On each wooden tablet, open up a paper-clip and place one end under the centre drawing pin. In this way, the paper-clip can be moved to touch either of the other two drawing pins.

3 Using the electric cable, connect up the switches with the battery and the bulb, as shown in the bottom picture.

4 Try out different positions of the switches to light up or to extinguish the bulbs.

What happens?

The bulb can be lit or extinguished by either of the two switches.

Because...

... when both switches and the wire form an unbroken circuit, the current passes through the circuit and the bulb lights up. Each time one of the two paper-clips are moved, this opens the circuit and makes the light go out.

Electric switches in the home

When a room has two doors, it may be necessary to switch the same light on and off from different points – for instance, near to each door. In this case, an electrical installation must be equipped with a two-way switch, like the one which you made in the last experiment. The same system can be used to switch the light on and off both at the bottom and the top of a staircase.

Switches and micro-circuits

Inside a computer there are complicated electrical circuits called integrated circuits (shown in the photograph), built on a coating of silicon (a material which is very light and resistant) just a few millimetres thick. The tiny little switches of these circuits are called transistors and these allow the current to pass from one circuit to another and to make a connection. Transistors are like little doors which open and close according to the impulses which we transmit through the computer. Each time we tap in a command on the keyboard, the computer 'translates' it into an electrical impulse which becomes introduced into the computer. When the impulse arrives at the transistor this stores it, and according to its density, activates or de-activates the circuit to which it is connected. Through this circulation of electrical impulses the computer works out the data which we input and gives us the answers. Transistors are not only the smallest switches ever invented, they are also the fastest. They can open and close thousands of times in one minute!

A current gate allows an electrical circuit to open or close in one of two different directions.

Effects of the Electrical Current

Can you imagine what everyday life would be like without electricity? Try to think how many jobs are made possible only because of electrical current! We use electricity for lighting, for heating, refrigeration and air conditioning, to power motors, for travel in trains and trams, in our play... so many things around us work by using the many effects of electricity. You already know how an electric light bulb heats up soon after it is lit. But did you also know that, by a little electric shock, some substances can be transformed into others? The next section of experiments will show you how this happens.

How does a bulb light up?

GLOWING WIRE

You need:

- a tablet of wood
- two thin nails
- steel filament (you can unravel this from a pan scourer)
- two pieces of electric cable with the plastic stripped off the ends
- a 4.5 volt battery

What to do

1 Stick the two nails in the wood. Wind an end of the steel filament around the base of each nail.

2 Wind one end of a length of electric cable around a battery contact, and the other end around a nail, above the filament. Connect a second length of wiring to the other battery contact. Touch the other nail with the free end of the wire.

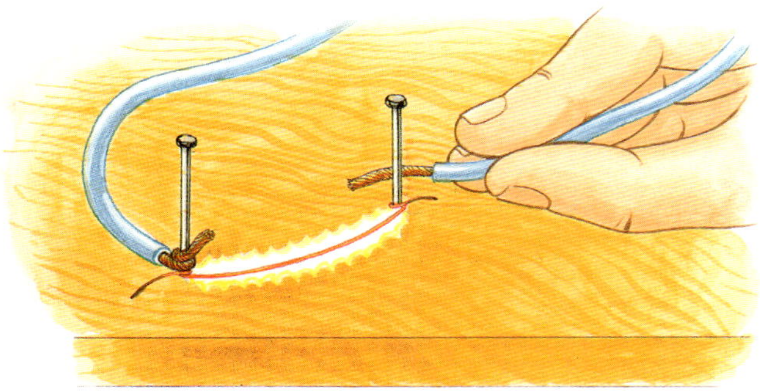

What happens?

The steel filament becomes red.

Because...

... the electrical current flows easily through the electric cable. But it is more difficult for it to flow through the steel filament. That is why the flow of electricity heats up the filament and makes it change colour.

BRIGHTNESS WHICH VANISHES

You need:

- one 4.5 volt battery
- one bulb, with bulb-holder
- electric cable, with uncovered ends
- a new pencil with both ends sharpened to a point
- sticky tape

What to do

1 Connect the bulb to the battery with the electric cable, as before. Take note of the light.

2 Insert the pencil into the circuit, connecting the wire to the lead of the point.

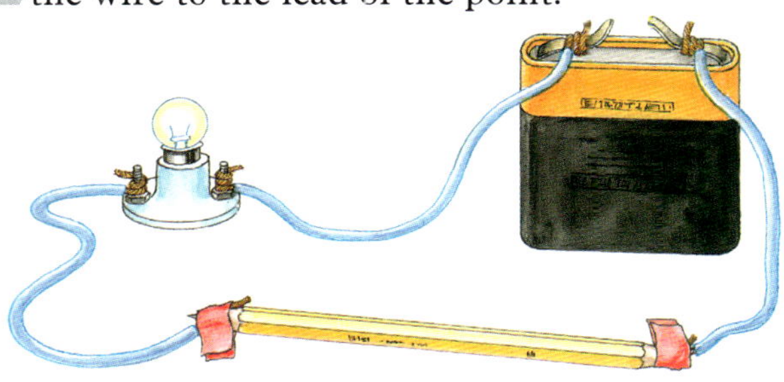

What happens?

The light from the bulb is not so bright.

Because...

... the lead conducts the current, but offers some resistance to the flow. As it resists the flow, the lead absorbs part of the electricity and so the bulb dims.

How a light bulb is made

Inside an electric light bulb can be seen a thin metal spiral, supported by two filaments which are also made of metal. The electricity enters the bulb through the wire and then flows. But the spiral wire does not let the electricity pass through easily, both because of its size and also the material of which it is made. The force of the current to pass through causes the filament to heat up, and this heating-up gives off a white light.

The filament inside a bulb offers some resistance to the passage of the current. So the filament heats up and gives off light.

Does electricity always produce heat?

THE HEAT OF ELECTRICITY

You need:

- a mercury thermometer
- a 4.5 volt battery
- a length of thin copper wire
- insulating tape

What to do

1 Wind the copper wire around the bulb of the thermometer, so that the spirals do not touch and the end of the wire is fairly long. If necessary, you can fasten down the wire with the insulating tape.

2 Wind the ends of the wire around the battery contacts.

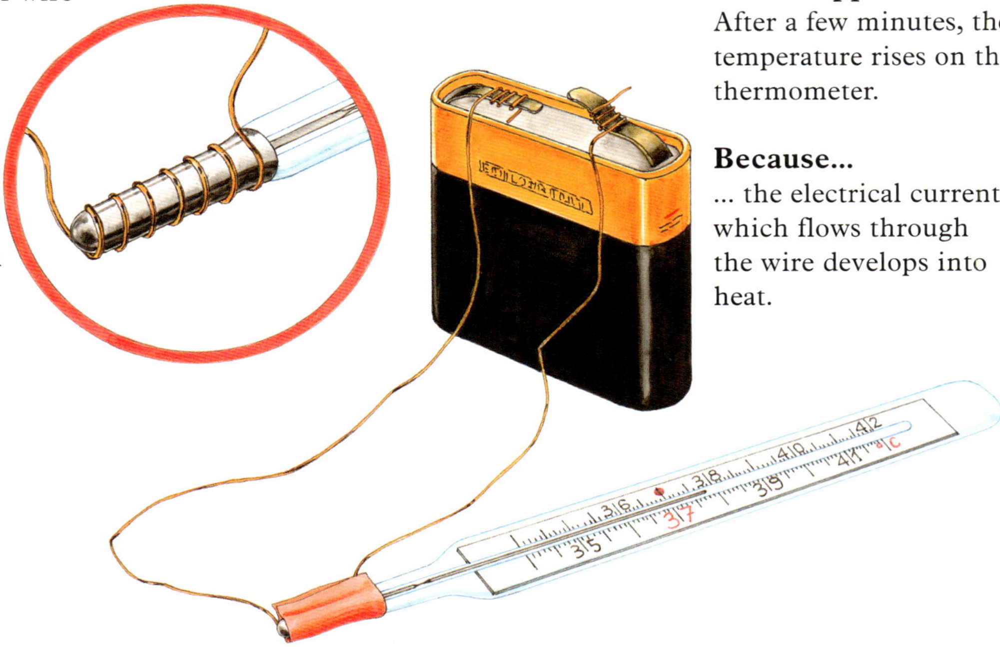

What happens?
After a few minutes, the temperature rises on the thermometer.

Because...
... the electrical current which flows through the wire develops into heat.

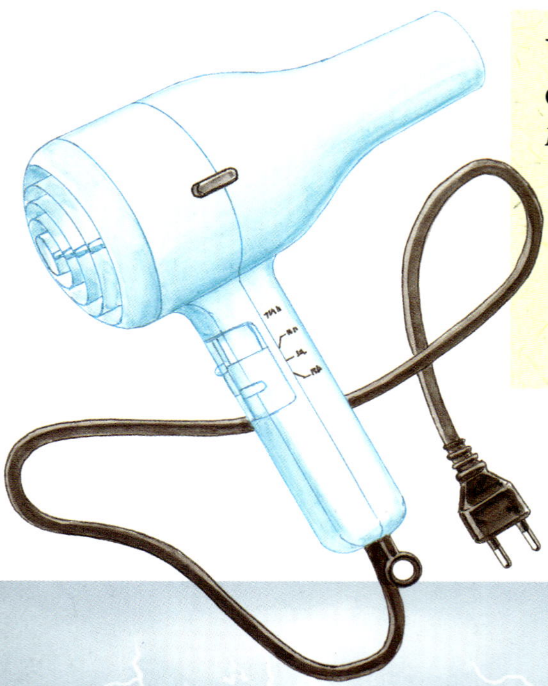

Using the heating effects of electricity

Many electrical goods which we use in our homes have inside them an electrical resistance which heats up with the passage of the current and changes the electrical energy into thermal (heat) energy. This is what happens with things like electric irons, electric cookers, toasters, electric blankets and hair-dryers.

TRANSFORMATION OF ENERGY

You need:

- three 4.5 volt batteries
- electric cable, with the ends uncovered, as before
- a tablet of wood with two drawing pins
- a strip of aluminium foil

What to do

1 Connect the three batteries and the wooden tablet with the drawing pins as illustrated in the picture. (Take care not to have positive and negative poles of the batteries next to each other.)

2 Place the strip of foil on the two drawing pins.

3 Now cut the foil to make it thinner. Put the foil on the drawing pins once again.

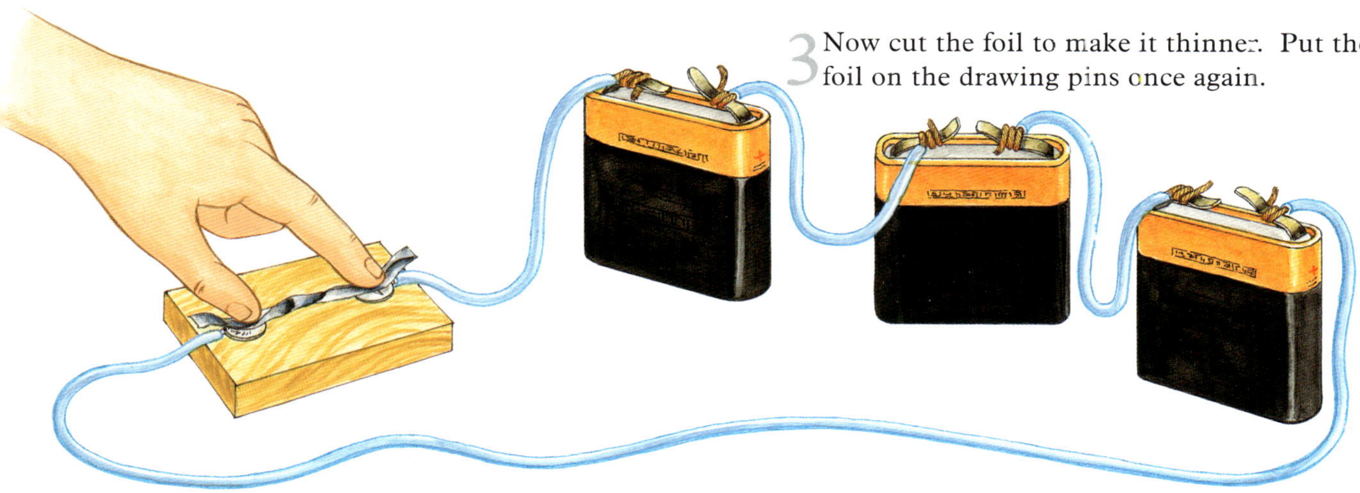

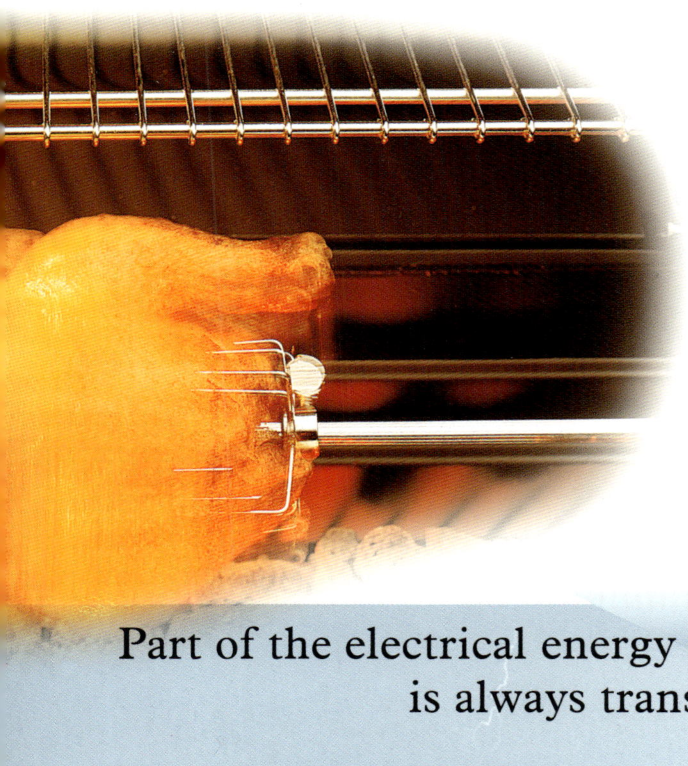

What happens?

The aluminium heats up. It becomes even hotter when it is thinner.

Because...

... the strip of foil offers resistance to the passage of current and transforms part of the electrical energy into heat. The thinner the strip, the more difficult the passage of the electrical current, and so the more heat this generates. Even in normal electric bulbs, brightness comes from the energy which flows through the filament into the bulb and becomes transformed into heat. That is why it is impossible to touch a bulb only moments after the power has been switched on.

Part of the electrical energy which goes through a conductor is always transformed into heat.

What does the brightness of light depend on?

VARIATION IN BRIGHTNESS

You need:
- a 4.5 volt battery
- a bulb with bulb-holder
- electric cable
- a lead pencil
- sticky tape

What to do

1 Connect the wire to the battery and to the bulb, as in the last experiment.

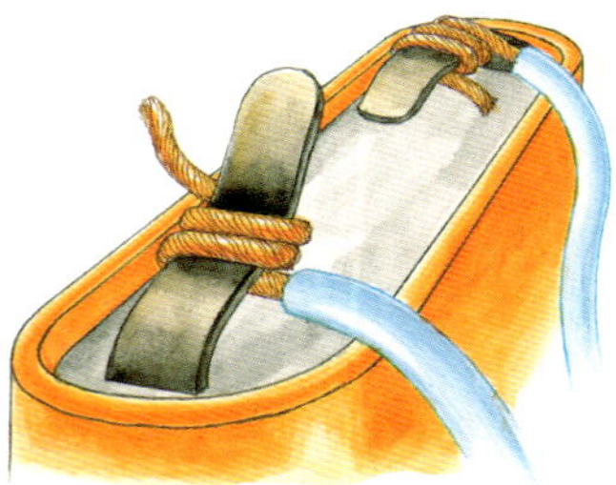

2 Open up the pencil. Take out the lead.

3 Fix the end of the wire to one end of the lead. Run the end of the other wire along the length of the lead.

What happens?
When the end of the wire is run along the length of the lead, the light in the bulb varies in brightness.

Because...
... as we have already seen, lead offers resistance to the passage of the electrical current. The longer the length of the lead which is part of the circuit, the more the energy which is absorbed, and the less the brightness of the bulb.

Fuses

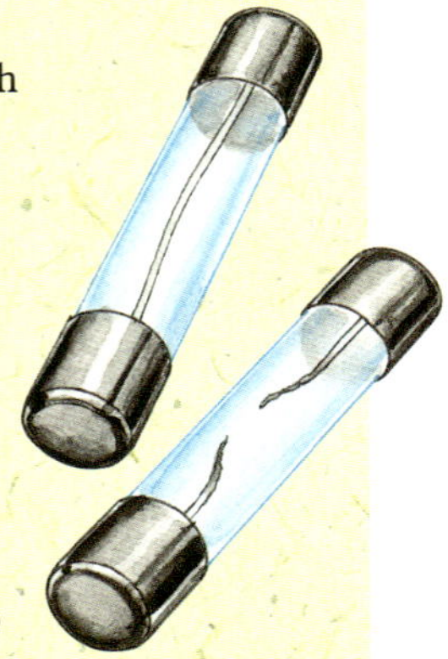

Electrical items are equipped with small safety devices called fuses. Inside a fuse there is a thin filament which breaks when a current which is stronger than the circuit can support,tries to flow through. As the filament breaks, the fuse opens the circuit and so interrupts the flow of current. Fuses are like automatic switches and they stop the flow of electricity. Otherwise the excessive heating-up of a circuit could cause a fire.

Volts and amps

The electrical tension – that is the speed with which the electrical charge passes through a conductor – is measured in volts. On the batteries used in experiments and on those which power electrical items and toys, the number of volts is always indicated, (1.5v, 4.5v or 9v). Batteries are not dangerous because of their low voltage. But in the wires of electrical installations in the home, the tension of 230 volts can kill a man. The high-tension pylons which transport electricity across long distances have a tension which can exceed 250,000 volts. Also, by the speed with which electricity flows through wires it is possible to measure its intensity.

We use as a unit of measurement of intensity the term ampère (amp for short). An amp meter indicates how many electrical charges are passing through a conductor at a certain time.

LIKE A FUSE

You need:
- three 4.5 volt batteries
- a low-wattage light bulb with bulb-holder
- electric cable, with ends uncovered as before
- a wooden tablet
- two drawing pins
- a strip of tinfoil
- a pencil sharpened at both ends

What to do

1 Connect the batteries together with the wiring. Make sure that the negative and positive poles are not next to each other.

2 Push the drawing pins into the wood. Connect these to the outer battery contacts and to the bulbs.

3 With the other two lengths of wiring, connect the two drawing pins to the points of the pencil.

What happens?
The bulb gives out a rather dim light.

Because...
... the lead of the pencil keeps back some of the electrical energy and so resists the passage of the current.

4 Connect the two drawing pins to the strip of tinfoil.

What happens?
The bulb produces a dim light and then goes out.

Because...
... the strip of tinfoil directly connects the bulb to the battery, as a parallel circuit. Therefore the bulb lights up with considerable brightness. However, the three batteries (each 4.7 volt) provides the low wattage bulb with a current which is too strong. Therefore the bulb filament fuses, interrupting the circuit.

The brightness of a light depends on the speed with which the electrical charge flows through the conducting wires.

What changes does electricity cause in water?

CHEMICAL REACTIONS

You need:
- electric cable (with ends stripped)
- two 4.5 volt batteries
- two large screws
- a glass
- water
- salt
- an old postcard

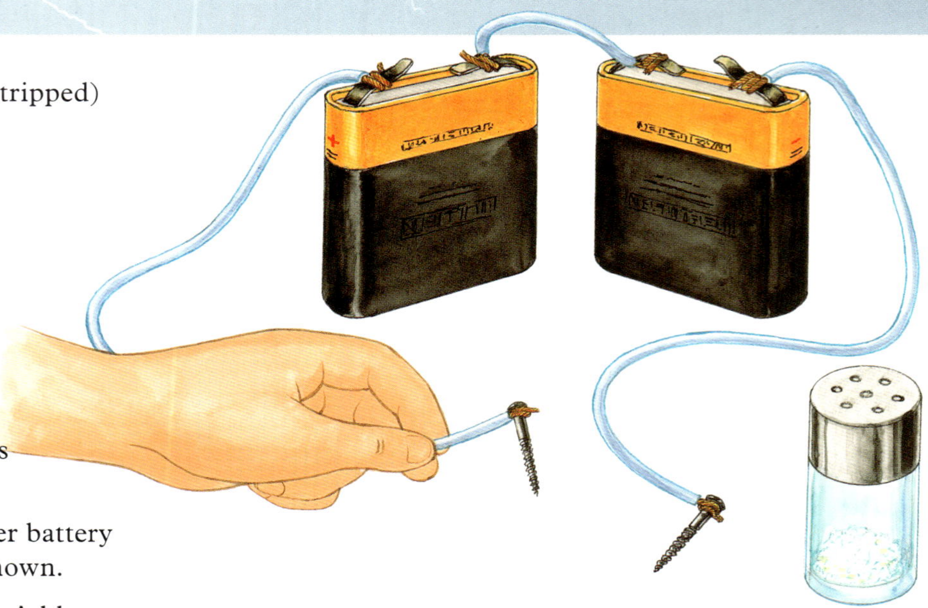

What to do
1 Connect the batteries with a piece of wire. (Negative and positive poles must not be together.)

2 Connect each of the outer battery contacts to a screw, as shown.

3 Fill the glass with water. Add the salt.

4 Make two holes in the card, a short distance apart. Place the card on the glass. Thread the screws through the holes.

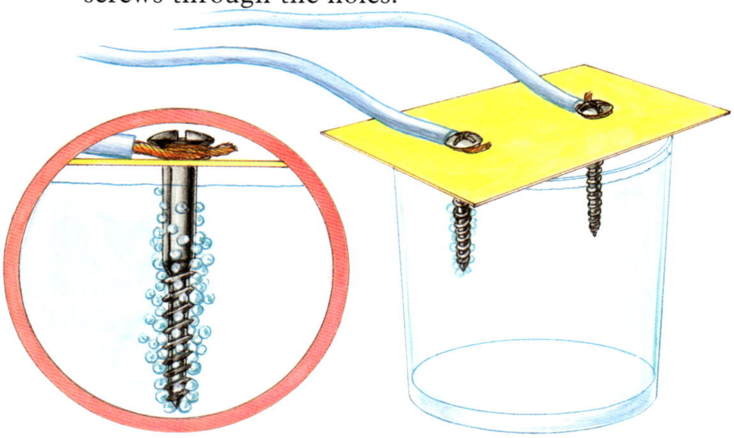

What happens?
Bubbles form around one of the screws.

5 Leave the screws in the water for a few minutes.

6 Take the screws out of the water.

What happens?
There is a deposit of green substance on the bottom of the glass.

Because...
... chemical changes are caused by the passage of electrical current in water. The current breaks up the water (the bubbles are full of hydrogen, a component of water). The electricity also changes the salt and the iron from the screws into other substances. This is the reason for the discolouration of the water and the deposit on the bottom of the glass.

Electrolysis

The term electrolysis means 'breaking down through electricity'. This is what we call the phenomenon by which the elements of a chemical composition can be separated by the passage of the current.

In industry, electrolysis is used to coat metal objects with a layer of another ornamental or protective metal, like gold, silver or chrome. The object being covered, such as a teaspoon to be silver-plated, is suspended by an electrode (one of the terminals of an electrical circuit) and immersed in a liquid solution which contains silver. In the liquid is also immersed another electrode. With the passage of the current, the particles of silver become separated into the solution and get fixed to the teaspoon. Electrolysis is also used to extract aluminium from rocks and to purify metals, separating the metal particles from anything which is impure. In car batteries, electrolysis enables the transformation of electrical energy into chemical energy which is stored in an accumulator. Often the steel bodywork of a car is plated with a thin layer of metal such as zinc to protect it from rust.

The steel bodywork of cars are often coated with a thin layer of metal such as zinc as protection against rust.

When electricity passes through water it can break up and change the substances which the water contains.

Fact-Finder

How a battery is made

The ordinary dry cell battery, although very different today, works on the same principle as the battery invented by Volta. The acid solution by which the battery functions consists of a chemical substance of a natural solid (manganese oxide) called electrolyte. The coating of the battery is made of zinc and this constitutes the negative pole. At the centre of the battery there is a stick of carbon which works as the positive pole and connection is made by the metal cap at the top of the battery. When the battery is connected to a circuit, the chemical substances inside react with one another. This chemical reaction causes the separation of the negative charges from the positive charges, and this makes it possible to build up a flow of current. When the substance inside the battery is exhausted, the battery is 'dead' and unusable, unless it is a battery of the rechargeable type.

An electric shock in the sea

The stingray is a fish with a special defence – an electric shock. On the sides of its body, the stingray has two organs made of a special muscle fibre which can accumulate electricity and give off a considerable electric shock, enough to kill or to stun a fish. The stingray is not the only 'electric fish'. There is also the manta ray, the electric eel and other species which have organs which can give electric shocks. A shock from an electric eel is strong enough to kill a man.

Inside the plug

An electrical plug is covered with insulating rubber. But the metal prongs allow the current to flow through, along the wire and to power whatever is connected to the electrical supply.

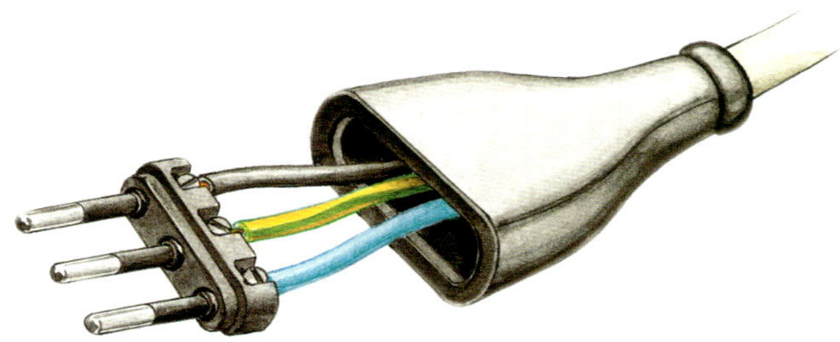

Why we need to strip the ends of wiring

In some of the experiments, you were told to ask an adult to uncover the ends of the electric cable, so that you could connect it to the battery or a light bulb. Electric cable is always covered with insulating plastic. The thin copper filaments inside conduct the current. So, if the plastic at the ends of the wire are not stripped off, the copper will not make contact with the battery contacts, nor with the metal parts of the light bulb. Therefore, the current would not be able to pass through, because it would be blocked by the plastic.
Some other advice:
If you twist the uncovered ends of the copper wire to obtain a stiff and tight end, this will make it easier to work with. If you need to connect the wire to the battery for only a short while, try twisting the copper filaments together, then wind them into a small ring which you can thread on and off the battery contact.

Chemistry

Does heat change a substance? When do two substances form a compound? Why do nails go rusty? What is the purpose of chemical analysis? How does the human stomach digest food? You will find the answers to these and many more questions by doing the experiments in this section, under the following headings:

Solids, Liquids and Gases • Mixtures, Solutions and Compounds
Chemical Reactions • Analysing Substances
Chemistry Around Us

Solids, Liquids and Gases

Everything around us is made up of atoms. These are tiny, little particles of matter which, with other atoms, either the same or of different types, form molecules. But what makes the difference between liquid, solid and gas substances? The state of the matter – liquid, solid or gas – depends on the movement of the molecules. In solids, the force which holds the molecules together, called the force of cohesion, is very strong and the molecules can only vibrate without changing position. In liquids, the molecules can slide one on the other, continually changing position, but keeping very close. In gas, the molecules, kept together by a very weak force, move in all directions and there is a lot of space between one molecule and another (that is why a gas can be compressed).

The following experiments will show you the effects of heat on molecules and how it is possible for a substance to change from one state to another.

All the experiments are safe to do, but an adult must be on hand to use some of the tools required.

Does heat change a substance?

DILATION OF LIQUIDS

You need:

- three identical glass jars with stoppers
- scissors
- three thin glass tubes, about 20-30cm long
- plasticine and sticky tape
- water, olive oil, methylated spirit
- a rectangular oven-dish
- a saucepan

What to do

1 Fill one jar with water, the second with oil, the third with methylated spirit. Label the jars with sticky tape.

2 Make a hole in the centre of each stopper. Push the glass tubes through, each one to the same depth in the jar, but not touching the bottom. Put plasticine around the tube at the top to hold it firmly.

3 Pour water into the oven-dish. Stand the three jars in the water. Ask an adult to put the oven-dish on the hot-plate.

What happens?

In a little while, the level of water in the three jars rises at different levels according to the substance.

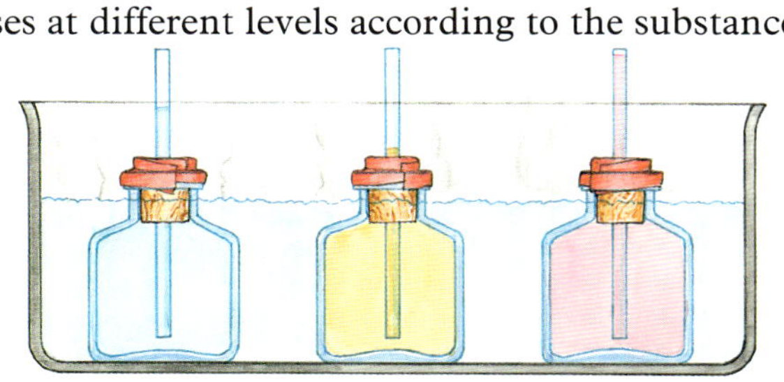

Because...

... the heat of the water in which the jars stand causes the dilation (enlargement or spreading) of the liquid they contain. (Dilation varies according to the density of each liquid.) There is not enough space inside the jars for the spread of the liquid, and so it rises up into the glass tubes.

HEAT UP A SOLID

You need:

- a coin
- a length of iron wire
- a clothes peg
- a lit candle

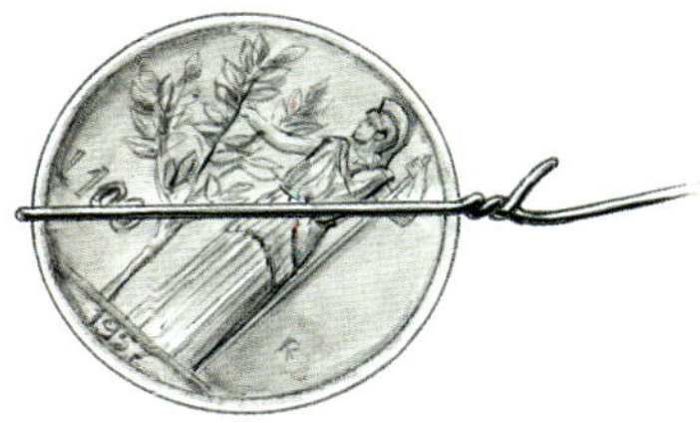

What to do

1 Make a ring from the wire. This must be the same diameter as the coin, so that the ring goes exactly over the coin.

2 Grip the coin with the clothes peg. Hold it over the flame of the candle for a few minutes.

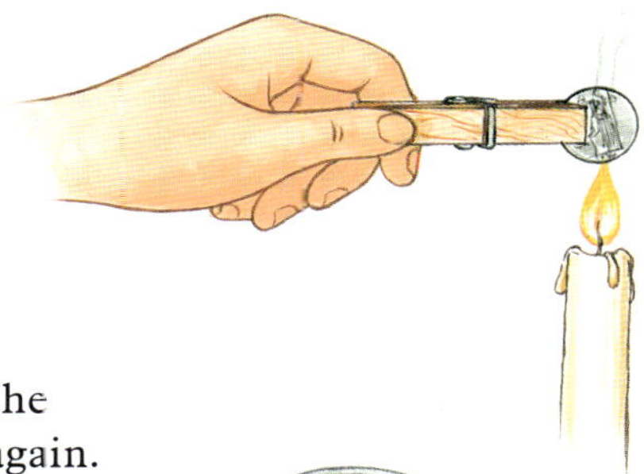

3 Now try to thread the ring over the coin again.

What happens?

The coin no longer passes through.

Because...

... the heat of the flame has temporarily dilated (enlarged) the coin. If you leave it to cool down, you will be able to thread it through the ring once more.

Railway lines can dilate because of excessive heat. That is why between one track and another, there is a space. This space is reduced when a railway line dilates.

Solids, liquids and gases can dilate (enlarge) with the effect of heat.

How does matter react to cooling?

AIR WHICH SHRINKS

You need:
- a glass bottle
- a balloon
- a sink with hot and cold water

What to do

1 With the help of an adult, pour very hot water into the bottle.

2 After a few minutes, empty the bottle. Put the neck of the balloon over the top of the bottle at once.

3 Turn the hot water tap on the outside of the bottle.

What happens?
The balloon sinks inside the bottle.

Because...
... the hot air inside the bottle contracts (shrinks) when it is cold, which means that it reduces in volume. As the air outside enters into the bottle and occupies the space which is left, it also pushes the balloon to the inside. The contraction of the air is due to the slowing-down of the speed of its molecules, resulting from the lowering of the temperature.

A special component

Have you ever frozen water to make ice? Then you will have seen that ice takes up more space than liquid water. That is why a tightly-closed bottle full of water in the refrigerator will break. This expansion of ice is due to the structure of the water molecules. When the temperature falls below 4°C these molecules change into rather cumbersome hexagon structures which need more space. This is the reason why leakages of water can cause trouble during the winter – as water freezes, the ice takes up more space, and can cause splits in stonework and broken roof tiles.

A COLLAPSING BOTTLE

You need:
- some cubes of ice
- a meat tenderizer
- a table napkin
- a plastic bottle with a screw-top

What to do

1 Put some ice cubes in the napkin. Ask an adult to crush the cubes with the meat tenderizer.

2 Put the crushed ice cubes in the bottle. Put the screw-top on.

3 Shake the bottle, so that the inside is thoroughly chilled. Then put it down.

What happens?
The bottle curls up.

Because...
... inside the bottle, the ice causes a rapid reduction of temperature of the air. This means that the air inside is reduced in volume. The air outside presses down on the bottle and squashes it.

With the exception of water, when things become cold, they undergo a contraction (become smaller).

Can substances change their physical state?

MOLECULES IN MOVEMENT

You need:
- an ice cube
- half a bar of chocolate
- a radiator
- a hot-plate
- a saucepan
- two small plates

What to do

1 Pour a little water in one plate. Place the ice cube in the other plate.

2 Place the two plates on the radiator.

3 Put the chocolate in the saucepan. With the help of an adult, heat it up gently on the hot-plate.

What happens?

After a few hours, the water disappears. But in a short time, the ice has changed into water. And on the hot-plate, the chocolate melts and changes into a thick liquid.

Because...

... the heat of the radiator makes the water evaporate. This means that the molecules increase their speed, spreading away from each other and dispersing among the molecules of the air in the form of water vapour. The heat of the radiator also transforms the ice, which is water in its solid state. In the same way, the heat of the hot-plate makes the chocolate change from its solid state to liquid.

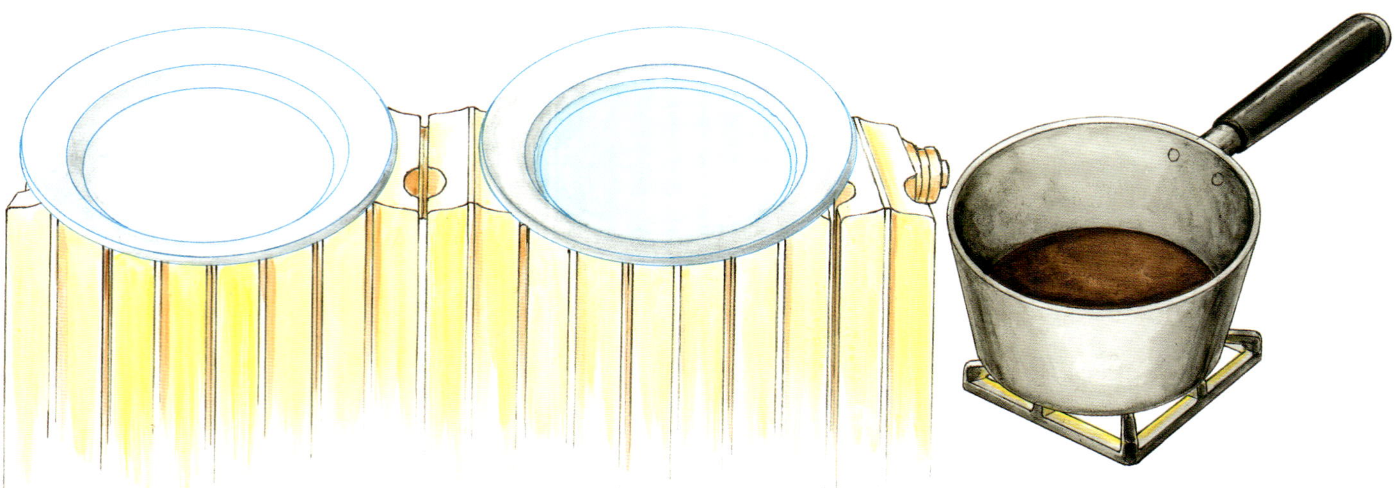

The path of state

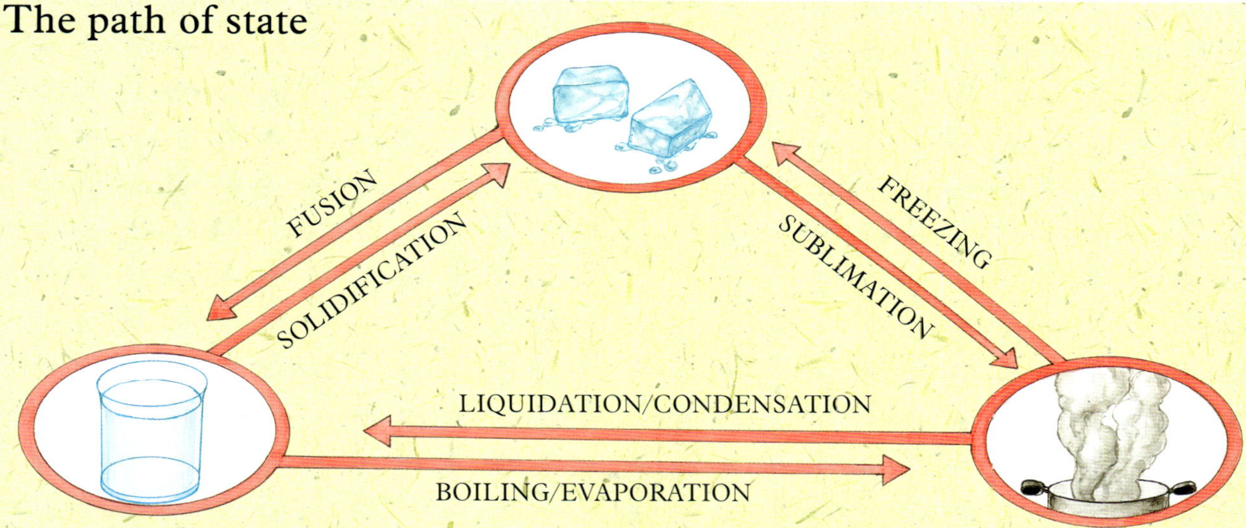

The passage from the liquid state to the gas (or vapour) state is due to the increase in temperature. In boiling this happens rapidly and involves the whole mass of liquid. Evaporation, on the other hand, is a slow process, which affects only the surface layer of the liquid.

Water vapour is a gas. When it meets a cold surface, it forms into tiny little drops (this process is called condensation). But all gases can be changed into liquids. Their liquidation is obtained by a powerful cooling (air becomes liquid at minus 195°C) or with considerable compression. (A cylinder spray often contains pressurized gas substances in a liquid state.)

The fusion (melting) of ice happens at a room temperature and water freezes at below 0°C. When a volcano erupts, it expels lava, solid rock which has become liquid due to an extraordinarily high temperature. As it cools, the lava returns to its solid state (solidification).

Dry ice is carbon dioxide in its solid state. When this comes in contact with the air or water, these substances help it to pass directly into a gaseous state (sublimation). The reverse passage, from vapour to solid, is called freezing. Frost forms on very cold days, when water vapour in the air freezes.

The effects of pressure

As well as temperature, pressure also influences the passage of a substance from one state to another. When pressure is increased, this makes the molecules stay close and tied to each other. In the pressure cooker, the steam which is created inside pushes on the surface of the water. As a result, the water reaches boiling point at a higher temperature (because it needs more heat to overcome the resistance of pressure) and the food gets cooked more quickly.

Variations in temperature or pressure can cause the passage of a substance from one physical state to another.

Mixtures, solutions and compounds

Scientists have identified 109 pure substances which are called elements. Each element is made up of the same atoms – which means there are 109 different types of atoms.

Atoms combine together to form molecules. The combinations are endless and create an enormous amount of substances which compose the whole Universe. But, is it enough to mix two elements to produce a new substance? What is the difference between a mixture, like sand and a solution of water and salt, and a chemical compound, like rust?

Do substances change in mixtures?

UNION AND SEPARATION

You need:
- fine salt
- white flour
- a spoon
- blotting paper
- a funnel
- a jug
- a large see-through container

What to do

1 In the jug, mix together an equal quantity of fine salt and white flour.

What happens?
In the mixture, the two substances, flour and salt, cannot be distinguished, one from the other.

2 Pour water into the jug. Mix again. Then wait a little while.

What happens?
After a few minutes, the flour settles on the bottom of the jug.

3 Fold the blotting paper into quarters. Take three of the corners and pull them back together. Pull the fourth corner back in the opposite direction, to make a filter. Now put the base of the filter in the funnel.

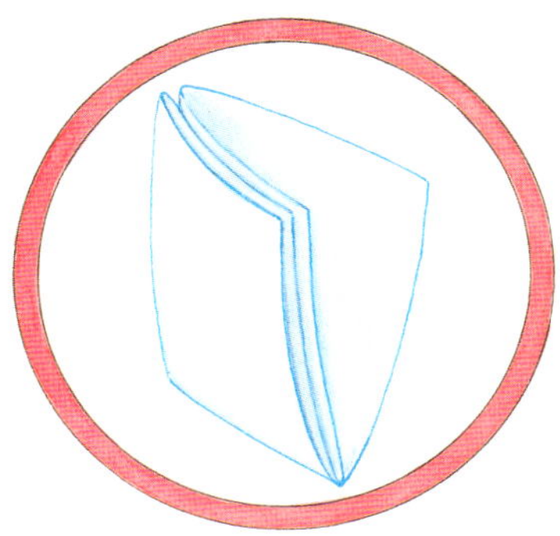

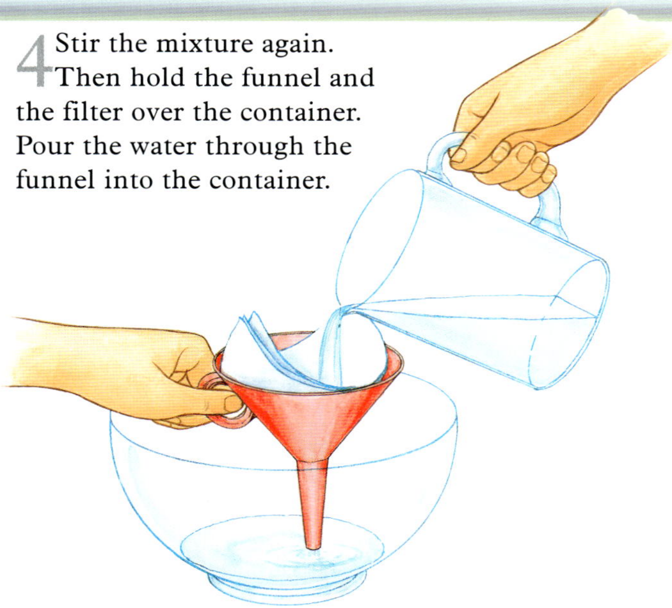

4 Stir the mixture again. Then hold the funnel and the filter over the container. Pour the water through the funnel into the container.

5 Take the filter out of the funnel. Leave the filter to dry.

6 Put the container with the filtered water in a cold place. Wait until the water evaporates.

What happens?

Flour has gathered on the filter. In the container, when all the water has evaporated, there remains a thin layer of salt crystals.

Because...

... flour does not dissolve in water. Instead, it tends to separate from it and settles on the bottom. This phenomenon is called decantation. Also, the particles of flour are too big to pass through the blotting paper, so that they stay on the filter. This system of separation from substances is called filtration. The salt has also dissolved in the water. It remains dissolved until the heat makes the water evaporate. Then, the salt returns to its solid state in the form of crystals. This method of separation of the components of a solution is called crystallization.

Substances which form a mixture do not change and can be easily separated.

Chemical Reactions

In chemical reactions, the elements or compound to begin with are called *reactants*, (which means they can undergo a reaction) and the end results *products*. There are chemical compounds of *synthesis* in which the reactants unite to create a new compound, and chemical reactions of *analysis* in which the reactants and compounds divide into the elements which they constitute. Then there are the reactions of substitution in which one or more elements of the compound change partners. By doing the following experiments, you can try different types of chemical reactions with air, heat and electricity.

Why do nails go rusty?

IRON OXIDIZES

You need:
- iron filings
- a test tube
- a see-through bowl
- a pen which can write on glass
- water

What to do

1 Dampen the inside of the tube. Then shake in a few iron filings, so that they stick to the inside.

2 Pour about 3cm of cold water into the bowl.

3 Turn the test tube upside down and place at the bottom of the bowl. Do this so that the level of water inside the test tube is level with that inside the bowl. (To do this, tip the test tube just a little as you place it in the water.)

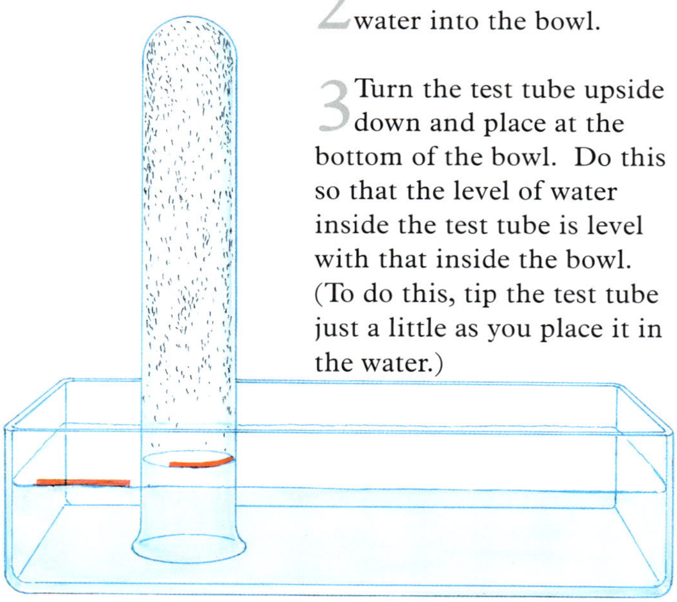

4 Use the pen to mark the level of the water, both on the test tube and on the bowl. Then leave the experiment for two days.

What happens?

The iron filings become brown. The level of water in the test tube has risen. The level of water in the bowl has gone down.

Because...

... the iron, by combining with the oxygen in the air inside the test tube, has formed rust. The chemical name for rust is iron oxide. In this chemical reaction, which we call oxidization, the oxygen has left the air and clustered on the iron. This means that the air inside the test tube has diminished in volume. The air outside presses on the surface of the water in the bowl, pushing it up inside the test tube, so that this occupies the space left by the oxygen.

Reactions of oxidization

The rust which forms on iron objects deeply corrodes (eats into) those objects, making them weaker. Once rust has formed, it remains on the object, making it crumble and exposing the layers of metal underneath to the air. These layers also become oxidized, (forming rust) in their turn. Another example of the reaction of oxidization is when slices of apple become brown, because the substance which the apple contains combines with the oxygen in the air. The blackening of silver things is also caused by the same chemical reaction.

Mars is distinguished from other heavenly bodies by its chesnut-red colour. This is due to the oxidization of iron on its surface.

In the chemical reaction of oxidization, the oxygen bonds with the iron, creating a new substance – iron oxide, or rust.

Do chemical reactions change compounds?

A LITTLE BANG

You need:
- iron filings
- copper sulphate
- two test tubes
- hot water
- vinegar
- a match

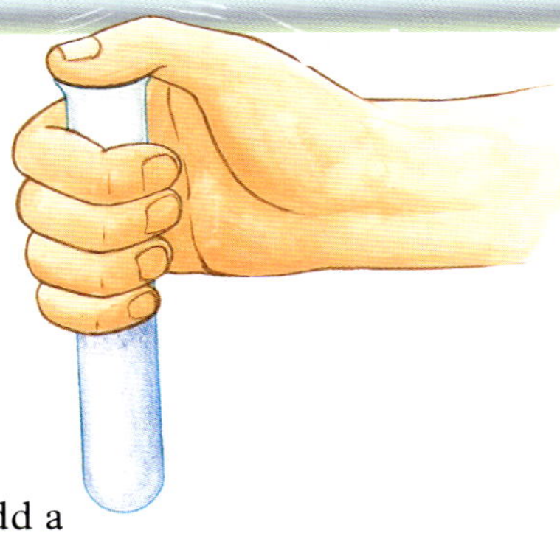

What to do

1 Pour some hot water into the test tube. Add a little copper sulphate. Shake the test tube to mix the two substances.

2 Put some iron filings in the other test tube. Then half fill with vinegar. Carefully put two drops of this solution into the first test tube.

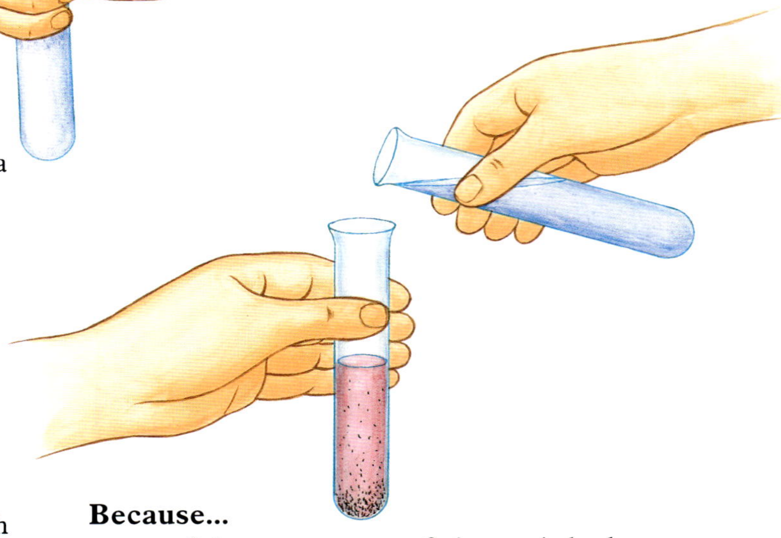

3 When you see bubbles forming, close the test tube with your thumb.

4 Ask an adult to strike a match near the mouth of the test tube.

5 When you feel the pressure of gas inside the test tube, remove your thumb.

What happens?
The flame makes a little bang.

Because...
... one of the components of vinegar is hydrogen, a gas. When the hydrogen reacts with iron, vinegar and copper sulphate, it is set free and remains isolated. So when the hydrogen escapes from the test tube, the match makes it burst into flame with a little bang and there is a brief increase in the flame.

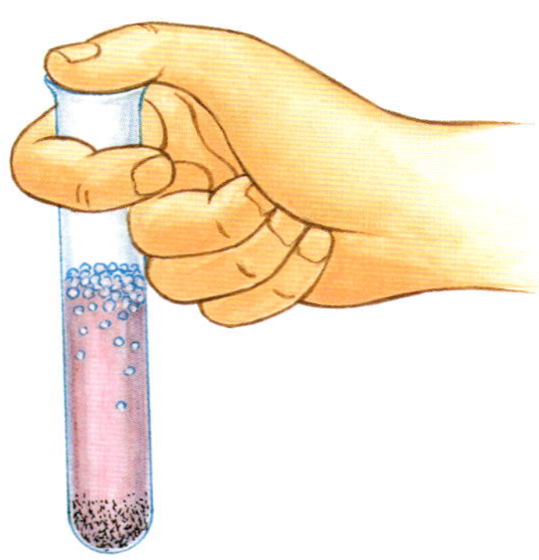

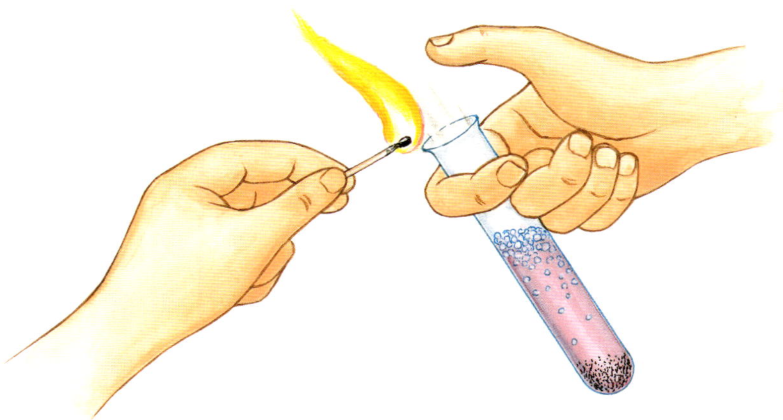

A GAS SET FREE

You need:
- bicarbonate of soda
- a teaspoon
- vinegar
- water
- a glass, tall and straight, if possible
- a match

What to do

1 Pour a finger's width of water into the glass.

2 Add a teaspoon of bicarbonate of soda and a little vinegar.

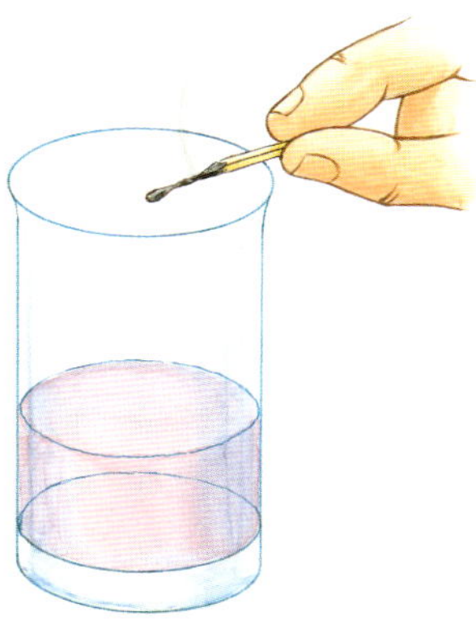

3 Ask an adult to light a match and to hold it down into the glass.

What happens?
The flame goes out.

Because...
... the bicarbonate of soda is a compound of sodium, hydrogen, carbon and oxygen. In the chemical reaction, it breaks up in contact with the vinegar. The carbon and oxygen separate from the other elements. Together they form a gas, carbon dioxide, which puts out the flame.

CHANGES IN THE ELEMENTS

You need:
- a test tube
- water
- copper sulphate
- iron filings

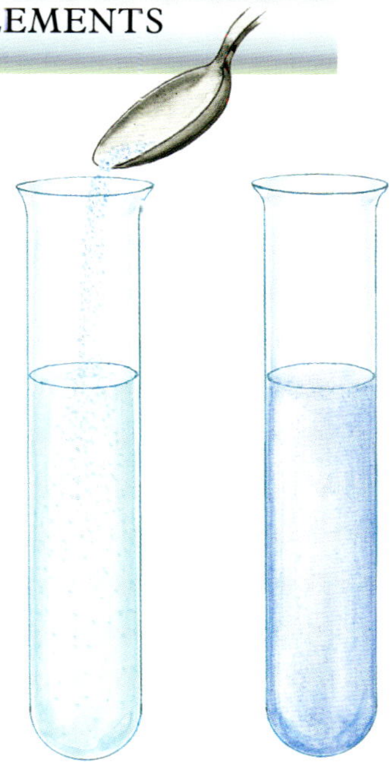

What to do

1 Fill two thirds of the test tube with water.

2 Add the copper sulphate.

What happens?
You get a blue solution.

3 Add the iron filings. Gently shake the test tube, keeping it closed with your finger.

What happens?
A red-coloured substance settles on the bottom of the test tube. The solution becomes clear green.

Because...
... the copper sulphate contains sulphur and copper. When you add the iron filings, the iron and the copper change places. The iron bonds to the sulphur, forming iron sulphur, which gives the solution a green colour. The copper remains isolated and this settles at the bottom of the test tube.

Chemical reactions can separate, unite or combine differently the elements of a compound.

Is combustion a chemical reaction?

A CANDLE DOES NOT ONLY GIVE LIGHT

You need:
- a candle
- candle holder
- a match
- a knife
- a microscope slide
- a clothes peg

What to do

1 Put the candle in the candle holder. Ask an adult to light it.

2 Hold the blade of the knife at the centre of the flame for a few seconds.

What happens?
The blade is covered with soot, tiny particles of carbon.

Because...
... these particles are found in the most central part of the flame. They are caused by the decomposition of the paraffin of which the candle is made.

3 Holding it steady with a clothes peg, hold the microscope slide above the flame, at the very tip of the wick, for about 10-15 seconds. Then allow the slide to cool.

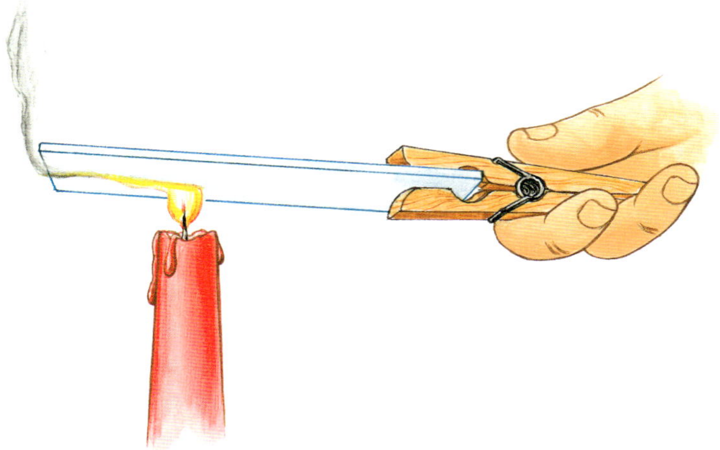

What happens?
There are traces of wax on the slide.

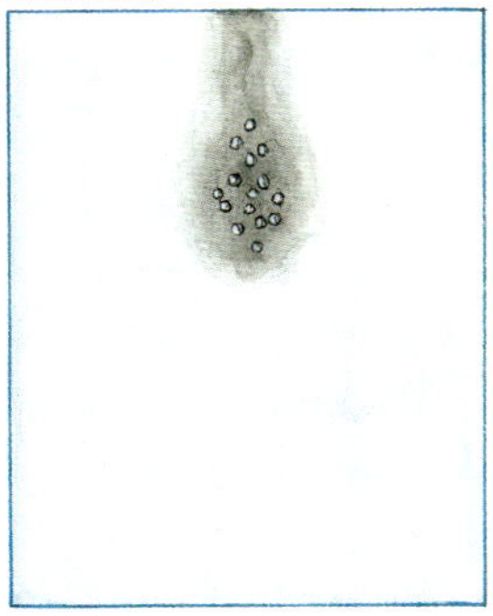

Because...
... not all the wax decomposes when the flame burns. Some particles are drawn up by the rising heat. On contact with the surface of the slide, these particles clot together again.

When a candle burns

The body of a candle is made of solid paraffin, which is made of hydrogen and carbon, and a paraffin-soaked wick. The flame which begins when the wick is lit is not equal in all its parts. In the outermost zone of the flame, due to the contact with the oxygen in the air, the burning of the paraffin begins and this gives off heat. In the central zone of the flame, where there is no oxygen, the paraffin divides into hydrogen and carbon. The heat makes the carbon become incandescent (luminous) making the flame bright.

The heat coming from combustion melts some of the wax, which drips down the sides of the candle and then solidifies.

Fire

Combustion is a chemical reaction which is often accompanied by the phenomenon of the flame. Therefore, a combustible, (for example, the sulphur of a match) combines with a combustive agent (for example, oxygen) to give heat.
Combustion usually happens by using a flame or a spark with which to light the combustible substance, then heat results and this adds to the combustion.
The vital elements of combustion are – the combustible, the combustive agent and heat. When any of these three elements are missing, the fire will go out.
Smoke, cinders and soot are all possible products to show that a chemical transformation takes place when something burns.

Combustion is a chemical reaction. When a substance burns, it changes and originates new substances.

Can electricity cause a chemical reaction?

DISAPPEARING WATER

You need:

- one 4.5 volt battery
- two pieces of electrical cable, with the plastic stripped off the ends (ask an adult to do this for you.)
- the lead from a pencil
- sticky tape
- two test tubes
- vinegar
- water
- a see-through glass container
- two clothes pegs
- matches

What to do

1 Break the pencil lead into two. Wind one end of wire around each battery contact. Wind each free end of wire around the pieces of lead. Wrap the join with sticky tape to hold firm, as shown in the picture. You have now made two electrodes.

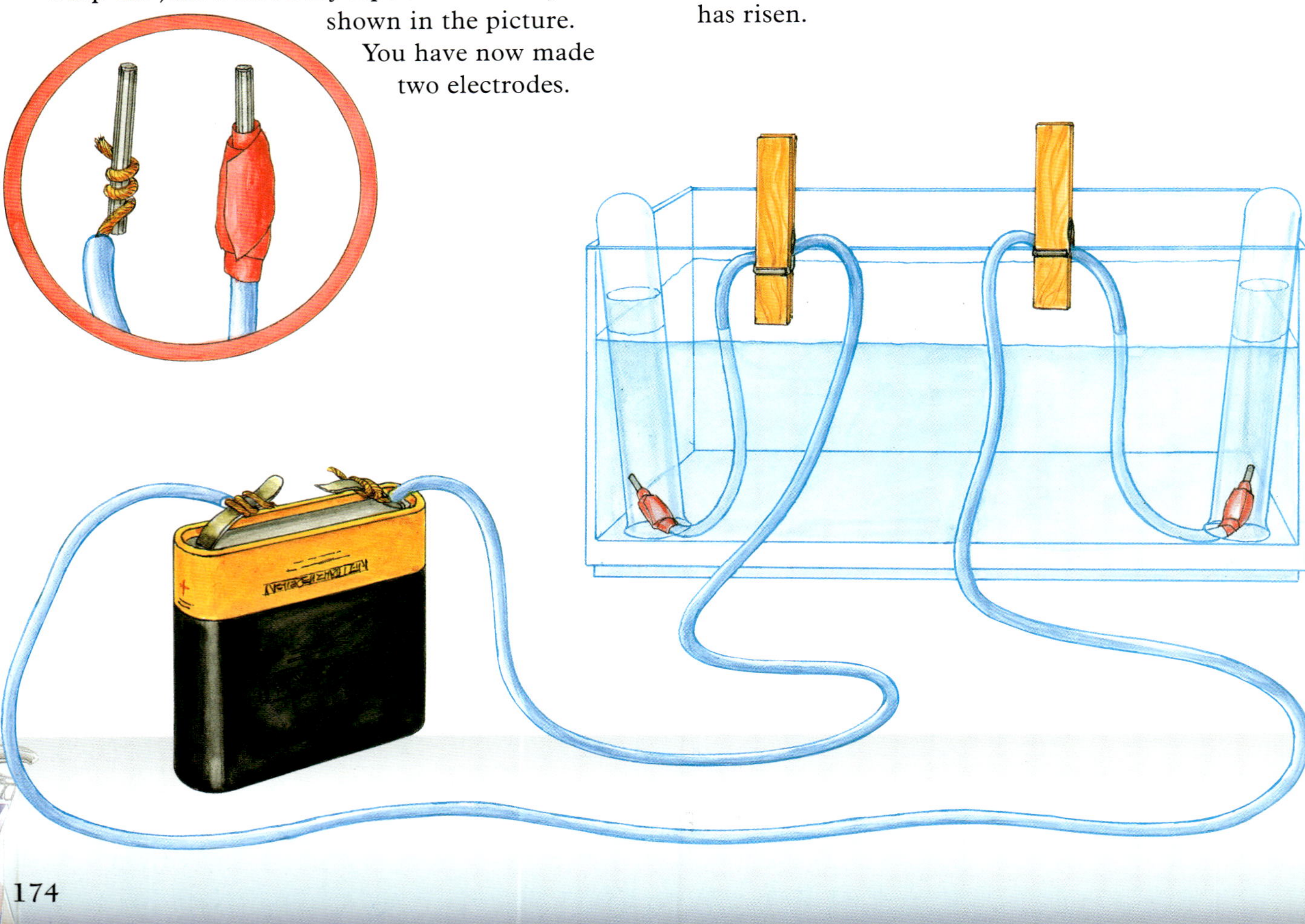

2 Fill the container with water. Put in the two electrodes, so that they touch the bottom. Fix the electric cable to the edges of the container with the two clothes pegs.

3 Fill the test tube with water, and hold your finger over the top. Turn the tube upside down into the container. Then take away your finger, so that you can put the tube over the top of the electrode. Do the same with the other test tube and put the second electrode in place.

4 Pour vinegar into the container. Then wait a few hours.

What happens?

Bubbles have formed in the test tubes. After a few hours, the level of water inside the test tubes has risen.

5 Disconnect the wire ends from the battery.

6 Take the test tube with the lowest level of water out of the container, keeping your thumb over the top.

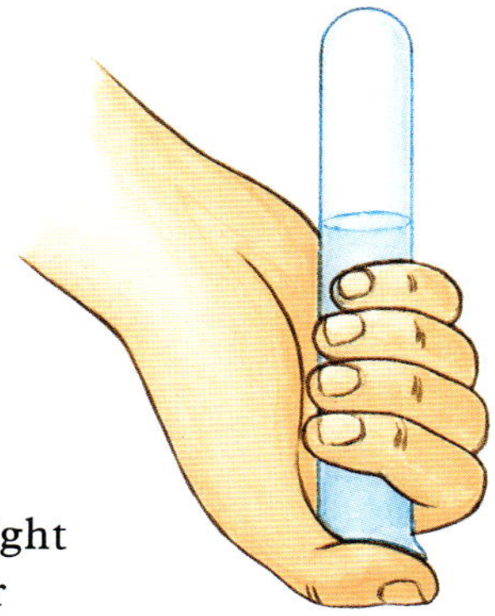

7 Turn the test tube the right way up. Take away your thumb and ask an adult to hold a match near the mouth.

What happens?
There is a little bang.

8 Now take the other test tube from the container in the same way. Ask an adult to light a match, then put it out, and put it into the test tube as soon as you take your finger away.

What happens?
The match bursts into flame again.

Because...
... the first test tube contains hydrogen, which, with the heat of the flame, explodes. The second test tube contains oxygen, which is able to re-activate the combustion of the match (makes it burn) once again. The passage of electricity (provided by the battery) has caused a chemical reaction in which the components of water, hydrogen and oxygen, are separated. This process is called electrolysis and is also used to separate the compounds dissolved in water.

Chemical reactions can generate electricity

Inside the batteries which we use to power toys and electrical equipment is a chemical substance called ammonium chloride paste. When the metal cap of the battery touches the metal tabs in a battery compartment, a chemical reaction begins inside the battery and it is this which generates electricity. Little by little, as the current is produced, the ammonium chloride paste is used up and the battery is finally exhausted.

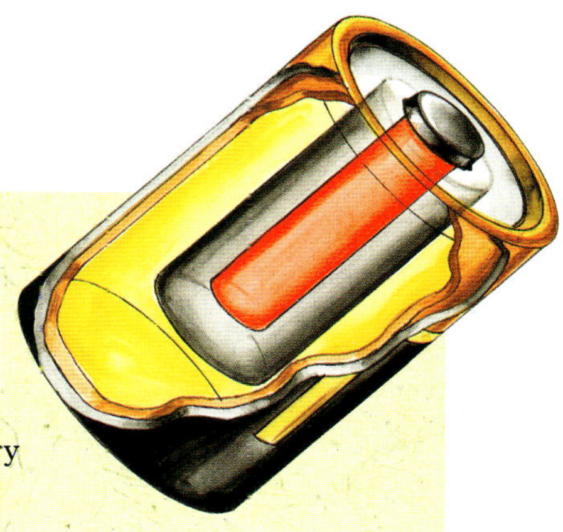

The passage of electrical current can break up water as well as the substances dissolved in it.

Do chemical reactions produce heat?

HEAT FROM NOTHING

You need:
- plaster powder
- water
- a deep plastic tray
- a spoon

What to do

1 Empty the plaster powder into the tray. Add water and mix with the plaster to make a stiff, thick paste.

2 Leave the paste for about an hour.

What happens?

The plaster hardens and the sides of the plastic tray become hot.

Because...

... the process of hardening of the plaster is due to the chemical reaction of the plaster powder with the components of water. One of the products of this reaction is heat.

The conservation of matter

French chemist Antoine Lavoisier lived in the 18th century. He was the first to understand that, in chemical reactions, matter is neither created nor destroyed, but undergoes transformation.
He demonstrated that the complex mass of the original substance is equal to the complex mass of compounds which are obtained, but the number of atoms present at the beginning of the reaction does not change. Instead, the atoms change their arrangement and the atomic bonds by which they are formed. Today it is accepted that the principle of 'Conservation of Mass' (or the 'Lavoisier Principle') does not apply to nuclear reactions, in which the matter which is destroyed is transformed into energy. But the destroyed matter still remains the basis of a common chemical reaction when heat is produced. The quantity of matter which is destroyed transforms itself into heat (thermal) energy and as such cannot be measured.

A portrait of Lavoiser, and, above, a reconstruction of his scientific laboratory.

HEAT RETURNS

You need:
- copper sulphate crystals
- a test tube
- water
- a hot-plate
- an eye-dropper
- a piece of paper

What to do

1 Fold the paper into a thick strip to make a test tube holder.

2 Put some copper sulphate crystals into the test tube. Ask an adult to hold it over the hot-plate, holding it carefully with the paper holder.

What happens?
The crystals become white. Drops of water form in the upper part of the test tube.

3 Leave the test tube to cool. Then add two drops of water.

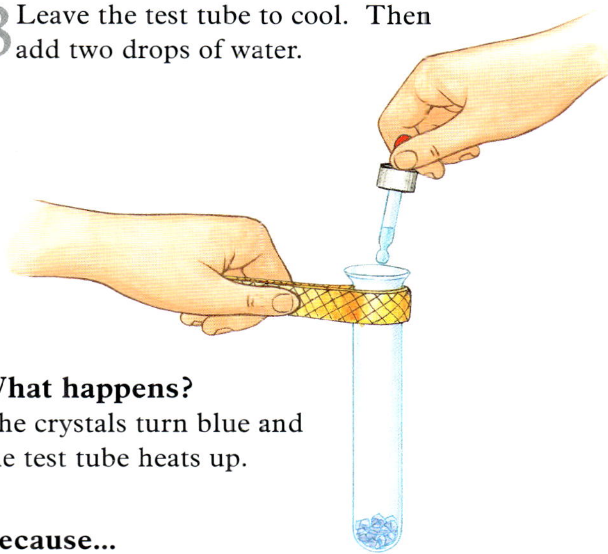

What happens?
The crystals turn blue and the test tube heats up.

Because...
... the copper sulphate crystals contain molecules of water which, with the effect of heat, evaporate and make the crystals lose their blue colour. When you add water again, the water molecules return to the crystals. This chemical reaction, reversing the result before, comes from the same amount of heat which was absorbed before.

Copper sulphate crystals

During some chemical reactions the energy contained in the reactants are set free in the form of heat.

Analysing substances

Some characteristics of substances with which we come into contact each day are immediately recognizable by our senses – taste, smell, colours, the consistency of materials or foods enable us to distinguish, classify, use or avoid them. However, in some cases, we cannot recognize characteristics by our senses. And although at times some people may try to find out by tasting or touching, this can often be very dangerous. There are many safe methods to discover the chemical nature of substances. In these pages, we shall discover some of the most simple.

Is it possible to discover one substance present in another?

AIR IN AIR

You need:
- lime water (obtainable from a pharmacy or a shop which stocks chemical products)
- a drinking straw
- a glass
- a bicycle pump

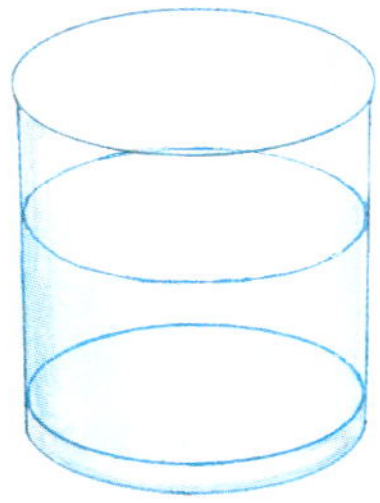

What to do

1 Pour the lime water into the glass.

2 Put the tube of the bicycle pump into the glass. Pump in a little air.

3 Now put the straw into the glass. Blow into the water.

What happens?

When the pump gives off air into the water, bubbles form, but the lime water remains clear. But when you blow into the water, it becomes cloudy.

Because...

... the lime water becomes cloudy when it comes into contact with carbon dioxide. This shows that this carbon dioxide (a compound) is present in the air which we breathe out, but not in the air which comes from the bicycle pump. In the process of breathing, we inhale pure air, but breathe out mostly carbon dioxide.

WHERE IS THE STARCH?

You need:
- samples of bread, rice, pasta, meat, an apple, a potato, white flour
- tincture of iodine
- water
- a glass
- an eye-dropper
- starch powder
- seven little plates

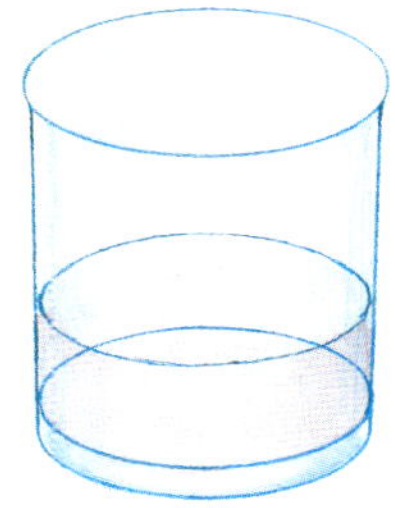

What to do

1 Fill the glass one third full with water. Add six drops of iodine.

2 With the eye-dropper, add a few drops of this solution on the starch powder.

What happens?

The starch turns blue.

3 Set out each food sample on a plate. Dampen each one with water. Using the eye-dropper, add a few drops of the water and iodine solution.

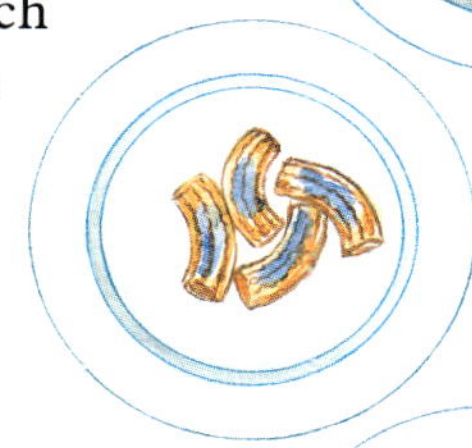

What happens?

Some of the food has turned blue where you added the iodine solution.

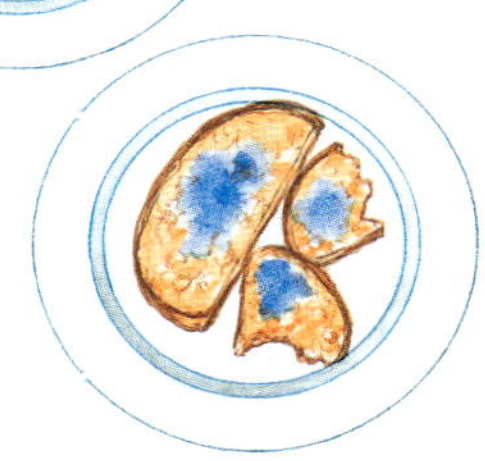

Because...

... the blue colour is the sign that in some of the foods there is starch. This is a sugar very common in vegetables, which they produce and store in seeds and in roots. The iodine solution functions as a discloser.

Some substances change colour when they come into contact with others, and this reveals their presence.

What is the purpose of chemical analysis?

CORROSIVE VINEGAR

You need:
- an egg shell
- flakes of wall plaster
- vinegar
- two glasses

What to do

1 Put the egg shell into one glass. Put the flakes of plaster into the other glass.

2 Half fill each glass with vinegar. Check the contents every twelve hours.

What happens?

First the egg shell and then the flakes of wall plaster dissolve in the vinegar.

Because...

... the vinegar is a substance which in chemistry is defined as an acid. This means it is able to corrode (eat away) at some substances, such as calcium, which is a component both of the egg shell and the plaster.

Acid substances and base substances

Acids and bases are two important types of chemical substances. Finding out whether a substance is an acid or a base is the first thing to do, in order to define the composition of a substance and the effects of contact with other substances.
Some acids have a sour taste (such as lemons and vinegar) and are virtually harmless. More powerful acids are dangerous enough to burn skin on contact. Bases are substances which are often present in detergents; but strong bases can be dangerous because they are corrosive. When a base can be dissolved in water it is called an alkali.

Pure water is neither acid nor a base; it is neutral. In order to distinguish an acid from a base, it is important to control the degree of acidity and base in different substances. That is why there is a Ph scale in which all substances are listed. The value of Ph7 indicates a neutral substance such as pure water. Acids have a Ph value lower than 7, and the lower the Ph, the stronger the acid. Bases have a Ph value higher than 7, and the greater the Ph the stronger the base. Even in the human body there are substances with different levels of Ph. Gastric juices have a Ph lower than 3 and the blood a Ph little higher than 7.

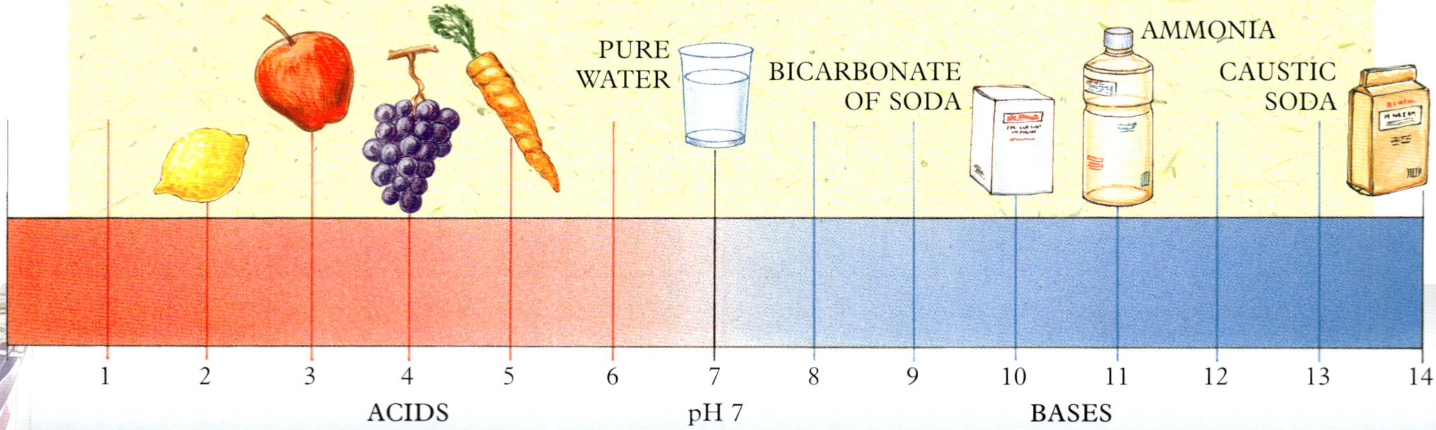

A LIQUID INDICATOR

You need:

- half a red cabbage
- a knife
- a saucepan
- a hot-plate
- water
- a strainer
- a glass jar
- three glasses
- a lemon
- bicarbonate of soda
- a spoon

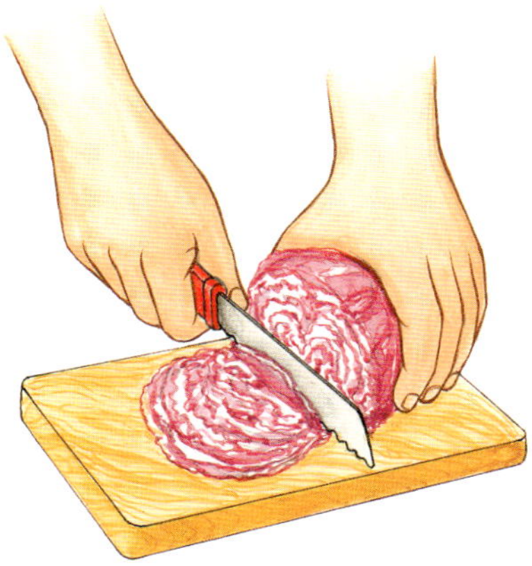

What to do

1 Ask an adult to cut the red cabbage into thin slices. Put these in the saucepan and cover with water. Place on the hot-plate to cook.

2 When the water begins to boil, stir the cabbage, then turn off the heat and leave for half an hour.

3 Put the strainer on the jar. Pour the cabbage into the strainer, so that the water filters through into the jar. You now have a liquid indicator.

4 Pour some water with the juice of a lemon into a glass. In another glass pour water with bicarbonate of soda. In the third glass, plain water.

5 Add a spoonful of the liquid indicator to each glass.

What happens?

The water with the lemon goes red. The glass containing water with bicarbonate of soda takes on a colour between blue and green. The plain water is only just slightly tinged with the same colour as the liquid indicator.

Because...

... the liquid which you obtained by boiling the red cabbage is an indicator, a substance which has a special ability to take on a different colour according to whether it comes into contact with an acid (when it becomes red) or an alkali (becoming green or blue).

In this experiment, the liquid indicator has shown you that lemon juice is an acid substance, bicarbonate of soda is an alkali substance, and the water is neither acid nor base, but neutral, shown by the way it keeps its colour.

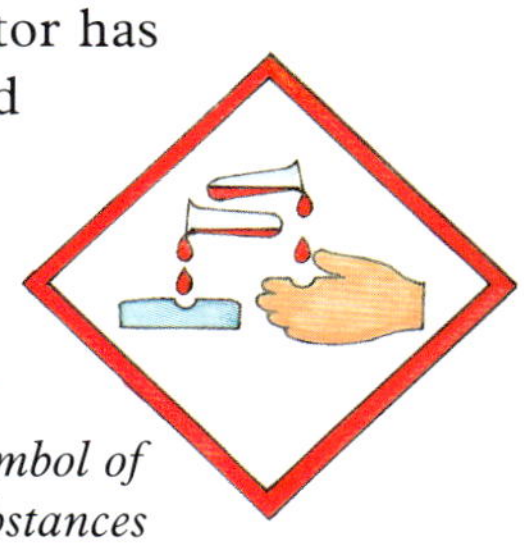

The international symbol of acid substances

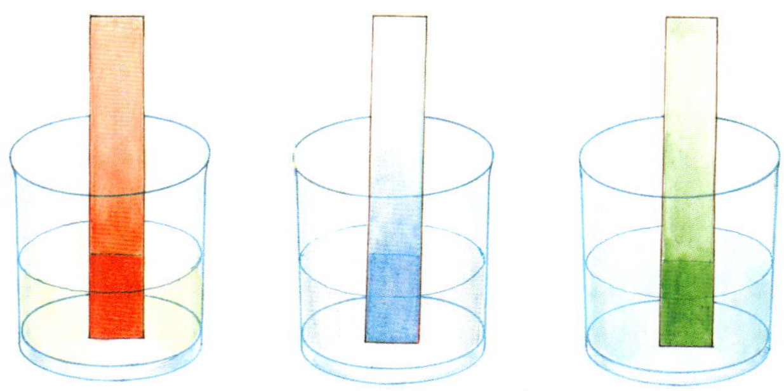

Different indicators are used in chemical laboratories. Among these are litmus papers – strips of paper soaked in a special substance which change colour when they come into contact with an acid or an alkali – and methyl orange, which reveals the presence of an alkali by going red.

Indicators used in chemical analysis reveal characteristics which are not immediately obvious in substances.

Chemistry around us

Many chemical reactions happen all around us. Chemistry comes into play every time we cook an egg or bake a cake, when we breathe, when we chew, when we digest our food.
In these pages you will find some simple experiments which will give you some idea about what happens to food when it is being prepared and when it is tasted.

How does yeast make the dough rise?

THE FORCE OF THE BUBBLES

You need:

- a plastic bottle
- about 150ml of warm water
- yeast
- sugar
- a teaspoon
- a balloon

What to do

1 Put three teaspoons of yeast into the bottle. Add two teaspoons of sugar.

2 Slowly half fill the bottle with warm water.

3 Place the balloon on the neck of the bottle. Wait for about an hour.

What happens?
The liquid becomes frothy and the balloon inflates.

Because...
... the yeast is a microscopic fungus which feeds on the natural sugar contained in flour. As this happens, a gas – carbon dioxide – is produced. This gas forms lots of bubbles which rise up towards the surface (that is why the liquid becomes frothy) and expands into the air above, inflating the balloon.

The rising of dough

In bread-making, the yeast feeds on the sugar contained in the flour and produces carbon dioxide which makes the dough rise. During the baking, this carbon dioxide is released into the air, and as this happens, it leaves behind the little holes which we see in bread.

Chemical substances in foods

The foods which we eat are generally formed of natural chemical substances, which we get from plants and from animals.

The substances which we must eat to maintain a healthy body can be subdivided into three categories:

- carbohydrates (found particularly in pasta, bread, sugar, fruit and green vegetables) which give us immediate energy, because they are burned up quickly by our bodies.
- fats (such as cooking oil, butter and margarine) which also give us energy, but at a more slower rate.
- proteins (found in meat, fish, eggs and cheese) and which constitute the material needed for growth, healthy bones and the maintenance of the body.

Foods also provide us with other vital substances – vitamins, mineral salts and a part of the water which we need every day.

As yeast converts the sugar contained in flour, it gives off a gas, carbon dioxide, which makes dough rise.

How does the stomach break up food?

ENZYMES AT WORK

You need:

- two glass jars
- two hard-boiled eggs (shelled)
- ordinary detergent
- biological detergent with enzymes
- warm water
- a spoon
- a pen
- two labels

What to do

1 Put a spoonful of normal detergent in one jar. Put a spoonful of biological detergent with enzymes in the other jar.

2 Label the jars to show which is which.

3 Pour water in both jars. Mix thoroughly until the detergent is dissolved.

4 Put a hard-boiled egg in each jar. Place the jars in a warm place, but not in direct contact with a source of heat. Leave for a few days.

Biochemistry

Inside the human body, as in all living organisms, countless chemical reactions take place. The study of these phenomena is the science of biochemistry. Biochemists carry out research to discover how molecules of inanimate (non-living) substances react together, to keep organisms (living things) alive.

Biochemistry is very important in the field of medicine. Studies of bodily functions such as breathing, digestion and the transmission of nerve impulses, have made it possible to develop new medicines for many diseases and afflictions.

The food industry has also used the knowledge gained by biochemistry, especially in the preservation of foods and the manufacture of foods for babies.

What happens?

In the jar with the normal detergent, the egg has not changed. In the jar with the biological detergent, the egg looks as if it has been partly eaten.

Because...

... the biological detergent contains enzymes. An enzyme is a special chemical substance which either makes a chemical reaction possible or speeds up a chemical reaction. The enzymes in the biological detergent 'eat' at the egg in the same way as they do with a speck of dirt, by separating the molecules and making them soluble in water. Our body also produces enzymes to break up food into very small particles which the digestive system can use more easily.

THE ACTION OF SALIVA

You need:

- iodine solution (as made for the experiment to detect starch)
- white flour
- cold water, lukewarm water and hot water
- a spoon
- a teaspoon
- a cup
- a test tube
- a glass jar
- an eye-dropper
- a plate

What to do

1 In the cup, mix a spoonful of flour with a little cold water. Then fill the cup with hot water.

2 Leave the mixture to cool. Then spoon a little on to a plate. Add one or two drops of the iodine solution.

What happens?
The water and flour mixture has turned blue, revealing the presence of starch.

3 Put as much saliva as you can into a test tube. Add a spoonful of the water and flour mixture. Shake vigorously, keeping the test tube closed with your thumb.

4 Pour the lukewarm water into the jar. Then put in the test tube. (Take care not to let any water get inside the test tube.)

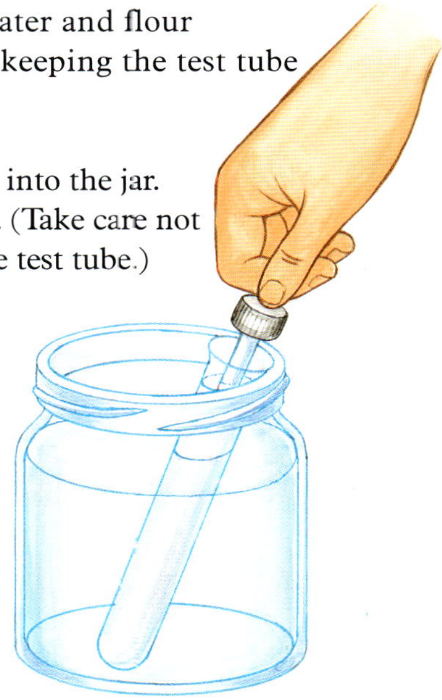

5 Every half an hour, remove a little of the contents of the test tube with the eye-dropper and repeat the test with the iodine solution. Do not forget to wash the plate each time.

What happens?
Little by little, as time passes, the iodine solution causes a change of colour in the flour mixture. Changes are always slightly evident, until the colour has changed completely.

Because...
... the saliva contains an enzyme (amylase) which is able to transform the starch into malt, a sugar which is more easily digested by the body. Try to chew a little piece of bread very slowly. At first, it tastes salty, then sweet. That change happens because of the action of the amylase.

Our bodies produce enzymes which transform foods into substances which are easier to digest.

Fact-Finder

What are mixtures?

Mixtures are obtained by mixing substances which keep their characteristics (which means, they do not change) and are easily separated. Sometimes, these substances can be recognized by the naked eye. At other times, the components of a mixture can be seen only with a special microscope. There are many types of mixtures in which the components are solids, liquids or glasses.

Here are a few examples.

solid with solid
- metal alloys such as bronze (made of copper and tin) and brass (copper and zinc) are mixtures obtained by melting the metals together at high temperatures and then leaving them to solidify;
- sand is a mixture of grains of different minerals;

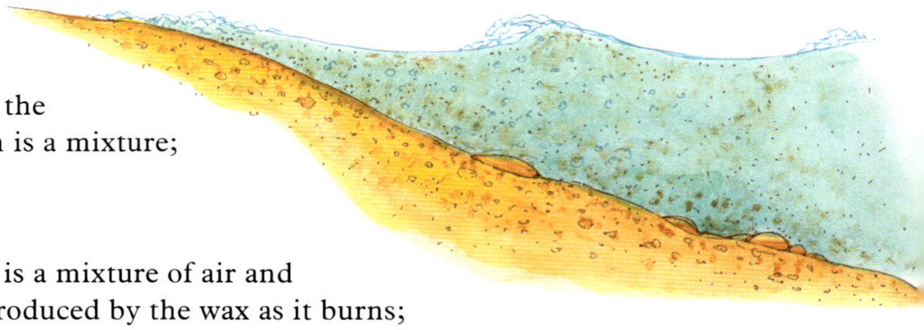

solid with liquid
-the water soaking into the sand during a sea storm is a mixture;

solid with gas
- the smoke of a candle is a mixture of air and microscopic particles produced by the wax as it burns;

liquid with liquid
- oil mixes with water to form a mixture called an emulsion. These two liquids never mix perfectly together;
- milk is an emulsion of water and fat;

liquid with gas
- mist is formed by tiny little particles of water mixed with the air.

Metals and non-metals

Natural chemical elements can be grouped into categories according to the characteristics which they show. An important subdivision distinguishes metals from non-metals. Metals are mostly solid, except for mercury which is a liquid, and is very light, most often with a colour similar to silver. Copper is red, and gold is yellow. All these are good conductors, both of electrical current and heat. They are easy to work with (we say they are adaptable and malleable). Other examples of metal are iron, aluminium and uranium.

Non-metals have characteristics which are more changeable. These might be gases, like oxygen, nitrogen and helium, or solids, such as sulphur and carbon. Non-metals do not have the typical sheen of metals, and do not conduct electricity or heat. They are fragile and are not so adaptable or so malleable as metals.

Glossary

Aerodynamics Study of the movement of objects through the air

Altimeter Instrument used to estimate heights, by means of comparing differences in atmospheric pressure

Ampere (or amp) Unit of measurement of intensity of electrical current

Arch Curved architectural structure with which it is possible to heighten an empty space

Archimedes' Principle Law of science which states that an object totally or partly submerged in a liquid displaces a volume of fluid which weighs the same as the object appears to have lost. Otherwise referred to as displacement

Atmosphere Layer of gas which surrounds the Earth

Atmospheric pressure Force exerted by gas which surrounds the Earth on its surface

Atom Tiniest particle of a substance which keeps its physical characteristics and chemicals; it is composed of a nucleus containing neutrons (with no electrical charge) and protons (with a positive charge) around which orbit the electrons (with a negative electrical charge)

Attraction Force which compels the mutual movement of two objects to make contact

Barometer Instrument to measure atmospheric pressure

Boiling The passage of a substance from a liquid state to a vapour state and involving all the substance

Centrifugal Force Force which pushes an object away from the centre of an orbit in a rotating movement

Centripetal Force Force which allows the rotating movement of an object, pushing it towards the centre of the orbit

Chemical reaction Transformation in which one or more substances (reagants) are transformed into difference substances (products) following the formation or the breaking down of chemical bonds

Chemistry Science which studies the properties (or characteristics) of substances, their composition, their possible transformations and their structure

Clouds Masses of air and water which form by atmospheric condensation

Combustion Chemical reaction; the oxidization of a combustible (such as a match) with a combustive agent (e.g. oxygen) with a supply of heat (fuel)

Combustible A substance which can ignite a flame, such as a match

Combustive agent A substance which feeds the flames, enabling them to burn (e.g. oxygen)

Compass Instrument which indicates position by use of the Earth's magnetic poles

Compound Substance obtained by a chemical union of other substances which present new characteristics in respect to those of the original substance

Compressed air Air which is rapidly diminished in volume by strong pressure

Concentric Tendency to meet at a central point (e.g. concentric circles)

Condensation Path from a vapour state to a liquid state

Conductor of heat Something which allows the flow of heat

Conductor of electricity Something which allows the flow of electrical current

Convection Propagation of heat in a liquid or vapour state through movement of the molecules from the bottom to the top and vice versa

Cyclone Stormy atmosphere, generally characterized by a whirlwind of air at high velocity and accompanied by an intense rainfall and violent wind

Density Weight and shape (mass) of an object contained within its volume (the space it takes up)

Dilation Variation of the dimensions of an object by the effect of heat

Dynamo Electrical machine which generates electrical current as it rotates

Dynamometer Instrument used to measure strength

Earth's Gravity Force which attracts objects towards the centre of the Earth

Earth's Magnetic Field Magnetic field of the Earth

Elasticity Property by which an object under the effect of a force is crumpled and at the end of the stimulus returns to its original form

Electrical charge Quantity of electricity which an object has

Electrical circuit Series of electrical components and conductors through which electrical current can flow

Electrical current Phenomenon due to an electrical charge which flows through conductive materials (for example, electrical cable)

Electromagnetism Electricity and magnetism used together as a source of power. e.g. electricity working a magnet, a magnet providing part of an electrical circuit

Electroscope Device for revealing the type of electrical charge (positive or negative)

Element Substance formed of atoms of one type

Energy Capacity to produce power

Evaporation Passage of a substance from a liquid state to a gas state; involves only the surface layer of a substance

Flame Mass of gas within which combustion takes place, producing heat and light

Freezing Direct passage from a vapour to a solid

Fusion Passage of a substance from a solid to a liquid state

Gas State of matter, in which the molecules are tied weakly, and so tend to occupy all the space available and can be easily compressed.

Geyser Intermittent, (non-continuous) natural spring (source) of hot water and steam

Heat Form of energy which is transmitted from one object or one body to another when there is a difference in temperature between them

Humidity Amount of air present in the atmosphere

Hydroelectric station Installation to produce electrical energy by using the force of falling water

Ice Water in its solid state

Impervious Cannot be penetrated

Insulator Material which does not let heat or electricity pass through

Kilogram Unit of measuring mass (symbol kg)

Laser Instrument to produce a very thin and intense beam of light which is capable of great energy

Lift Force which sustains an aircraft in flight, determined by the stronger pressure of air (under the wings) in respect to that in the air in movement (above the wings)

Lightning Atmospheric phenomenon caused by an electrical charge between one stormy cloud and another, or between a cloud and the Earth's surface

Liquidation Passage of a substance from a gas state to a liquid state

Magnet Material which attracts iron materials and those which contain cobalt or nickel; a magnet also enables a person to calculate their position by following the direction of the needle towards the Earth's magnetic poles

Magnetic Field Area in which a magnet is able to exert its force of attraction on an object of iron

Membrane A fine, thin surface skin

Metals Chemical elements characterized by a good ability to conduct heat and electricity, hard wearing qualities, the sheen and the fact that they are easy to work with

Mist Mass of very small drops of water suspended in the air near the ground

Mixture Two or more elements or compounds mixed together but not united chemically

Molecule Particle formed by two or more atoms tied chemically; the smallest part of the substance which maintains its own characteristics

Newton Unit of measurement of force (symbol N)

Non-metals Chemical elements characterized by a low capacity to conduct heat and electricity and often breakable

Opaque Cannot be seen through

Orbit Journey, usually in circular or oval form, along which a body (such a planet, satellite or electron) moves around another

Orientation Ability to determine the right position in a space, or the right direction

Oxidization Chemical reaction in which a chemical element combines with oxygen

Phenomenon Something happening naturally, which we can see, feel or hear

Photosynthesis Process in which plants absorb sunlight and carbon dioxide, which they use with water absorbed from the ground and chlorophyll contained in their leaves to produce glucose, a sugar on which plants feed

Prism Triangular-shaped solid glass, through which white light can be divided into the seven colours of the spectrum

Rain Atmospheric fall of liquid formed of drops of water

Rainbow Luminous arch made up of the seven colours of the spectrum in succession and caused by the refraction of the sunlight on raindrops

Reflection Phenomenon in which rays of light change direction when hitting a reflective surface (like a mirror)

Refraction Dividing up of a ray of light

Resistance Quality of a component of an electrical circuit. Resistance against the passage of electrical energy determines its transformation into heat and light

Respiration Biological function which enables the absorption of oxygen used in the internal process of combustion and expulsion of waste substances, such as carbon dioxide

Sea current A mass of sea water in movement

Shadow Zone in which the rays of lights do not reach because of an opaque object

Snow Atmospheric fall of ice crystals

Solid State of matter in which the molecules are joined tightly to each other; solid matter forms a proper shape and a permanent volume

Solidification Passage of a substance from a liquid to a solid state

Solution Mixture of one or more substances, obtained by dissolving a liquid, solid or gas (solute) in a liquid (solvent)

Solute A substance which can be dissolved

Solvent Substance in which other substances can be dissolved

Sound Audible disturbance which is produced within a space (for example, in the air) and which generates an audible sensation

Spectrum All the colours together which form white light

State of matter Physical state presented by matter (liquid, solid or gas), and which depends on the speed of the molecules which constitute it

Static electricity Phenomenon due to electrical charges in a state of rest in the presence of an object or person

Sublimation Passage of a substance directly from a solid state to a gas state

Surface tension Force which makes the surface layer of a liquid like a thin elastic skin, capable of supporting an object

Switch Electrical device which opens or closes a circuit, interrupting or reactivating the flow of electrical current

Telescope Instrument used to observe objects at a distance and which uses a system of lenses

Translucent Partly allowing light to pass through

Tuning Fork Instrument which produces a tone with which to tune musical instruments

Universal Gravity Force by which all objects with a mass are attracted

Weight Force of gravitational attraction exerted on a body

Wind Movement of a mass of air in the atmosphere caused by variations of temperature and air pressure

Wind farm Installation for the production of electrical energy which uses the force of the wind

Vapour Gas state of matter which is obtained by the sublimation of a solid, or by evaporation or boiling a liquid

Vibration Periodic movement of an object around a position of balance

Volt Unit of measuring electrical tension (symbol V)

Index

Air 3

Air is everywhere 4
The pressure of air 8
Hot and cold air 14
Flight 22
Air and combustion 26
Sounds 30
FACT-FINDER 34

Water 35

The force of water 36
Surface tension of water 42
To float or not to float? 48
The transformation of water 54
Water solutions 60
FACT-FINDER 64

Light 65

Rays of light 66
Reflection 72
Refraction 78
Colours 84
Capture an image 92
FACT-FINDER 96

Magnetism 97

Magnets 98
The Magnetic Poles 106
Magnetic Force 112
Magnetism and Electricity 120
FACT-FINDER 128

Electricity 129

Static Electricity 130
The Electric Current 138
Circuits and Switches 144
Effects of the Electrical Current 150
FACT-FINDER 158

Chemistry 159

Solids, liquids and gas 160
Mixtures, solutions and compounds 166
Chemical Reactions 168
Analyzing substances 178
Chemistry around us 182
FACT-FINDER 186

Glossary 187

Acknowledgements: Photographs

Archivio IGDA: 20, 32, 76, 82, 86-87, 95a, 99, 106, 119, 130, title page, Electricity; Bertaggia,E. 59b, Buss, W. 95c, 138-139, 168; Carfagna, G. 72-73; Castano, P. 84-85; Castiglioni, A. e.A. 79; Chasseria, N. 184; Ciccione, 176b; Cigolini, G. 103,152, 169a, 177-178; Cirani, N. 55b; Dagli Orti A. 157a; Dagli Orti G.111, 141, 176a; Dani, C. 33, 95b, 148; De Gregorio, A. 60; Donati, A. 54-55a; Gellie, Y. 109; Ghislandi, R, 11; Jaccod, P. 22-23, title page, Water; Ledoux, T. 48; Liaci, P. 71; Picard, 38; Pidello, G. 8-9, 65; Pozzoni, C. 149, 161; Prato, S. 90-91; Quemere, E. 21; Rives, C. 41; Rizzi, A. 77m 83b; Romano, L. 57b, 88, 129; Sappa, C. 16, 163; Sioen, G. 35, 36, 52-53, 117, title page, Light; Staquet, D. 58-59a; Tessore, A. 66; Veggi, G. 57a, 62; Vergani, A. 3, 63, 157b, 160, 166-167; Wright, G. 14-15, title page Air, Contrast 97; Farabolafoto; 112, Ba92; Revy, J.C, 59c; Wysocki, 26; Fotoservice/Filser, W. 159; Grazia Neri/M.Agliolo 142-143; R. Hansen, 155; Laura Ronchi, 25, 85a, 95d; Cade, P. 4, Galante, D. title page, Magnetism; Massey Teatro alla Scala/Lelli-Masotti. 30-31; Zefa-Boden-Ledlingham; title page, Chemistry;
Cover page: Zefa/Anderson, B.